The Low-Carb Cookbook

D0037211

The Low-Carb Cookbook

The Complete Guide to the Healthy

Low-Carbohydrate Lifestyle—with over 250

Delicious Recipes, Everything You Need to

Know about Stocking the Pantry, and

Sources for the Best Prepared

Foods and Ingredients

Fran McCullough

Foreword by Michael R. Eades, M.D.,
and Mary Dan Eades, M.D.

HYPERION
New York

Copyright © 1997 Frances McCullough
Foreword Copyright © 1997 Michael R. Eades and Mary Dan Eades

Georgian Egg Salad from *The Georgian Feast* by Darra Goldstein.
Copyright © 1993 by Darra Goldstein. Reprinted by permission of
HarperCollins Publishers, Inc.

All rights reserved. No part of this book may be used or reproduced
in any manner whatsoever without the written permission of the
Publisher. Printed in the United States of America. For information
address Hyperion, 77 West 66th Street, New York, New York
10023-6298.

LIBRARY OF CONGRESS CATALOGING-IN-PUBLICATION DATA

McCullough, Frances Monson
     The low-carb cookbook : the complete guide to the
healthy low-carbohydrate lifestyle : with over 250 delicious
recipes, everything you need to know about stocking the
pantry, and sources for the best prepared foods and ingredients / by Fran McCullough ; foreword by Michael R. Eades
and Mary Dan Eades.—1st ed.
     p. cm.
     Includes index.
     ISBN 0-7868-6273-4
     1. Cookery. 2. Low-carbohydrate diet—Recipes. I. Title
TX714.M3793   1997
641.5'638—dc21   96–49343
                                              CIP

Mass Market ISBN: 0-7868-8991-8

FIRST EDITION

10 9 8 7 6 5 4 3 2 1

ALSO BY THE AUTHOR, WITH BARBARA WITT

Great Food Without Fuss

Great Feasts Without Fuss

Classic American Food Without Fuss

Acknowledgments

I like to think that Doctors Michael and Mary Dan Eades have actually saved my life—certainly their low-carb diet has brought my formerly high blood pressure, high cholesterol, and high triglycerides into the normal range, and dramatically reversed my ominous health profile. I can't thank them enough.

I'm grateful to my wise agent, Irene Skolnick, and my unflappable editor, Rick Kot, who made this book happen in record time. Big thanks to Lisa Kitei, who "got it" right away and put her great enthusiasm to work for the book.

Even with all this support, and the unflagging spirits of my husband, David, who had to literally eat the mistakes, this book wouldn't exist without the help of my endlessly generous cook friends: Bruce Aidells, Colman Andrews, Jo Bettoja, JoAnn Clevenger, Doe Coover, Elaine Corn, Susan Costner, Alice Doyle, Suzanne Hamlin, Ken Haedrich (my dessert guru), Diana Kennedy, Deborah Madison, Norma Marshall, Priscilla Martell, Michael Roberts, Alice Rosengard, Martha Rose Shulman, David Soohoo, Martin and Sally Stone, John Taylor, Sylvia Thompson, James Villas, Eileen Weinberg, Faith Willinger, Barbara Witt, Diane Worthington, and Rob Wynne.

Finally, thanks to Irwyn Applebaum, for his brilliant sense of timing in setting me free to finish this book.

Contents

Foreword

April 22 and 23, 1996, were red-letter days in the annals of nutritional medicine. It was on these days that a group of internationally renowned experts met in Dallas to focus on the topic of the role of dietary fat in human health and disease. Many of them concluded that the low-fat, high–complex-carbohydrate diet has been a dismal failure in addressing the problems of obesity, cardiovascular disease, and diabetes. These leading researchers had spent years investigating all aspects of fat's role in health and discovered that many of the dietary truisms we've been taught to accept uncritically in the last two decades are in fact not only incorrect but actually dangerous in their implications for our health. For instance, no doubt remains that the low-fat high-carbohydrate diet raises triglycerides—a type of fat found in the blood that was once thought to be a harmless bystander, but is now turning out to be the single best predictor for heart disease risk. No doubt remains that the low-fat high-carbohydrate diet lowers the level of HDL—the so-called good cholesterol that protects against heart disease. And although it's true that the low-fat, high–complex-carbohydrate diet has accomplished a modest lowering of LDL cholesterol (the so-called bad kind) levels, as it turns out, even this apparent benefit evaporates under closer scrutiny. Although the levels do fall a bit, the LDL particles that remain are smaller and denser and therefore more prone to cause heart disease—in effect, a much stronger negative factor than a somewhat higher LDL level.

But as useless as the low-fat, high-carbohydrate diet has proven to be for cardiac risk, it's an even bigger flop as a treatment for obesity or diabetes. During the last decade—the heyday of the low-fat diet—the nation has gotten substantially fatter (by a third) and the incidence of adult-onset diabetes has *tripled*.

Such dismal statistics come as no surprise to us, since we've seen the same results in disappointed low-fat dieters who've come to our practice. During the last decade, we've devoted our professional lives to treating these disorders nutritionally. But we have not used the standard USDA Food Pyramid low-fat, high-carbohydrate approach. We tried that model very early in our medical careers and met the same high rates of failure that frustrate physicians and patients today. So we stepped back and took a fresh look at what works biochemically and what simply doesn't. That led us to develop the Protein Power program, which we've used successfully to help thousands of patients in our clinical practice reclaim their health as well as lose weight.

The approach we take is to control the hormone insulin, which not only causes the fat cells to store fat but also has a key role in high blood pressure, vascular disease, and diabetes. Of the three dietary elements—protein, fat, and carbohydrate—only carbohydrate increases the production of insulin, which then sets off these adverse effects in people with hyperinsulinemia (insulin resistance). And curiously enough, the *only* way to cut back on insulin production is through diet, by cutting back the carbohydrates, the very sugars and starches emphasized on the low-fat diet. The several low-carbohydrate diets differ a little in specifics, but they all restrict carbohydrates to achieve their health benefits and weight loss.

Given our success in bringing down our patients' cholesterol and triglycerides, controlling their blood sugars, virtually reversing adult diabetes, and helping people to achieve weight loss who had failed again and again with the low-fat diets, we are amused when nutritional "experts" trot out worn clichés in an effort to discredit our higher-protein, moderate-fat, restricted-carbohydrate approach. Among these tired warnings are that a low-carbohydrate diet will damage your kidneys and weaken your bones, and that all the weight you lose is simply water that will be gained right back. While our own experience belies these myths—in ten years of practice with thousands of patients, we've never seen a single person develop kidney damage or weak bones (and we check their blood regularly to be sure)—even the peer-review medical literature abounds in work that disproves them.

Dr. Miriam Blum laid to rest the myth that higher-protein diets damage the kidneys in a classic paper published in the *Archives of Internal Medicine* in 1987. Her research team identified adult subjects who currently ate and had eaten a high-protein diet—including meat of all kinds—for most of their lives and matched them by age and sex to a second group of adults who were long-term vegetarians. The second group (who had been vegetarians for an average of 13.3 years) consumed very little protein, and what they did eat was entirely of vegetable origin. The team then measured the natural "age-related decline" in kidney function (a condition that unfortunately occurs in all humans as we age) and found that there was absolutely no difference between the two groups across the entire spectrum of ages. This study shows that eating meat or eating a diet of high protein carries with it no risk of damage to normal, healthy kidneys. A much more recent study by the German research team of Remer and Mantz, published in the *Journal of Nutritional Biochemistry* in 1995, showed that weightlifters who consumed excessive amounts of protein actually experienced *improved* kidney function.

Similar studies have disproved the argument that protein causes osteoporosis. According to this theory, increased protein intake should cause increased acidity of the blood, as a result of an elevation of protein breakdown products. To maintain the proper acid level, the body must therefore "neutralize" the acid excess by leaching calcium out of the bones to act as the buffer. The calcium would then pass into the urine, at the expense of the bones. In fact, Herta Spencer, M.D., considered the foremost calcium research expert in the world, has published a number of papers showing absolutely no correlation between meat consumption and loss of calcium in the urine.

Some medical writers have suggested that the low-carbohydrate diet increases uric acid levels in the blood—a major factor in gout—but in fact the diet *lowers* uric acid levels.

We, our patients, a growing number of physicians of all specialties across the country, and millions of dieters are convinced of the safety and efficacy of a low-carbohydrate nutritional regimen. The most common reason that people do abandon this program is not that it damages their health, or fails to correct their problems—quite the contrary. One of the statements we hear most often from patients coming into our office is: "The only time I ever really lost weight and felt good was on a high-protein diet." When we inquire why they abandoned a regimen that by their own admission worked, they usually reply, "I just got tired of eating nothing but meat. And I just didn't know what else to cook." How can one follow a nutritional program of any kind for the long term without variety in texture, in flavor, and in food choices? To say the least, overcoming this monotony has been a challenge.

Since the publication of our book *Protein Power* in early 1996, we have been besieged by readers wanting more how-to advice on low-carbohydrate meal preparation. They've discovered the same thing we have: There's just not much information out there on the practical aspects of maintaining the low-carb lifestyle. We made a foray to our local chain bookstore and encountered a plethora of books on vegetarian cooking, fat-free cooking, high-carbohydrate cooking, and fat-removal modifications of virtually every kind of ethnic cooking in existence. All in all, we found 617 different titles on some aspects of low-fat cooking, but not even *one* low-carbohydrate cookbook. Not a single one! Over the years we've gathered recipes from patients, friends, the Internet (an active low-carb newsgroup creates and exchanges recipes), and from our own experimentation and modification of published recipes that we've adapted for low-carbohydrate cooking. With such slim offerings available, we even included a mini-cookbook in *Protein Power*, but space constraints limited the number of recipes we could offer.

Finally, however, comes Fran McCullough to the rescue, offering us a tour de force for low-carbohydrate cooking. Fran is uniquely qualified to this task. She is a fabulous cook herself, with a discriminating palate, an inventive mind, and a love of good food; she has several previous cookbooks to her credit; and she has edited award-winning cookbooks by other authors. Most importantly, she herself has lived a lifelong battle with her

weight and the health issues related to it. She has walked
the walk, and knows firsthand the culinary dilemmas that
bedevil people trying to adapt to a low-carbohydrate life
in a high-carbohydrate world. And what she offers in *The
Low-Carb Cookbook* is more than just a collection of
recipes—it's a complete primer on how to modify your
kitchen, stock your pantry, alter your cooking methods,
and change your life to accommodate your new dietary
regimen. She's packed her book full of helpful ideas and
suggestions for navigating the minefield of carbohydrates.
Because of her own health problems and sensitivity to
carbohydrates, she's acutely aware of the way that even
tiny bits of carbohydrate can add up to sabotage good in-
tentions. She understands that carb grams are much like
long-distance phone calls—each one costs only a few
pennies, but at the end of the month, the bill can be out-
rageously high. Her own struggle has helped to define
this book and make sticking to a lower carbohydrate regimen a snap. She's packed *The Low-Carb Cookbook* with
complete and easy-to-understand instructions on how to
prepare exceptional dishes, from appetizers to soups and
salads to entrees, snacks, and desserts—everything you
could need to cook well for yourself while at the same
time preparing meals that will satisfy your family and will
be impressive enough for entertaining friends.

Fran also loves to travel, and her journeys have given
her a familiarity with cuisines around the world. Many of
her delicious recipes reflect these rich influences. Her
knowledge of specialty stores and food purveyors across
the country—even around the globe—is encyclopedic.
When we travel, we always check with Fran for tips on
local specialties that will fit into our eating plan. Whether
she was guiding us through a farmer's market in Seattle,
cooking low-carbohydrate waffles for us in the eclectic

kitchen of her rambling Hudson River Valley house, helping us nosh our way through the delis of Manhattan, or taking us on a wild $25 taxi ride to find the only decent barbecue in Las Vegas, Fran's food instincts have been unfailingly on the mark.

And although her recipes sometimes call for a certain unusual spice or piquant flavor, she's savvy enough to recognize that access to such delicacies could present a problem in many cities and small towns across the country, and she comes to the rescue again with an extensive listing of sources that will bring the world of great food to your door, wherever it is.

With *The Low-Carb Cookbook* boredom will never again be a valid excuse for straying from the path of low-carbohydrate righteousness. Thanks, Fran!

—MICHAEL AND MARY DAN EADES

Introduction

As I have almost every year, I spent most of 1995 dieting. But this time there was a big surprise: For the first time in a lifetime of try-and-fail yo-yo dieting, I know that the weight loss I've already sustained (over 60 pounds) will continue and that I'll end up sometime soon as a normal-weight person who is no longer at the mercy of food. Finally, I got it. It's not that I've solved an emotional problem centered around food—although simply being fat and failing over and over again to solve the problem certainly creates major anxiety—but rather that I discovered I have a metabolic problem, specifically an insulin problem. And now I know what to do about it, with a new way of eating so simple and so enjoyable that there's no question of losing control. The only question is how to adapt this new way of eating to the rest of my life—which is how I came to write this book.

I'm sure my diet history will be familiar to anyone who's been overweight. Weight Watchers was a great struggle, and then the few lost pounds would come right back. The liquid diet was easy and worked like crazy, though it left me with a strange "wasted-but-still-fat" look. But after four months of liquid dieting my hair started falling out around my shoulders, and I panicked. When I came off the diet, all I wanted to eat was sugar and fat, preferably together. I would eat an entire batch of cookies and then make another one and eat the dough right from the bowl—followed by a walk to keep myself from eating ice cream. My cravings were simply overwhelming and not to be denied. In desperation I turned to a version of the old Atkins diet, the only diet that ever really worked for me. After my doctors told me I'd ruin my kidneys if I stayed on it (not true, as it turned out), I resigned myself to simply gaining back more weight. Next, I gave low-fat dieting a big try with a famous doctor, whom I loved. First I gained 10 pounds, as I'd been assured I might (not to worry—they'd come off soon), and though it was a lot of fun to eat all that bread and pasta, I didn't really feel good and I didn't lose any weight. And I started to develop gout.

One day my favorite diet counselor pointed out that there is a typical dieting pattern. She drew a lozenge on a blackboard that showed where anxiety levels typically peaked after regaining weight, then intensive dieting began, then slacking off, and then the anxiety again, etc. I was aware of this cycle, of course, but seeing it so starkly represented had a big effect on me: I knew I had to stop doing this to myself. Either I would solve this problem and lose weight or I'd ignore it and just get fatter.

My first clue to a solution came from a nutritionist who told me I had a big difficulty with carbohydrates. "Your metabolism just can't handle them," she said. She put me on a very restricted diet, limiting my carbs to a few green vegetables, rice, and apples. This diet seemed right to me, and in fact it worked very well. But the routine was so bleak—a harsh sentence for a cookbook editor who passionately loves food—that I couldn't stand more than four months of it. And my hair was falling out again. On to another famous doctor who put me on his low-carb salmon and salad diet—another success, but then the gout returned. So I began searching for something similar but better, something I could live with that didn't have these alarming side effects.

At that point I got really lucky: Into my life walked doctors Michael and Mary Dan Eades with the manuscript for their book, *Protein Power*, for me to edit, and I knew right away that here was the answer. The Eadeses explained that the carbohydrate-intolerance problem is actually a genetic insulin problem, and that it contributes to a cluster of chronic diseases, including hypertension, heart disease, gout, and diabetes. I already had gout and occasional high blood pressure, which runs in my family, as does heart disease. My bloodwork looked terrible, with extremely high triglycerides and low HDL, the good cholesterol. I had all the signs of pre-diabetes plus a good 80 pounds to lose. In the course of editing *Protein Power*, I became a convert. Not only does their theory make excellent medical sense, but their diet offers a broad range of foods. Now my blood looks terrific, with model numbers for cholesterol and triglycerides and very low insulin. Beyond that, I have enormous amounts of reliable, steady energy, a new mental clarity, and a strong new body with muscles. For those things alone I'd keep on this diet for life.

But there were other surprises: My husband, just to be companionable, joined me on the low-carb diet and promptly lost the 30 pounds he'd slowly put on over the years. Our daughter, a wilderness instructor in her mid-twenties, had been unable to shake an extra 20 pounds despite careful low-fat eating and vigorous exercise. She was intrigued by our dramatic weight loss and tried a modified version of it herself by just cutting out obvious carbohydrates. At the end of a summer of turning away from bread, pasta, potatoes, and sugar, she found that the

20 pounds were gone. All of us, of course, have the insulin problem, and all of us will be on some form of the low-carb diet for the rest of our lives.

In the months that followed I watched other people go on the diet for entirely different reasons with equal success. One friend just wanted to lose a few pounds and have more energy; another wanted to recompose her body in the direction of muscles (a great side effect of the diet); another was a panicked, newly diagnosed diabetic. The broad health benefits of this way of eating continue to amaze me.

In the end, I learned the hard way (which may be the only way) that you have to trust your own instincts about your body. Despite my lack of results with it, I stayed with the low-fat program for far too long because it seemed the entire medical establishment insisted—and still does—that it is the only effective way to lose weight. If you stay tuned to yourself, and keep conscious about what you eat and how you feel, you'll begin to have a sense of what works for you. For me, this is hardest at wonderful dinners where the champagne and wine are flowing freely and after two glasses I simply don't care what I eat. But basically such temptations come up every day, and although my eating is almost automatic now, I still have to remember to watch the boundaries.

When you're trying to lose weight, it's a lot easier if the food on a given diet is very simple and not all that interesting; when you're maintaining your weight for life, though, if the food you're eating is boring, you almost certainly won't stay on the regimen. You can easily fall into a pattern of making boring meals. For instance, protein in the low-carb way of eating is so satisfying that sometimes it's hard to remember to make the side dishes and salads that put the meal together—but that gets tiresome, and such limited repasts will eventually send you off the diet. So make an effort to have regular meals.

Once I understood that I'd been given the tools to solve my weight problem——finally!——I realized that I was going to have to do some serious thinking about what to eat for the rest of my life. As a cookbook editor and author, I'd managed to make food the center of my professional life, as well as my personal life, and I was losing my favorite part, the carbohydrates. No more grits casseroles with jalapenos and cheese, no more wild mushroom risotto, no more pecan pies or chocolate hazelnut tortes or homemade bread or waffles. Granted, when you're dieting you assume you'll give up those things, but not forever. And you also assume you'll go off the diet——but not this one.

Instead, I'd entered an odd new world of food: sometimes I'd pretend I was a cavewoman browsing through the supermarket; anything I couldn't have dragged into my cave wouldn't make it into my cart. I was so used to dieting in general that things like carrots would just jump into the cart by themselves before I remembered they're a little pricey in carbs. But slowly I began to get it; I even found myself, as the editor of *Protein Power*, taking phone calls from strangers who wanted to know what to eat. Well, I'd say encouragingly, you could take that piece of fish and do this or that to it and serve it with some spinach that you'd tossed with butter and toasted sesame seeds and . . . Butter! They'd get excited all over again, and so would I——what a great diet!

That was all fine, but I knew I was going to have to come to terms with real low-carb life: sort out the various sweeteners, find some substitutes for the things we were all missing, see what I could do to make real food, delicious food, fit into this context. I wanted everything in one place: I could never remember things like how much the onions were costing me or whether a certain cracker had worked as bread crumbs last time I tried it. I was always meaning to spend a few hours cruising the specialty stores for seasonings that were carb bargains. And if I, with so many resources at my fingertips, had these problems, what about busy home cooks who had families to feed?

There would be holidays, and dinner parties, and houseguests for breakfast—you don't factor such things into your usual diet, but for your lifetime diet, you must.

In short, I needed this book, so I had to write it, since there was nothing like it on the market. With the help of my wonderful cook friends and a lot of research, I solved at least some of these problems. But in the same way everyone's cooking repertoire changes from year to year, so will our low-carb cooking, as we grow more comfortable with its limitations and more inventive in overcoming them. So I think of this as a primer on the subject—there's a great deal more to come, and I'm eagerly awaiting it.

It can be hard to defend the low-carb diet in the face of such overwhelming endorsement of the opposing low-fat diet on all sides. My kinder friends say things like, "Aren't you worried that you'll get cancer?" Am I worried that I'll get cancer because I don't eat sugar and starch? Well, no. In fact, there aren't extensive studies that compare the two diets, and there are unlikely to be any anytime soon. (See the Foreword, which recounts the latest science on the subject.) But a good general guideline is to trust your own bloodwork. While the low-fat diet isn't dangerous on its own, if you do have hyperinsulinemia, it could indeed be dangerous for you.

Finally, I know that everyone has to work out an indi-

vidual way of dealing with this or any diet—a version
that works for him or her. With its emphasis on real food
and its de-emphasis on ersatz starches and sugars, *The
Low-Carb Cookbook* reflects my way of dealing with it. Of
course, it's not the only way, but I hope that with these
recipes you'll always look forward to the next meal with
the joy of knowing you're going to eat well in all senses
of the word.

How We Got Here:
A Little History

> Be reassured, I shall map out a diet for you, and prove
> to you that there are still a few pleasures left for you
> here on this earth where we live to eat. . . . Shun any-
> thing made with flour, no matter in what form it hides;
> do you not still have the roast, the salad, the leafy veg-
> etables?
>
> —Jean Anthelme Brillat-Savarin, Meditation XXII on
> Obesity from *The Physiology of Taste*, 1825

You may be reading this book because you're already a successful low-carb dieter who needs help figuring out what to eat, or because you're thinking about taking the plunge. You may be unsure of the medical underpinnings of the low-carb approach, you may wonder how to choose among the various versions of the diet, you may think you'll never eat a good meal again—but read on; all of these questions have answers.

The very idea of a low-carbohydrate cookbook seems startling in this era of low-fat eating—which has necessarily meant low-protein as well, since meat, poultry, fish, eggs, and cheese, the major sources of protein, also contain fat. As we've struggled to follow the government's low-fat recommendations since 1988, we've actually increased our carbohydrate levels, consuming more pasta, grains, bread, beans, and fruit, just as prescribed by the model of the nutritional pyramid. Because there are only three basic elements of food—fat, protein, and carbohydrate—when one element is reduced, another must go up. In the case of the low-fat diet, since both protein and fat are down, the only alternative is for carbohydrates to take up the slack.

Although we don't think of them that way, the hundreds of low-fat cookbooks on the market are in effect *high*-carbohydrate cookbooks. While most people scarcely think about carbs at all, for those who do tend to gain weight and have the family constellation of hereditary health problems associated with obesity—heart disease, high blood pressure, diabetes—the sugars and starches that make up carbohydrates are a big part of the problem. For them, carbohydrates trigger excess insulin production, which initiates fat storage, vascular damage that can lead to heart disease, and high blood pressure. In addition, if the pancreas keeps frantically overproducing insulin to stabilize blood sugar in response to the presence of more and more carbohydrates, the insulin receptor cells can become exhausted, developing a state called insulin resistance. And insulin resistance can easily lead to Type II diabetes.

For people who have this underlying metabolic disorder, the low-fat prescription has been a disaster, not only because it doesn't work very well for weight loss, but also because it actually makes the associated health problems worse. Many dieters make the crucial mistake of regarding the low-carb diet (low-sugar, low-starch) as simply a quick fix for weight loss, and once the pounds are off they return to their old ways of eating—even to the recommended "healthy" low-fat diet. But they find that along with the pounds return the health problems, including a raised LDL or "bad" cholesterol level, a lowered HDL or "good" cholesterol level, and a dramatic increase in triglycerides, a dangerous blood fat thought to be predictive of heart disease.

Although the low-carb theory may seem new and radical and unproven, it's the basis of our ancient hunter-gatherer diet, and in fact has been the main approach to weight loss for well over a hundred years. The French gourmand Brillat-Savarin observed in 1825 what so many of us have noticed on our own: that certain people seem destined to be fat. The only way around this, he advised his readers, was to stop eating starch and sugar (he also distrusted eggs for some reason) and stick to protein, salad, and vegetables—especially radishes, asparagus, and celery (all extremely low-carb). He noted that one could eat very well on such a regimen—remember, he was a gourmand. He also recommended wearing a snug belt and drinking lots of water, ideas that have passed into contemporary diet lore.

In our own century, low-carb diets became popular in the 1960s and 1970s, featured in books like *The Stillman Diet*, *The Scarsdale Diet*, *The Drinking Man's Diet*, and of course, Dr. Atkins, the all-time bestseller. Though there are differences between them, these diets all restrict carbohydrates more or less drastically and emphasize protein (to maintain lean body mass) and fat. The diets were all wildly successful, partly because they were fun and satisfying and especially because they worked. (Some, in fact, are still in print.) They have a counterpart in England in the work of Dr. John Yudkin, a true pioneer in the field whose popular books on "slimming" were never published in this country. Yudkin's regimens were based not on hard science (because no one understood why they worked) but on Brillat-Savarin's system—simple observation. For

years it was a diet commonplace to eschew bread, potatoes, and dessert and stop worrying about calories.

In the 1980s, around the time Dr. Dean Ornish began
to publish his work on heart disease and the minimal-fat
diet, however, the thinking moved in a new direction.
Protein and fat became suspect, and the low-carb diets
were seen as dangerous—bad for the kidneys and bad for
the blood vessels. Though there are now plenty of studies to refute these allegations (see the Foreword), the
low-carb diets fell into disfavor and the low-fat regimen
won the official endorsement of the government, not to
mention the media. Suddenly there were "bad" foods that
could kill you—eggs, butter, red meat—and forget the
salt. When cholesterol hysteria hit hard, we chose margarine. Entire industries sprang up around these dietary
principles, and some extraordinary careers were made
touting them. But little by little the program has begun to
fall apart.

In the spring of 1996 Dr. Walter Willett of Harvard,
a leading researcher in the field, remarked at the Second
International Conference on Fats and Oil Consumption in
Health and Disease that it was time for the scientific com-
munity to acknowledge that the results of the low-fat
prescription have been a disappointment. According to
the latest government statistics, for the first time, more
than half the American population is overweight, and extreme obesity has doubled in the last ten years—the era
of low-fat. Dr. Tim Byers of the University of Colorado
says, "It's been clear for several years that Americans are
getting fatter, and it's accelerating." Meanwhile, the
overemphasis on cholesterol has begun to be corrected,
and even the reputation of much-maligned eggs has been
rehabilitated—thanks to discoveries that they don't have

as much cholesterol as originally thought, and that most cholesterol is in fact made in the body itself, not ingested. The ratio of HDL to LDL has come to be seen as a much more important index of vascular health than the total cholesterol number, and the triglyceride level and its relative ratio to HDL looks as though it's going to be even more critical. Margarine has been revealed as not only a fake food, but a dangerous trans fat. Salt isn't much of an issue anymore, and even red meat has some positive benefits in its stearic acid content. But consider this: If it's true that 25 percent of the population has a metabolic problem with carbohydrates (which is just a guess on the part of the medical experts), that's an even larger percentage than the group that's salt-sensitive—and it's on their behalf that we were all supposed to stop using salt. Couldn't the government just as easily have recommended a low-carb diet for everyone to be sure that we were as protected as the salt-sensitive people?

Merely posing this question points up one of the great fallacies in making dietary policy: There isn't a single diet that's right for everyone. Legislating diet was simply an experiment that didn't work for one of the target groups in the population it was meant to address: the unhealthy overweight. While the low-fat diet works well for people with normal metabolisms who just eat a little too much and exercise not enough, it's been dramatically demonstrated that the rest of us need something else. And something else was waiting in the wings: the new generation of low-carb diet books.

Right at the epicenter of this group is the same old Dr. Atkins, much reviled by the medical establishment but much beloved by his desperate readers. Although he fell out of the media's sights in the eighties, his loyal readers continued to pass the word, and in 1996 his new book sold over a million copies. Hard on his heels came the Hellers, authors of *The Carbohydrate Addict's Diet*, *Healthy for Life*, and *The Carbohydrate Addict's Lifespan Program*. The Hellers focused on the addictive nature of carbs but tried to help their readers ingest as many carbs as possible in a scheme that gave over an hour a day to pleasurable eating of just about anything. In *Healthy for Life*, they drop the one-hour prescription but add more carbs in general for very slow weight loss, a system they recommend over Atkins's speedy results. Barry Sears's *The Zone* (and its sequel, *Mastering the Zone*), another stunning bestseller, isn't really geared for weight loss, but it does recommend cutting the carbs back and balancing them with protein and fat intake to get into the optimum state of performance, both mental and physical. (Note: Despite the white coats on most of these book jackets, not all of these authors are real doctors with real patients. Look for the M.D. degree for reliable clinical experience.)

Finally there's *Protein Power* by Doctors Michael and Mary Dan Eades, who wrote the Foreword to this book. When the Eadeses discovered that the low-fat diet was not a success for their overweight patients, they returned to the literature to see if there might be a better approach. They were intrigued by the strong history of the low-carb approach and decided to try the regimen, first on themselves and then on their patients. The results were amazingly successful, but they were puzzled about why. Going back to their biochemistry textbooks, they figured out how it worked and why, which meant they could play a little with the parameters of the diet and give their readers more carbs—more healthy carbs, not more sugar and starch.

Essentially, say the Eadeses, all carbohydrates are basically sugar—that's what they're broken down into, and that's how the body receives them. For people with the metabolic disorder we've been talking about—hyperinsulinemia or Syndrome X—*any* form of sugar, whether it's a candy bar or rice, triggers an outpouring of insulin, the master hormone without which no fat is stored. The more carbs you eat, especially simple sugars, the more insulin pours into your bloodstream, and the more fat you store (assuming you have consumed more calories than you've burned). Through some very elaborate mechanisms explained in *Protein Power*, excess insulin initiates a cascade of health problems: you make more triglycerides, more bad cholesterol, have higher blood pressure—and you're likelier to develop gout and diabetes. As the Eadeses point out in their book, the diet the government wants you to follow gives your body a full two cups of sugar a day to handle—fine if you don't have the genetic tendency to the insulin problem, but a true disaster if you do.

How do you know if you're a candidate for this diet? Your family history is a good guide: If obesity, heart disease, diabetes, gout, and high blood pressure run in your family, there's an excellent chance you have this problem. If you are overweight and can't overcome it with a simple diet and exercise program, this is probably the reason why. You can have your fasting insulin level tested; anything above 10 is abnormal for men and most women, though some women test normal despite having hyperinsulinemia. According to the Eadeses, a high triglyceride level all by itself is almost enough to diagnose hyperinsulinemia.

But try Brillat-Savarin's idea: Just observe yourself. Do you crave sweets? Once you start eating bread, or pasta, or dessert, is it hard to stop? Do you actually feel better, free from cravings and energy swings, when you cut the carbs back? (Give yourself a week to test this, since it will take you several days to start producing the right enzymes to digest your new diet.) Remember, if this is in fact your problem, it's a health problem as well as a weight problem, and it's important to address it for the long term, not just as a quick weight-loss scheme. Diet is the *only* way you can control your insulin output, and it's amazingly effective.

It's always a good idea to see your doctor before you start on *any* regimen—and in this case there's a real bonus, since you can compare your bloodwork before and after and see for yourself what an excellent favor you've done your health. Many a skeptical doctor, including mine, has been won over by the amazing results. If you're taking any medication it's *essential* to check with your doctor, since this diet has such profound effects it can play havoc with your medications.

As Dr. Atkins explains, there are many gradations of insulin sensitivity within the hyperinsulinemia population—some people do very well with cutting carbs back just a little once they've reached their ideal weight; for others, carbs will always have to be kept at a bare minimum for life. The only person who can figure this out is you: Once you reach your goal weight, you'll have to increase the carbs bit by bit—5 grams a week, and then hold for a week—and see how you feel. When the scale begins to drift upward, you'll know exactly what your level is, and that's where you should try to stay for life.

If you have more than 15 pounds to lose, it's a good idea to read one of these diet books, choosing the program that seems to make the most sense to you. (See the box on Sorting Out the Low-Carb Gurus, page 17.) Then you'll have a program to follow and answers to your many questions, which will make the diet much easier to live with for months. You can fit most of the recipes in this book into your program—just check the level of protein, fat, and carbohydrates you require and look for the recipes that match it.

In the same way that low-fat has become a lifestyle choice, low-carb eating will take its place as the diet of choice for those of us with a metabolic problem, because it's essential for our continued good health as well as weight control. Although most of the recipes in this cookbook work perfectly well for the quick-fix weight-loss plans of the low-carb diet books, they're really designed for the long haul, on the assumption that if you're seriously concerned about your health and your weight, you'll need to watch the carbs for the rest of your life. But you'll also need to be able to entertain, to serve holiday meals, to move easily from one season to the next, taking advantage of farm-fresh produce. You'll need to know how to stock your pantry in this new and unfamiliar way of looking at the kitchen. And you'll probably prefer to avoid eating bizarre diet versions of familiar foods. Because I'm a cookbook editor and author myself, it's very important to me to eat well, and to serve food that's as much like traditional good food as possible while staying within the diet guidelines. That's my mission here: simple food, real food that works to solve some of the problems of cutting back the carbs.

Does taking the low-carb leap mean you'll never eat another doughnut, another plate of pasta, another slice of your own birthday cake? Of course not—life is too cruel, and these foods are too wonderful to forswear them entirely. A little treat every now and then works wonders (but *only* every now and then), and a special occasion becomes truly special when it involves an indulgence. Once your insulin is well under control, you'll probably notice

Sorting Out the Low-Carb Gurus

All the popular low-carb diet programs agree that excess insulin production is the real problem in weight gain, and they all take a low-carb approach to controlling it, but there are lots of differences in the diets themselves. Here are some of the significant ones, plus their ideas on how to divvy up the three major elements of food: protein, fat, and carbohydrate. It's useful for comparison to remember that the average American diet contains at least 300 grams of carbohydrate a day, and the government's food pyramid recommends even more. Do calories count? Not in these schemes, but if you're having trouble losing weight, you may also need to cut back the total calories, which usually means cutting back the fat. The diets have in common a stricter phase for weight loss and a more generous one for weight maintenance.

- Robert C. Atkins, M.D., Dr. Atkins' New Diet Revolution (M. Evans, 1992). Dr. Atkins is the grand old man of low-carb dieting. His millions of readers have been losing weight on this restricted diet for decades. Dr. Atkins insists his patients go into ketosis, a state reached by extreme carb restriction in which ketones—a product of fat breakdown—are produced in abundance. The diet has two phases: induction (15 grams of carbohydrate per day for 2 weeks), followed by a gradual increase of not more than 5 grams per week until maintenance level is reached (i.e., the level of ideal weight). For most people, that's between 25 (below diet level for Protein Power) and 90 carb grams per day, or less than a third of the average American diet. You can have all the protein and fat you want and almost all the macadamia nuts you can afford, but Atkins never allows sugar or starches like potatoes and pasta. He also frowns on alcohol.

• Michael R. Eades, M.D. and Mary Dan Eades, M.D., Protein Power (Bantam Books, 1996). The Doctors Eades key protein requirements to individual needs in a formula explained in their book. More lean protein is okay; less is not. The intensive weight-loss phase is restricted to 30 grams of carbohydrate per day. (Because the Eadeses calculate the carbs by subtracting the metabolically inactive fiber content of food, their carb allowance is actually quite a bit more generous than Atkins's.) For a long-term diet, the carbs go up to 40 per day after the first three or four weeks. The Eadeses don't worry about fat, except for unhealthy trans fats, and warn that too much rich cheese will stop weight loss. At ideal weight, dieters proceed 5 carb grams per week until they reach the magic number where weight is maintained. Although the doctors acknowledge that some carbs like flour and fructose have more dramatic effects on insulin than others, they basically see all carbs as essentially sugar. They allow small amounts of actual sugar and starch as long as they're accounted for in the carb budget. Their way of counting carbs steers dieters toward fiber-rich, vitamin-loaded vegetables and fruits.

• Rachel F. Heller, Ph.D., and Richard F. Heller, Ph.D., Healthy for Life (Dutton, 1995), The Car-

bohydrate Addict's Diet (Signet, 1993) and The
Carbohydrate Addict's Lifespan Program (Dutton,
1996). He's a pathologist, she's a therapist. The
Hellers' first book was a huge amount of fun: as long
as you restricted your carbs in the other two meals
of the day, you could eat whatever you wanted for
dinner, even many desserts, as long as you ate it all
within an hour. The strategy was to avoid extra insulin production, which would occur at exactly 1
hour 15 minutes after eating began. That approach
has been dropped in Healthy for Life, which lets you
have only one quarter of your day's carbs for dinner.
But the Hellers still feel that high-carbohydrate
foods such as fruit juice and pasta are valuable "for
essential balance" and should constitute at least 50
percent of the diet once you're beyond initial weight
loss. This makes for very slow weight loss, if any, but
the Hellers think that's sounder in the end. They feel
it's unwise to lose more than 1½ pounds a week.
Their program has three different levels of weight
loss with a lot of options and add-ons. The Hellers
are against alcohol and caffeine on the grounds that
they raise insulin levels.

- Barry Sears, Ph.D., with Bill Lawren, The Zone
(Regan Books, 1995), and Mastering the Zone
(Regan Books, 1997). This long-lived bestseller (and
its how-to successor) is based on Sears's expertise in
drug delivery. He's figured out how to use food as a
drug to manipulate the hormonal system into producing optimal performance, both mental and physical—a state he calls "the zone." Elite athletes who

use his program swear by it. Although it's not designed for weight loss, this system does often reduce weight because the protein levels are higher and the carb and fat levels lower than the standard American diet. Of all these diets, Sears's is closest to the standard low-fat nutritional advice, but the establishment doesn't like his program any more than the others.

Sears insists that everyone has an exact individual protein requirement—no more, no less—that must be met every day and matched with carbohydrates, eaten together in a system of blocks. Monounsaturated fats form the rest of the diet. In terms of calories, it's 40 percent from carbs, 30 percent each from protein and fat. If you're very small, this way of eating will leave you with very few calories; if you're very large, it will leave you with too many carbohydrates, which will keep you large. If you have a lot of weight to lose, this may be too many carbs for you.

• Oddly enough, all these diets aren't drastically different from the old Overeaters Anonymous diet (OA no longer has a diet), which has been around for years (its fruit-for-breakfast prescription would seem to fit the hypothesis that insulin is better able to handle carbs in the morning):

Breakfast: 1 fruit, 4 ounces of protein
Lunch: 2 cups of vegetables, 4 ounces of protein
Dinner: 3 cups of vegetables, 4 ounces of protein

that an occasional piece of cake——once or twice a month, say——has no effect whatsoever, possibly because you lack the enzymes to properly digest the sugar.

However, do not, under any circumstances, take a major holiday from your diet. I did this one Christmas for two weeks, thinking I'd just deal with the few pounds I gained later, and it would all be worth it. My weight loss stopped cold, and it took me six months of strict dieting to get back to where I was, never mind to get the momentum going again. Your body has a built-in survival mechanism that actually promotes fat storage once you've come off a diet, and it's frighteningly effective.

So stay conscious, watch the scale, and remember: You're doing this for your good health as well as to lose weight, so you don't want to sabotage all your hard work. A weekend is about the maximum debauchery you can easily handle——just jump right back on a strict version of the diet, consuming as few carbs as you can manage, until you lose the extra weight. And even that will be hard; the Hellers are right, for people with insulin problems, carbohydrates really are addictive.

But the good news is that this diet is a snap to follow, because the terrible cravings for food, especially sweet and starchy food, disappear quickly. You'll have an amazing take-it-or-leave-it-alone attitude about food, you'll drop all the anxiety and guilt and shame you may have felt about it, and you'll feel so good and so energized that sticking with it seems a very minimal price to pay.

The Nitty-Gritty on Carbs

ᛟ

Starting Out:
What *Is* a Carbohydrate?
And What *Do* You Eat?

A carbohydrate is one of the three basic food elements (the other two being protein and fat), and it's composed of carbon, hydrogen, and oxygen. But essentially it's sugar, and that's how your body processes it, which is where the insulin problem comes in. As the *Oxford American Dictionary* notes in its "carbohydrate" entry, carbs are "considered to be fattening." It's easy enough to get rid of the obvious sweets when you're dieting, but carbohydrates also lurk in starchy foods like potatoes, pasta, bread, grains, popcorn, pretzels, beans, and bananas—not to mention raisins, yogurt, and many other surprising places. In the low-fat era, these foods have been extolled as the healthiest, and as we've noted, they're fine for people who don't have an insulin problem. But for those of us who do, they're always going to be a problem that we need to control. And in terms of nutrition, they come close to being high-class junk food. The nutritious part of the potato is not the starchy white but the skin—and that you can have (see page 306). The zucchini pasta on page 278 has many more nutrients than plain old white-flour pasta.

A rule of thumb is to ditch the whites in your diet—potatoes, pasta, bread—and go for the greens and reds: virtually anything green, plus tomatoes and red peppers. Sugar is completely out, except for tiny amounts that make a big difference in desserts. In this new way of eating, protein, whether it's meat, fish, eggs, poultry, cheese, or tofu, is the heart of your meal, accompanied by vegetables and perhaps fruit. (See the chapter titled "Your New Best Friends.") And yes, you get to have fat—good fats from nuts, seeds, butter, and oils, even cheese. (If you're trying to lose weight, though, too much fat will sabotage your efforts.)

But once you get beyond the delirious joy of having steak and brie all the time, how do you ease into this diet as a way of life? That's what this book is all about—how to stock your pantry, how to deal with holidays and entertaining, how to satisfy your cravings beyond sweets. (These will disappear in a matter of days or weeks—I promise—but until they do you may find yourself hovering over bowls of sugar-free gelatin.)

Does It Matter When You Eat These Carbs?

The Hellers' *Carbohydrate Addict's Diet* suggests eating anything you like for dinner, as long as you eat it within one hour, so your insulin doesn't get overstimulated. My own experience is that their approach doesn't work for weight loss, though it's an interesting way to indulge without paying the piper too much. (Since the Hellers dropped the idea in their latest book, *Healthy for Life*, they've probably come to the same conclusion.) A much better bet is to eat your major carbs for breakfast, as the Eadeses advise, because that's when your insulin is most sensitive, and you won't be launching the craving and bingeing cycle you'd get later in the day. Try this for yourself: See if you can have a banana, say, for breakfast without sabotaging your weight. Otherwise, spread the carbs as evenly as you can throughout the day.

Getting Back What You're Missing

The low-carb way of eating is so inherently satisfying that it may take a while before you realize you're missing anything. You may even forget to eat the vegetables and the occasional fruit, which you do need for both their vitamins and their fiber. But sooner or later you're going to miss one or all of the following textures and tastes. Here's what to do about those cravings:

Crispy

This may be the favorite American food characteristic, the reason we love French fries and chips and deep-fried everything. Everyone else in the world loves it too, but we love it more.

- Have just a little: A few potato chips contain only a few carbs; get a tiny package of Cape Cods for 10 carbs.

- If you don't think you can control yourself, try pork rinds. They're practically all protein, not fat as you might think, and you can eat a lot of

If the Diet Isn't Working for You

Everyone hits plateaus, but if from the very beginning you don't feel good eating fewer carbs and more protein, chances are it's because you're sensitive to arachidonic acid—a subject discussed in both <u>Protein Power</u> and <u>The Zone</u>. This substance is found in red meat and eggs. If you're sensitive to it, arachidonic acid can make you feel lousy. If that's the case, you have two choices: Either drop red meat and eggs from your diet and see what happens, or add three to four 1000 mg capsules of cholesterol-free EPA oils with each meal when you consume those foods. The EPA solution is such a good fix that you'll feel better within 15 minutes.

Another possibility: your blood type may be a crucial metabolic factor. Get a copy of Dr. Peter D'Adamo's <u>Eat Right for Your Type</u> (Putnam) and check it out. The diet for type O is low-carb. According to D'Adamo, each blood type has different diet and exercise requirements for optimum health. If you're Type O, though, you're on the right diet: Os are the oldest blood type, and they flourish on a low-carb hunter-gatherer diet. We Os may just be less evolved than the newer blood types, who've adapted to the "new" agricultural diet (just 8,000 years old, a mere blip in human history).

them for no carbs at all. This is the choice for the freakout binge.

- For an elegant crisp, try the frico, page 130, for almost no carbs. Good as these are, they're selfcontrolling—you can't eat an endless amount of them.

- Corn crisps, page 131.

- Nuts: Try one of the roasted nut recipes in the Appetizers chapter.

- Make some fried chicken with a pork rind crust—incredibly crunchy.

- Sizzle a few croutons in olive oil and scatter them over a salad for the crunch factor and just a couple of extra carbs.

- Sizzle a few croutons in some melted butter and stir them into your scrambled eggs.

Creamy

If you find yourself missing mashed potatoes see potatoes, below. Creamy in general isn't such a big problem, since you can actually have cream, though mainly for dessert.

- Vegetable purées with cream: Cauliflower, broccoli, and creamed spinach head the list.

- Quiche and frittatas: Although these usually form the main course, a little sliver of either can be served along with dinner as a creamy accent.

- Avocados: Whether they're stuffed with, say, shrimp salad, or just sliced as part of a salad or mashed into guacamole, these highly nutritious tropical treats are luxuriously creamy.

- Coconut milk: Unsweetened canned coconut milk is a good thing to keep on hand for making instant Thai curry sauces, drinks, and ice cream.

Potatoes

At a restaurant you can always snatch a few French fries off a friend's plate to get your fix. Beyond that, try substituting cauliflower for potatoes—an amazing impostor. And try small, pointy-tipped sweet potatoes, with their skins left on, which are much lower in carbs than you'd think—about 13 grams.

- Real baked potatoes: Eat just the skin and a little of the white (see page 293). These are unbelievably good and satisfying. You won't miss potatoes anymore.

- Cauliflower purée: You can hardly believe you're not having mashed potatoes. Page 302.

- Cauliflower vichysoisse: No one will guess you're not serving potato soup. Page 107.

- Cauliflower potato salad: Another completely satisfying masquerade. Page 122.

Bread

This one's tough. Again, the cravings leave quickly. A bite of bread out of the basket at the restaurant may be all you need to remember that it really wasn't all that wonderful. Although low-carb diet program books are full of ersatz bread recipes, and supermarkets carry low-carb breads, I find them all distinctly unappealing. Much better to buy a loaf of multi-grain bread—such as Ezekiel bread from the natural foods store freezer, 12 g carbs—and have only a slice or two for breakfast.

The fat-free whole wheat tortillas from La Tortilla Factory (see Sources) are great with eggs or as a sandwich wrapper—just 3 carb grams.

Pasta

Now that pasta's become our national dish, abandoning it is especially hard. Save it for your birthday, and have the best imported Italian pasta you can get your hands on. Low-carb noodles are surely on the way, but until they get here, you'll need to make do with squash and greens.

- ◆ Zucchini pasta: This is pretty delicious, and faster than actual pasta. Page 267.

- ◆ Spaghetti squash: Use the basic recipe, page 311, and toss with pesto sauce.

- ◆ Lasagne: Make your favorite lasagne recipe substituting savoy cabbage leaves or chard for the noodles. Just dunk the leaves in boiling water for 30 seconds, then in ice water to make them flexible. Dry them well before using and be sure to butter or oil the lasagne dish so the leaves won't stick, then proceed as usual.

Understanding the Tradeoff System

Once you figure out what your carbohydrate level is—which will depend on which diet system you're using, or your own careful monitoring to see what works for you (i.e., how your carb intake affects the scale)—you can work the specifics of your diet out any way you want to, as long as you're getting enough protein, fiber, and vitamins, or supplementing them. Remember, the carbs are all basically sugar, so these count as treats, even though they don't seem like treats.

If you'd die for a plate of risotto, have a little, and confine the rest of your meal to protein and salad. For any in-

dulgence, just figure out the carbs involved and how to incorporate them into your regimen. A glass of wine may
mean much more to you than some peanuts, so drink it
and plan accordingly.

My own system of tradeoffs turned out to be something of a surprise: I assumed I'd be saving up for bread
or pasta or sweets, but in fact I save my carbs for seasonal
fruit and vegetables. When corn season hits I'm in agony,
but I figured out that I can have two ears of corn on week-
ends if I have them for breakfast with some ham or
sausage. When crisp, tart apples are in the farmers' market, that's my treat; it's cherries in early summer; apricots
when they're great; pears when it's their moment. I love
these things so much that I'm willing to have just salmon
and salad or some other spartan meal so I can really enjoy
them. Other times when a craving hits, I have to have a
handful of chocolate-covered coffee beans after dinner.

To make tradeoffs work smoothly, you have to be conscious of what you're eating, and you need to have a good
idea of how many carbs are in your favorite foods—which
means you need a good carb-counting book (such as
Corinne T. Netzer's) that also lists fiber counts, since you
can subtract those grams from the total carb count. Of
course, you can go on automatic pilot and cut out almost
all the carbs, but that's a harsh and not very healthy way
to live over the long term. And once you get the hang of
it, this is one of the easiest regimens in the world to stay
on—easy to figure out and easy to live with. As your
hair and skin improve dramatically, your energy burns
evenly and reliably, you're no longer at the mercy of
food, your body begins to recompose, and your face re-
gains the flattering tiny muscles it lost over the years of
dieting, you will have every reason to keep eating this
way, and you will.

Hitting the Wall:
The Dreaded Plateau

All diets have plateaus, even the astonishingly effective
low-carb diet. The usual advice to up the exercise and cut
back on the treats is the first line of defense, but when
that doesn't work, you need more help. Here are some
possibilities.

- Check your actual carb level. Write down every
  morsel that goes into your mouth and check it on the
  charts. If you drink a lot of coffee, for instance, you
  could be adding some surprise carbs—a cup has only
  .8 grams (these are beans, remember), but if you
  have six cups a day you're getting almost 5 grams of
  carb, plus whatever you add to lighten it. If you're
  heavily invested in artificial sweeteners, it may come
  as a shock to learn that they all contain a little
  sugar—fractionally less than a gram per packet,
  true, but if you have a lot of them in a day it adds up.
  You may think those little pink and blue packages
  are free, and they are, in moderation, but if you're
  overdoing it you could be sabotaging your diet.

- Consider cutting out all artificial sweeteners, especially if you're drinking a lot of diet soda. There's a
  possibility that for extremely sensitive people even
  the sensation of sweetness can trigger a release of
  insulin—the same way that some people think that
  merely stepping into a bakery makes them gain
  weight. It may be true, in the sense that the antici-
  pation excites an insulin release.

- Check your thyroid. Low thyroid and insulin problems are old comrades, and they could be ganging up on you.

My very slow rate of weight loss speeded up once my deficiency was corrected. I discovered this myself, though my famous low-fat doctor had earlier diagnosed a goiter—but told me I didn't need to take thyroid if I didn't want to. Since I was completely clueless at the time, I decided not to. But thyroid deficiency is a very serious problem that often accompanies the metabolic disorder of hyperinsulinemia; it has a role to play in preventing heart disease, infertility, and a number of other serious conditions as well. And if you go on a low-carb regimen, you'll be requiring even more thyroid from your body just to deal with the extra protein, so you can easily become deficient.

You can check thyroid deficiency yourself using the Barnes Basal Temperature Method: for four consecutive days, before you get out of bed in the morning, put a glass thermometer under your armpit for 10 minutes (shifting hormones can skew the reading, so women should do this beginning the second day of their period). Anything below 98.2 is low. For further information, call or write the Broda Barnes Foundation (see Sources), a nonprofit organization that works with physicians and patients to further the work of Dr. Broda Barnes and other pioneers in the field of hormone research. According to Dr. Barnes, if you have red hair, you're by definition low-thyroid (due to a missing chromosome).

- Consider adding some supplements: Atkins recommends CoQ10 at the 100 mg level (also good for your heart and your gums, and widely used in Japan). If you've been off your diet recently, you may need to take chromium picolinate to curb cravings or take a more effective kind of chromium, such as Ultra-Chrome.

- The jump start: Sometimes when nothing will budge, a radically different diet will help. The low-carb gurus focus on a single food group for these adventures in metabolic chaos. Atkins has a Fat Fast—at its most basic, it involves eating only five handfuls of macadamia nuts throughout the day (about 1,000 calories) and nothing else—but warns not to do it for more than five days. Atkins also likes the Fruit Fast: eating nothing but fruit for a few days, especially if you've been feeling fruit-deprived. You'll probably gain a little weight, but you may satisfy your longing for fruit and shake things up when you go back on the diet. The Eadeses like a lean protein fast: Try eating just tofu and salad for a couple of days—again, this will be less than 1,000 calories.

- Drink more water. The more you drink, the more you'll lose. You may think you'll spend your life in the bathroom, but not so, says Phoenix diet-doctor Donald Peterson; the body adjusts after a couple of weeks.

- If all else fails, just hang in there. Eventually you'll start to lose again, and in the meantime you're getting all the health benefits of the low-carb diet, so don't worry too much about it.

The Sweet Question

This is perhaps the most vexing issue in low-carb cooking. Sugar is clearly out of the question, except in very small amounts, and none of the alternatives is entirely satisfactory, with the exception of SPLENDA® Low-Calorie Sweetener—a mix of dextrose, maltodextrin, and sucralose sold in Canada but not yet approved by the F.D.A. for sale in the U.S. Sucralose is made from sugar, modified so that it isn't absorbed by the body, and this slightly fluffy sweetener performs nearly the same way in the kitchen that sugar does, although it doesn't caramelize and does make chewy meringues. There's no bitter aftertaste and no known side effects, so there are no restrictions on its use in countries where it's approved, even for pregnant women. It's legal to bring in Splenda for your own personal use or have it sent in by a friend for your own use—just have it labeled "sweets." A packet of Splenda is equal to 2 teaspoons of sugar and has 1 carb gram. It also comes in bulk form; it's used and measured like sugar. All of the sweet recipes in this book have been tested with Splenda as well as aspartame, and it's definitely the preferred choice, if you can get it. If you have questions—not about availability, which is beyond their control—call McNeil Specialty Products Company, the producer, at 908-524-6336. The FDA has been looking at sucralose for more than six years, and they may approve it any day now. It's been in use in Canada and a number of other countries for more than seven years.

The number-two choice, if you can bear its bitter aftertaste (kindly described as licorice), is stevia *(stevia rebaudiana)*, a South American herb that's not approved for commercial use in food products but is available at the natural foods store. You can also grow your own. Stevia is a tender plant, a member of the daisy family that needs to be indoors in winter, and its leaves can simply be plucked and dried. Call the largest nursery in your area or mail order from Richter's (905-640-6677) or try Alice Doyle at Log House Plants, a commercial grower whose enthusiasm for stevia keeps her informed of other sources (541-942-2288). Stevia has had no complaints lodged against it with the FDA, and it passed a safety review with the Herb Research Foundation, who found no evidence of toxicity. Stevia's been used in soft drinks and elsewhere in the food supply in Japan since the 1970s with no ill effects.

Stevia is supposedly somewhere between 30 and 300 times as sweet as sugar, which is a somewhat meaningless rule of thumb. Unlike all the other ersatz sweeteners, it has no carbs. It comes in a green powder (which tastes more or less like pond scum), white powder (preferred), and dissolved in liquid, which can be very bitter. You can also buy dried leaves to make a sort of syrup: 1 teaspoon to a cup of water. It's best used in strongly flavored dishes, like cranberry sauce; in delicate desserts, such as custards, it can be far too intrusive. It's heat-stable to 400°, so it's also good for baking.

You can order powdered stevia from Body Ecology (1-800-4-STEVIA), which supplies a little kit to make it liquid; they also include recipes, but they're not low-carb.

A slightly more palatable powder comes from Stevita (see Sources).

Jean's Greens (518-239-8327) sells the dried leaves for about $1.00 an ounce.

Alice Doyle just breaks up a dried leaf of stevia into, say, lemonade, to sweeten it. She also has a freezer strawberry jam that's worth trying.

FREEZER STRAWBERRY JAM WITH STEVIA

1 pack no-sugar pectin (such as Kerr Fruit Pectin
    Lite)
2 tablespoons powdered stevia
1 cup cold water
5 cups sliced strawberries

Put the pectin, stevia, and water in a saucepan and stir
well while bringing to a boil over medium-high heat. Boil
the jam 1 minute, then add strawberries and freeze.

The next most palatable sweetener choice is aspartame, a blend of two amino acids that's packaged under
the Equal and NutraSweet brands. Aspartame has a chemical backtaste, but it's minimal. It doesn't perform well in
baking, especially if a dessert must stay in the oven for a
long time, and it won't caramelize or make meringues
easily. It makes rock-hard ice cream unless you add
gelatin. Aspartame is best added at the end of cooking,
when it has less chance to break down.

Although it has passed over 100 tests with the FDA,
who swear it's safe, there's been a recent groundswell of
paranoia about aspartame. If you're concerned, you can
easily access information by sending $1 to the Aspartame
Consumer Safety Network at Post Office Box 780634,
Dallas, Texas 75378. In some studies, it has caused brain
tumors in rats and is suspected of causing eye problems.
Because it's an excitotoxin, aspartame is also suspected of
causing brain damage, especially memory loss. It can de-
crease melatonin and serotonin, which some researchers
speculate may lead to increased cravings for, you guessed
it, sweets.

Aspartame has been used in this book as the lesser of

many evils just on the grounds of taste. If you're worried about the chemicals, swallow the bitter pill and use stevia. On the plus side for aspartame, it contains PEA, phenylethylamine, a natural amphetamine secreted in the brain during erotic arousal. (See *The Alchemy of Love and Lust*, by Theresa L. Crenshaw, M.D.)

Saccharine is still with us in the form of Sweet 'n Low, but it's strongly suspected of causing cancer and may be banned soon, as it has been for years in France and Germany. One teaspoon of saccharine replaces 1/4 cup of sugar and costs 5 carbs. Saccharine-fed lab animals get hungry and gain weight. Not a pleasant substance.

Moving right along, there's Sunette (Sweet One), which is stable for baking and tastes truly terrible. The chemical name is acesulfame potassium, and I don't recommend it.

You may believe, as so many nutritionists do, that natural sweeteners such as honey and maple syrup and rice syrup are big improvements over sugar, but they're all just sugar in the end, and they all have the same unfortunate effect in the body. Fructose, often touted as the best sugar, actually raises triglycerides, a dangerous marker in blood tests.

None of these substitutes manages to perform the same functions that sugar does in baking—which includes browning, and adding tenderness, texture, and volume. From both a taste and health perspective, you'd be best off avoiding sugar substitutes altogether, and that's the recommendation here. But human frailty being what it is, we all need a little something sweet from time to time, which means compromise, at least until Splenda gets the green light from the FDA. Or try mixing the various sweeteners to cancel out their drawbacks.

On the horizon is Alitame, 2000 times sweeter than

sugar, with no aftertaste. Alitame may be approved by the FDA in the next year or two—before the millennium—though it's been under review since 1986, an amazingly long time. Meanwhile it's approved in other countries such as Australia, China, and Mexico. Alitame is not totally heat-stable, and will first appear in food products before it's available to the home cook.

The Low-Carb Kitchen

If you haven't done so already, your first mission is to go through your cupboards, your refrigerator, and freezer and remove the following, many of which are staples of the low-fat diet world: rice cakes, popcorn, flour, grains, pasta, crackers, pretzels, powdered sugar, syrup, raisins, flavored yogurt, jams and jellies, and chocolate. Virtually anything labeled low-fat goes. Keep sugar around for your friends, and for your own use in minute amounts. Flour and cornmeal get used from time to time, but in very small measurements. A handful of rice or beans can be good in soups.

Crossovers from the old diet world—and there are precious few—are cottage cheese, celery, some other vegetables (but not carrots), and some fruits (but not bananas).

You'll be eating lots of grilled foods, salads, hearty soups and stews, stir-fries, vegetables, and—for special treats—fried foods and desserts. This food will be fresh, real food, uncomplicated and served with sauces, dressings, and marinades, which makes it important to keep a number of seasonings and condiments on hand.

The Pantry

Seasonings and Condiments

SALT: Number One is good salt—sea salt—both coarse and fine. You don't have to worry about salt on these regimens, and it plays such a big role in seasoning simple food (see Bringing Up Flavor, page 214) that it's worth the tiny investment to have good salt around. Best of all is Maldon salt from England, which has no additives. (Sea salt in the supermarket does contain them, but it's a good second choice.) Look for it in gourmet stores.

PEPPER: You need a peppermill, actually two—one for black pepper (Tellicherry peppercorns are especially good) and one for white. If you're not used to cooking with white pepper, try it; some cooks think it's more delicate than black, some think it's more assertive. It's absolutely delicious and different, and it adds another level of flavor to food.

PAPRIKA: Even regular supermarket paprika is useful and cheering in many dishes, but sweet Hungarian paprika is better yet.

CHILI: If you can get your hands on some good New Mexico chili powder (see Sources), by all means do so, and keep it in the freezer. If all you can get is the chili mix, get a good one, such as Gebhardt.

CHIPOTLE CHILE: A smoked jalapeño chile that will quickly become addictive. This comes three ways: dried, as powder, or canned in adobo paste. The canned chipotles should be rinsed and seeded, then spun into a paste in the food processor. The paste will keep for months tightly sealed in the refrigerator. Chipotles are great in mayonnaise and on grilled foods. A pinch of the powder on scrambled eggs is magical.

GREEN PEPPERCORNS: These are delicious with cream cheese on crackers. Look for the du Chef brand or Ets Moulin.

HOT PEPPER SAUCE: Essential for both meats and greens. Try Durkee's Red Hot or Crystal or good old Tabasco.

PICKAPEPPA SAUCE: The taste of Jamaica, and a great pick-me-up for almost any kind of protein for just 1 carb per teaspoon. Pickapeppa has lots of forbidden tastes—mangoes, raisins, tamarind, cane sugar—and it's especially great with ham. Make a little sauce with cream and Pickapeppa. It's also delicious spread over a block of good organic cream cheese, served with crackers.

SESAME SEEDS: Great for tossing on vegetables and salads, making a crust for fish, etc. You can buy Japanese toasted sesame seeds in a jar. Keep sesame seeds in the refrigerator; they turn rancid easily.

BACON BITS: There are several brands on the supermarket shelves. These are real bacon, not hydrolized protein, and they seem to keep forever. Good for tossing into egg salad, chef's salads, cooked greens, and scrambled eggs.

LIQUID SMOKE: Look for hickory smoke; this comes in a little bottle that will last the rest of your life.

CAPERS: Those in the know insist on salt-cured capers, which you can find at Italian specialty stores. They need a good rinse or a 15-minute soak to remove the extra salt. The salted capers last indefinitely. Otherwise look for Spanish nonpareil capers, the tiny ones in glass bottles.

ANCHOVIES: These are simply delicious if they're not too salty and aggressive-tasting. Look for the mild anchovies in glass jars from Sclafani, which are aged and don't need soaking in milk for 15 minutes to sweeten them, as other canned anchovies do. Keep them in the refrigerator. Or use anchovy paste in a tube.

SUN-DRIED TOMATOES: These give a lot of bang for their carb buck—just one piece of the oil-packed variety costs you about 1 carb. Sliver it and you have a lot of flavor.

HORSERADISH: This comes fresh in root form (well, around Christmas it does), but otherwise it's in the dairy case or in little jars on the supermarket shelf from Inglehoffer—endlessly useful. Cut away any green on fresh horseradish—it's bitter.

SOY SAUCE: Labels on the bottles claim it contains no carbs, but list wheat and soy on the ingredient list. Whatever the truth is, soy sauce is so useful for marinating steaks and other meats and fish and making stir-fries that it's hardly worth worrying about the phantom carbs. In Asian stores, look for mushroom soy to use in stir-fries.

OLIVE PASTE: Good for tucking into deviled eggs, adding to sautéed greens, spreading on salmon to be broiled, etc.

THAI RED CURRY PASTE: Added to canned unsweetened coconut milk, it makes a great curry sauce. Mae Ploy is a good brand. Just a little spoonful is all you need to enliven a stir-fry. Heat gently in oil for several minutes to bring out flavor.

MANGO FAT-FREE DRESSING & MARINADE: Made by Consorzio, this is a favorite condiment that delivers tropical taste and exuberant flourishes to a great variety of dishes from melon and prosciutto to coleslaw, for just 1 carb per teaspoon. Available at some supermarkets and Williams-Sonoma. A great secret ingredient.

CITRUS OILS: These come in lemon, lime, and orange under the Boyajian label (available at Williams-Sonoma and King Arthur Flour catalogue). They're intense and wonderful; use them by the drop. (Unfortunately, they don't come with a dropper, so just pick one up at the drugstore.) Start off with a sampler kit of all three flavors in small bottles. They save a lot of carbs in marinades, vinaigrettes, baking, and dozens of other uses. The same company makes a mint oil that's delicious in drinks.

CANDIED GINGER: Half-inch chunks are less than 3 carbs each. Good minced in or on ice cream.

ROASTED GARLIC PASTE: This staple of the low-fat kitchen has more carbs than you'd like if you use it generously—and roasting a whole head of garlic will leave you with too many cloves to use before they spoil. A better solution is to buy one of the pastes, like Consorzio's, and just use a little at a time for less than 1 carb per teaspoon. These are better with a little cream added; sometimes they develop an acrid bite, and the cream will smooth it out.

SWEET RED PEPPERS AND SWEET PEPPER SPREAD: Look for the Peloponnese brand, which contains no citric acid. The spread includes Greek sheep cheese, and it's delicious on grilled eggplant or crackers— less than 1 carb per tablespoon. Use the peppers in pepper soup or for antipasto.

CURRY POWDER: From eggs to chicken salad to soups and stews, curry powder is great to have on hand.

A mild, sweetly fragrant curry is the most useful—Ameer from Harrods in London is brilliant, but there are many others.

MAYONNAISE FLAVORED WITH DIJON MUSTARD: from Maille. Great for snacks and for punching up and smoothing a vinaigrette. Less than 1 carb per tablespoon. Or make your own by mixing mayonnaise (2 parts) with Dijon mustard (1 part).

DAVINCI SUGAR-FREE SYRUPS: These are the best I've found to date. They're actually meant for coffee and Italian soda drinks, but they work for fruit, pancakes, or almost anything that needs sweetening. You can even make snow cones with them. There are 18 sugar-free flavors, including interesting and odd ones like amaretto, buttered rum, Irish cream, and crème de menthe. Unfortunately, the chocolate is disappointing. You can find them in the coffee bar at your local Barnes and Noble superstore, or see Sources.

CRAB BOIL: These little sacks of intriguing spices are great for seasoning seafood, especially shrimp. Just drop them into a pot of boiling water along with a half lemon and some garlic and then add the seafood. Zatarain's is a good brand.

DRIED WILD MUSHROOMS: Best, and most expensive, are Italian porcini. You can either soak these and chop them before adding to soups and stews or just toss them in the food processor and grind them up into powder. If you soak them, save the liquid for soup; strain it first.

PAPPADUMS: Tamarind Tree's little 1½-inch disks of spicy lentil crisp—fry these in a little peanut oil, 2 for 1 carb gram, and a nice crunch.

Canned Goods

TUNA: A mainstay of the everyday low-carb diet. It's worth seeking out the best tuna on the market, Genova, from Italy, in the gold can. Genova is yellowtail tuna packed in olive oil, and is truly delicious. The brand is pricey as tuna goes (about 60 cents more per can), but not as protein sources go—and it's worth every penny. Genova is available in some supermarkets and specialty stores.

SARDINES: If you like sardines, they're also great for this diet. Best are the Norwegian brislings packed in olive oil and Sclafani's Portuguese sardines. These are good on Wasa crackers and they also make a good pâté, mashed with a little mayonnaise and lemon juice and a jolt of horseradish.

SALMON: Canned salmon varies from nearly inedible to quite delicious—price is a perfect index.

TOMATOES: Muir Glen organic tomatoes are the gold standard. The diced tomatoes, which have most of the bitter seeds already removed, are especially useful.

COCONUT MILK: The Thai unsweetened coconut milk in cans is a good alternative to the real thing. Good for ice cream and for making curry sauces. Store any leftovers in a glass jar in the refrigerator for up to 24 hours.

GREEN CHILES: Unless you live in chile country, canned whole chiles will be your only alternative. They're very low-carb, about 1 gram per chile, and they're good in chili con carne, eggs, and Southwestern-style stews. Ortega is a good brand.

PICKLES: Not sweet pickles, of course, which are very high in carbs, but dills and kosher pickles. Be sure to check the labels—you're looking for pickles that are a great carb bargain, about 1 carb per pickle.

JAMS AND JELLIES: You can find special dietetic versions of these in the supermarket, but I don't think they're very good. I'd rather poke around the shelves looking for a fruit-only spread and then have just a teaspoonful, which will run 3 to 4 carbs.

SYRUP: Another disappointment. The ersatz maple syrup from the Vermont label is the best of the breed, worth a try if you really crave maple.

MARINARA SAUCE: These run 12 to 14 carbs per ½ cup, but Rao's is only 4.

Shelf Items

SOY MILK: Good for making breakfast smoothies. Look for Pacific Wave or West Soy in natural foods stores. Nutrition counts vary, but what you want to avoid is sweetened soy milk, which is more common than you might think.

DRIED EGG WHITE: Just Whites brand, on the baking shelf at some supermakets, makes meringues and is a good emergency protein powder.

COCOA: Saco unsweetened cocoa is a carb bargain at 4 grams for 3 tablespoons.

HOT COCOA MIX: Carnation Fat-Free (but not the one with mini-marshmallows) is lowest in carbs. Add your own cream, and it's pretty good.

CROUTONS: Chatham Village brand is exemplary. These seem forbidden, but just a few will bring crunch to a salad or—sizzled in a little butter—scrambled eggs. Just 4 carbs for ¼ cup of croutons, which will be enough for two people.

PEANUT BUTTER: As long as you don't overdo it, you can have a lot of fun with peanut butter. Ordinary brands include dangerous trans fats and peanuts that are sometimes rancid, not to mention sugar. Look for a good unsweetened alternative like Arrowhead Mills or get your own fresh ground at the natural foods store. Or roast and grind your own, page 166.

ALMOND AND HAZELNUT BUTTERS: More delightful nut spreads. Roaster Fresh brand in natural foods stores is just 6 grams for 2 scant tablespoons.

WASA FIBER RYE OR SESAME CRACKERS: These should always be waiting on the shelf—at just 2 grams for a giant cracker that's also delicious, they're the obvious rafts for impromptu open-face sandwiches as well as the buttered base for smoked salmon. Grind up Wasas in the food processor for crispy toppings—mix them with a little grated Parmesan and a spoonful of wheat germ and drizzle melted butter on top.

HOUSE OF AULSEBROOKS: Crackers from New Zealand with pepper or sesame seeds. Very good, and just 3 carbs.

FIBER-RICH CRACKERS: These seem a little too good to be true; once you subtract the fiber grams, they have 0 carbs. On the other hand, they have a kind of horse-in-the-feed-bucket quality. For pig-out moods, they're a good choice. Both these and their clones, GG Crispbreads (1 carb) are unsalted, unfortunately.

PORK RINDS: The butt of many diet jokes, these are still pretty useful as snacks and comfort food when you need something crispy, or you just want something to dip into salsa. Pork rinds have been around at least since the Ming Dynasty (1358–1644) and the Chinese love them (avoid Chinese brands with added MSG). People think they're entirely made of fat, but they're almost entirely protein; check the label. You can crumble a good brand of pork rinds (see Sources) into stews and hearty soups, as the Mexicans do. In fact, if you live near or in a Mexican neighborhood, you can probably find fresh pork rinds, aka chicharrones. Pork rinds don't last forever on the shelf—check the labels for expiration dates.

CHOCOLATE-COVERED COFFEE BEANS: Lots of companies make these, but most don't give you a carb count. Starbucks does; their beans cost you a little over a gram of carb for 2 beans.

CHOCOLATE-COVERED ALMONDS: Trader Joe's on the East and West coasts makes a delicious cocoa-dusted version of these that's a little under 1.5 carbs each. A nice, slightly sweet finish to a meal.

PIZZELLE: These big Italian waffle cookies are crisp and satisfying, great-looking stuck in a dish of ice cream. Riko brand from Canada comes in anise and vanilla flavors and costs 4 carbs per big cookie. In supermarkets.

AMARETTINI: These are the miniature button versions of amaretti, the famous Italian cookies that come in the red tins. The babies have only 1 gram of carb for 3 little cookies. Good on their own or crumbled into fresh fruit compotes.

Flours

You might use a little regular flour from time to time but mostly you'll use Wondra, the instant flour, added by the teaspoon or tablespoon to thicken sauces and stews.

ALMOND AND HAZELNUT FLOURS: These slightly mealy flours are delicious and very useful in baking. The best is made by American Almond, distributed by King Arthur and by the Gluten-Free Pantry (see

Sources). It's worth calling American Almond to see if any of their other wonderful flours (such as peanut) are available to the consumer yet (see Sources). You can make your own if you have a flour mill (also from King Arthur); a food processor will produce oily nut butters, not flours. Refrigerate these flours, tightly sealed.

PEANUT FLOUR: Sometimes available in natural foods stores and African markets. Good for breading.

QUINOA FLOUR: Sometimes available in natural foods stores, this high-protein flour is tastier than soy flour for bread making—but still relatively high carb at just under 34g for ½ cup.

SOY FLOUR: I'm not a big fan of soy flour, and it doesn't figure in any of the recipes in this book—but for the record, it's 13.5 carbs for ½ cup. It tastes better if you toast it briefly in a skillet.

OAT FLOUR: This is delicious, and of course it has more carbs than we wish it did (24 grams per ½ cup). Still, if you have to bake something, it's a good alternative to white flour, which has twice as many carbs.

CHEESE POWDER: Available through King Arthur (see Sources), this product works like flour to bind elements together wherever cheese would work with the other flavors.

CORNMEAL: You'll need a little to make the corn crisp on page 131 and to enrich your chili. Get the best stone-ground cornmeal you can find and keep it in a glass jar in the freezer.

Fats and Oils

You'll just have to forget that these are the villains of the low-fat nutritional police. They're important for a number of reasons: if you don't have enough fat in your diet, you won't make enough hormones, your immune system will be compromised, your hair and skin will suffer, and you won't enjoy your food very much. Not all fats are good, certainly not margarine (which has been so manipulated that it's a dangerous trans fat), and not highly processed fats like solid vegetable shortening. Oils heated to the smoking point are damaged, as are oils that are fried more than twice even at the correct temperature. But pure oils like olive oil, nut oils, and even coconut oil (which isn't dangerous, media hype notwithstanding) are fine. And then there's lard, which has less cholesterol than butter. And finally there's butter.

BUTTER: This superb fat (see box) is just about irresistible, and there's no reason to resist. My choice is Plugra, a high-fat butter used by professional cooks, which doesn't need to be clarified for sautéing—just use it as it comes. Plugra is available at some supermarkets and specialty stores. Grab it when you see it and keep some in the freezer.

To clarify butter for sautéing: You'll be taking out the milk solids, the part that burns. To do this, melt unsalted butter slowly in a heavy pan over medium-low heat, or do it in the microwave. You definitely don't want the butter to boil. Skim off the foam at the top and carefully pour the clear yellow liquid into a clean jar, leaving the milk solids behind. You'll have about ¾ of what you started with. Store the clarified butter in a tightly sealed jar in the refrigerator; it will keep for many weeks. *To make ghee,* the nutty-tasting Indian clarified butter, keep cooking the butter until the milk solids turn golden. Strain the liquid through a coffee filter and store in the refrigerator.

OLIVE OIL: Rich in micronutrients and monounsaturated fat. Extra virgin is good for salads and vegetables; otherwise, regular old olive oil is fine. Spanish and Greek oils tend to be good bargains. Olive oil is excellent for frying, since it has a high smoking point and tastes delicious. For frying, use the cheapest olive oil.

FLAVORED OILS: These deliver some carby flavors with no extra carbs. Especially delicious are the line of roasted oils from Loriva, including sunflower, pumpkinseed, and walnut. Loriva's garlic oil is also excellent,

What's So Good About Butter?

According to Sally Fallon, author of <u>Nourishing Traditions</u> (ProMotion Publishing, 1995), a lot. Butter is a rich source of the essential fat-soluble vitamins A, D, and E, not easily found elsewhere in the diet in a simply assimilated form. Butter has a good supply of the X Factor, a catalyst that helps the body absorb minerals. Its short and medium-chain fatty acids are much less likely to cause fat storage than the long-chain acids in olive oil; they also have anti-microbial, anti-tumor, and immune system–supportive functions—especially 12-carbon lauric acid, which isn't found in other animal fats and is the one saturated fat the body doesn't make itself. Butter also contains conjugated linoleic acid, which has anti-cancer properties. It also supplies lecithin, which aids in the proper metabolism of cholesterol and other fats. On top of all that, it has a lot of trace minerals.

Why have we spent all these years eating margarine?

if pricey, and saves you the garlic carbs, which aren't insignificant. Or make your own no-carb garlic oil: Heat a clove of garlic, smashed, in a cup of olive oil until the first bubble appears. Remove the garlic and let the oil cool. Use it the same day or store it, tightly sealed, for up to 2 days in the refrigerator.

Fresh Food

You'll be eating a lot of truly fresh food in the form of seasonal produce, supplemented by a few frozen products. In the refrigerator at all times should be: celery, scallions (better carb bargains than storage onions), bell peppers, cabbage, cucumbers, citrus fruit (oranges, lemons, limes, but mainly for the zest—which you can peel and freeze). Herbs are wonderful for vegetables and salads; you can even make a whole salad out of mixed herbs if you have a garden. Sometimes when you're eating a lot of protein you crave something light and refreshing, and a lot of mint, parsley, and chives can do wonders to take a dish in that direction.

In the Refrigerator

MAYONNAISE: Hellmann's or Best Foods—no point in using Light. You can have an instant sauce, a marinade, a crunchy coating for chicken in seconds with this excellent product.

SOUR CREAM: A spoonful or two makes a big difference for very few carbs, and sour cream seems to have an inordinately long shelf life. Don't overheat sour cream or it will curdle.

CHEESE: Good cheeses for snacking are the relatively low-fat ones such as string cheese, mozzarella, and

Muenster. Parmesan, Cheddar, feta, and blue cheese are always useful. For treats, brie and cambozola and chèvre.

CREAM CHEESE: Exiled from the low-fat kitchen, cream cheese is back and welcome—all ready to be whipped into a cheesecake or spread on crackers with some interesting seasonings for a quick appetizer or snack. Whipped cream cheese is ready to spread, of course.

COTTAGE CHEESE: You want 2 percent or 4 percent-fat cottage cheese, which has fewer carbs. This can be breakfast or served on sliced tomatoes with lots of black pepper as lunch or a snack.

CREAM: It's up to you how much fat you want to use, but cream is luxurious and very useful. You'll quickly notice that half-and-half has many fewer carbs than the 1 percent or 2 percent milk you may be used to with your coffee.

NUTS: Forbidden though they are in most diets, nuts are welcomed in the low-carb world. You can't eat endless amounts of them, but you can have a few every day, and they're a reliable treat. They're also very good for you, full of essential nutrients such as calcium, phosphorus, magnesium, potassium, folacin, vitamin E, some of the Bs, and antioxidants. It may be because they have long roots reaching deep into the earth that they have such a motherlode of nutrients in their tiny packages. Macadamia nuts are lowest in carbs and high in the good fat, POA, palmitoleic acid, which some studies show helps the body metabolize fats and balance HDL and LDL cholesterol; it also helps break down the harmful fats surrounding the liver and heart.

Peanuts are, of course, in the bean family, not the nut clan, but they act like nuts and they have a very similar profile.

Know Your Onions

On low-calorie and low-fat diets, any kind of onion is virtually free, but in the low-carb world you pay a little price for their sweetness. Here's what it costs:

> chives: so low in carbs they're considered free
> garlic clove: 1 carb gram
> shallot: 3 carb grams
> onions: 5 carb grams per ½ cup
> scallions (green onions): 5 carb grams per cup
> leeks: 4 carb grams per ½ cup

If you're trying to lose weight, the carbs can add up. To flavor oil with garlic, use the trick on page 45 (see Flavored Oils), then discard the garlic. Chives are obviously the winners in this category, especially for salads and garnishes. Scallions are a good choice otherwise, but for flavoring a stew or other long-cooking dish, choose leeks, onions, or shallots.

If you store nuts properly—tightly sealed in the refrigerator—they'll keep from 9 months (pecans) to a year, so it's a good idea to find an excellent nut supplier and stock up (see Sources). You can also freeze them, especially macadamia nuts, but the texture suffers a bit.

To toast nuts: Put them on a baking sheet in a 350°F oven for 5 to 10 minutes, until they start to smell good.

To crisp pistachios that have been refrigerated: Put them on a baking sheet in a 200°F oven for 10 to 15 minutes, until they start to smell good.

To skin or not to skin: Don't buy skinned almonds; the skin protects them, and adds flavor and fiber. There's almost no point in skinning hazelnuts for the purposes of this book, but toasting them will make a big difference.

In the Freezer

FROZEN BERRIES, RHUBARB, AND GRAPES: You can provide these yourself when they're in season. Just freeze on a tray and store in tightly sealed bags.

SMOKED SALMON: For instant celebrations, just pull out the smoked salmon, defrost, and serve with Wasas, butter, and a little snipped dill.

BACON: Good bacon is one of the big treats on low-carb diets. The best I've found is Wright's Peppered Bacon from Vernon, Texas, and S. Edwards (see Sources). In the supermarket, Jones Country Bacon is good but a little salty. Microwave bacon to minimize the formation of dangerous nitrosamines—or eliminate them by buying nitrite-free bacon at the natural foods store.

SAUSAGE: Jimmy Dean and Jones and are two good brands to keep in the freezer.

VEGETABLES: Frozen spinach and other greens are your best bet.

OTHER FRUITS: Frozen unsweetened rhubarb, peaches, and melon balls are useful to have around.

TOFU: Freeze firm tofu right in the sealed carton for up to several months and defrost before using. The color will change to old ivory, but the texture just improves.

Equipment

You really don't need anything special, but a Benriner cutter or V-slicer is useful for making little vegetable shreds for salads, and a citrus zester for making elegant little ribbons of orange or lemon zest. A grill is endlessly useful for low-carb cooking, as is a smoker. Aficionados who are missing pasta may want to order the magical tool (almost $100) that turns vegetables into pasta from J. B. Prince Company (800-473-0577). An ice cream maker is a major convenience.

The Organic Question

A number of the low-carb fruits and vegetables—strawberries and broccoli, for instance—turn out to be on the list of those vulnerable to pesticide contamination. And of course the main protein sources—meat, dairy, and eggs—may harbor not only pesticide residues but also hormones and antibiotics. You can drive yourself crazy trying to sort out these issues, and the fact that the government doesn't have national standards to clarify what's what doesn't help. If you can afford to eat organic food, you probably should do so. If you can afford only some organic food, here are some suggestions.

My vote goes to strawberries, broccoli, potatoes (for their skins), and pumpkin. Veal and pork are not raised with hormones, so you don't have to worry about them for that reason. According to Dr. Samuel Epstein of the University of Chicago, the government has never tested a single animal for hormone levels so it has no idea what the actual levels are—but independent tests reveal levels 30 times the normal background levels for cattle. So beef may be the organic choice in the meat department, if you have just one.

Chickens are another story; free-range sounds wonderful, but in fact it means only that the chicken was able to stick its head out the door, not that it was frolicking on the farm. As long as chickens stop getting antibiotics and hormones two weeks before they meet their maker, they're certified as being raised without hormones or antibiotics. Small-farm chickens, in flocks of less than 20,000, have no regulation at all. So you might as well just choose a brand that consistently tastes good.

Remember that toxins like pesticides and excess hormones are stored in fat—if you cut off the visible fat, you'll be removing a lot of them. That's also a good reason to choose organic dairy products such as butter and cheese; as a rule, these also offer significant taste benefits.

NOTE: In this book, carbohydrates are counted as they are in Protein Power, which is minus the fiber content. This is a breakthrough, and in fact it's the way the government nutritionists understand carbohydrate composition: The fiber element is not metabolically active. This means you can eat much more of the fiber-rich carbs—vegetables, certain fruits, and high-density crackers and breads—which guides you toward naturally healthier choices and lets you enjoy a lot more carbs than more restricted programs.

In some cases, soy products particularly, there's disagreement among the authorities about what the actual carb content is. Don't worry about this too much; just go with what it says on the product you're buying.

Organic eggs are a relative bargain and much tastier than the generic product.

On Dr. Epstein's list of the Dirty Dozen most contaminated products in America in terms of known carcinogens, right up front are two brands of hot dogs: Oscar Meyer and Hebrew National.

As with everything else in the world of food, you'll have to consider the issues and make your own decisions. There are no easy answers, but there's also no reason to worry about all this excessively. Dropping sugar and junk food out of your diet will make a much bigger difference in your health than eating all-organic, however desirable that may be.

Appetizers

Of all the courses of a meal, this one offers the most variety to the low-carb gourmet. The traditional tidbits of nuts, cheese, olives, shrimp, crudités, etc., are all on our approved list. Even those on strict weight-loss diets can have a field day with appetizers, so it seems prudent to keep the carbs as low as possible here and spend them elsewhere in the meal, where they may be more useful.

To minimize the carbs, you may want to offer some cracker alternatives—with a rich pâté, for instance, a slice of daikon or French breakfast radish (or any radish that's not too bitter) makes a perfect base. Cucumber slices are good for lighter fare, such as fish. And radishes with soft sweet butter and a little bowl of sea salt to dip them in are simply terrific (but check to be sure they're not bitter). Cherry tomatoes scooped out with a melon baller and filled with something interesting like herbed goat cheese are always a hit, at about 1 carb gram each.

It may seem tempting to just put out the old cheese tray, but it really works much better to save it for the salad or dessert course—everyone will be too stuffed to eat dinner if they pig out on several kinds of cheese first. A little cheese is fine, of course, such as little balls of fresh mozzarella marinated in olive oil with garlic, parsley, hot pepper flakes, and salt and pepper (serve with toothpicks).

Nuts are also candidates for overconsumption; use one of the spiced nut recipes here, and your guests will be satisfied with just a few, not handful after handful.

As a good host, keep in mind that many of your guests will not only not be on your regimen, they'll be devotees of its polar opposite, the low-fat diet. Be sure you have enough elements that work for both regimens—crudités, for instance—so that everyone will feel comfortable.

ROASTED ALMONDS WITH
SOUTHWEST SPICES

Just a little hot, these are great with drinks. They'll keep a couple of weeks in a tightly sealed container.
MAKES 2½ CUPS, 10 SERVINGS

> 3 tablespoons olive oil
> 2½ cups almonds
> ½ teaspoon ground cumin
> ½ teaspoon chili powder
> Salt to taste

Per Serving: Protein: 6.7g   Fat: 21.7g   Carbohydrate: 3.2g

In a large skillet, heat the oil over medium heat, add the nuts, and sauté until they're golden, giving a stir from time to time. When they're golden, remove them with a slotted spoon to a bowl, then toss with the cumin, chili powder, and salt to taste. Spread on a baking sheet to dry.

ROSEMARY WALNUTS

This much-copied recipe seems to have first turned up in
The Pink Adobe Cookbook by Rosalea Murphy, where it's
made with butter. That's very good, but olive oil is even
better. MAKES 2 CUPS, 8 SERVINGS

> 2½ tablespoons extra-virgin olive oil
> 2 teaspoons crumbled dried rosemary
> 1 teaspoon salt
> ½ teaspoon ground red pepper (cayenne)
> 2 cups walnut halves

Per Serving: Protein: 7.6g   Fat: 22g   Carbohydrate: 2.2g

Preheat the oven to 350°F. Mix everything but the
walnuts together and toss the olive oil mixture with the
nuts to coat well. Scatter the nuts on a baking sheet and
roast for 10 minutes.

ROASTED PISTACHIOS WITH MACE
AND CINNAMON

Mace is the outer covering of nutmegs—a more delicate
version of the same spice. It's too fiddly to shell this many
pistachios yourself, so if you can't find shelled ones, just
skip it. MAKES 2½ CUPS, 10 SERVINGS

   2½ cups shelled pistachios
   1 teaspoon ground mace
   1 teaspoon cinnamon
   Salt to taste
   1 teaspoon sugar

Per Serving: Protein: 4.7g   Fat: 4.5g   Carbohydrate: 5.3g

In a large skillet over medium heat, heat the nuts—no
oil—until they're golden, stirring from time to time. It
will take about 5 minutes. Add the spices, sugar, and salt,
stir well to combine, and remove from the heat. Let the
nuts dry on a baking sheet.

GUACAMOLE WITH CAULIFLOWER

This dip-and-dipper combination may seem like a bizarre one, but in fact avocado and cauliflower are classic companions in Mexican cooking. Make the guacamole just before you serve it——or make it up to several hours ahead without adding the cilantro and tomato, cover it with a layer of plastic wrap directly on the surface, and refrigerate. Bring to room temperature before serving, stir, and add the final cilantro and tomato. Surround the guacamole with the cauliflower florets for dipping. SERVES 4

2 cups cauliflower florets

GUACAMOLE:

2 Hass avocados

2 tablespoons chopped onion

1 teaspoon coarse sea salt

1 serrano chile, seeded and minced

1 tablespoon chopped cilantro leaves

¼ cup diced tomato without seeds or diced
     radishes

Additional cilantro for decorating

Per Serving: Protein: 3.6g   Fat: 15g   Carbohydrate: 4.3g

The cauliflower: Drop the florets into a pan of boiling salted water and let cook for 3 minutes. Drain and let cool to room temperature.

The guacamole: Roughly mash the avocado in a bowl. Using the back of a fork in a small bowl, mash the onion with the salt until it begins to liquefy, then add the chile and chopped cilantro. Mix this into the avocado and taste for seasoning. Decorate with additional cilantro and tomato bits before serving with the cauliflower florets.

ISRAELI GUACAMOLE

The Israelis wisely add some protein to their avocado dip.
Serve this one with spears of Belgian endive for dipping.
(Cut out the bitter cores before you separate the leaves.)
If you can find some imported Italian tuna, that will be
the best; otherwise look for chunk light tuna. SERVES 8

　1 recipe guacamole, page 62, minus the cilantro
　1 (6-ounce) can tuna, drained and flaked
　3 Belgian endive

Per Serving: Protein: 8.2g   Fat: 18.7g   Carbohydrate: 4.1g

Mix the guacamole with the tuna and serve in a bowl
surrounded by spears of Belgian endive. Cut them off at
the base so they'll all be roughly the same size.

HAZELNUT CREAM CHEESE SPREAD

This is an interesting change from the common cream cheese spreads—and very useful to have on hand. Stuff celery with it, spread it on Wasa crackers, try it with smoked salmon. MAKES 1½ CUPS, ABOUT 12 SERVINGS

½ cup toasted hazelnuts (don't bother removing
   skins)
1 cup whipped cream cheese, at room temperature
1 teaspoon ground black pepper
½ teaspoon ground red pepper (cayenne)
2 tablespoons toasted sesame seeds, optional

Per Serving: Protein: 2g   Fat: 7.2g   Carbohydrate: 1.1g

Put the nuts in the food processor and chop—don't let them get too fine or you'll have hazelnut butter. Add the cream cheese and black and red pepper and beat until creamy. Chill for 2 hours to develop flavor. Remove from the refrigerator 1 hour before serving. Scatter sesame seeds over if you like.

Hazelnut Cream Cheese Spread in Cucumber Cups

Use a long hothouse cucumber and score it down the length of the skin with a fork to make skinny stripes. Cut crosswise into chunks at 1-inch intervals. Scoop out the center of each chunk. Fill the holes with the hazelnut spread, mounding it over the top. Sprinkle with toasted sesame seeds.

CUCUMBER DIP WITH CUMIN

Good for crudités when you can't stand to face another plate of them. SERVES 8

> 1 (8-ounce) package cream cheese, at room
>   temperature
> 2 tablespoons heavy cream
> ⅓ cup minced cucumber
> 1 tablespoon minced scallions
> ½ teaspoon salt
> ¼ teaspoon ground cumin

Per Serving: Protein: 3.5g   Fat: 7.5g   Carbohydrate: 1.2g

Mash the cream cheese with a fork until it's soft, then add the remaining ingredients and mix together well. Let stand for half an hour to develop flavor.

EGGPLANT AND PEPPER DIP

Known as ayvar (EYE-var) in the Balkans, where it's a
defining regional dish, this delectable dip appears in one
form or another all over the Middle East. This version,
which I learned from Margot Blair, is very easy and very
good; it may seem like the cumin is overkill, but it isn't.
And you'd swear it has garlic in it, but it doesn't.

Once you have this spread on hand, you'll think of
lots of uses for it beyond serving it as a dip (with endive
leaves or red pepper strips) or spreading it on Wasa
crackers or stirring it into scrambled eggs.

MAKES ABOUT 2 CUPS, 16 SERVINGS

    2 red bell peppers
    1 medium eggplant
    ⅓ cup olive oil or more to taste
    ½ teaspoon salt or more to taste
    1 tablespoon ground cumin or more to taste
    Optional additions: 1 tablespoon minced lemon zest
            with 1 teaspoon fresh lemon juice, 1 tablespoon
            chopped mint or basil, a shake of cinnamon

Per Serving: Protein: 0g   Fat: 4.6g   Carbohydrate: 2.4g

Preheat the oven to 350°F. Line a baking sheet (one
that has a small lip) with foil and put the vegetables on the
foil. Bake for 1 hour. Remove from the oven and let the
vegetables cool. Remove the stems from the vegetables
but not the seeds (adds fiber).

Put the oil in the workbowl of a food processor and
add the vegetables. Process until you have a rough purée,
adding more oil if necessary. Add the salt and cumin and
the other optional ingredients and blend well. Store in the
refrigerator for several days—it actually improves in flavor.

ENDIVE LEAVES WITH ROQUEFORT
AND WALNUTS

You can put all sorts of things in endive leaves and use them for dippers as well, but this particular combination of flavors is just right. SERVES 6

> 2 heads Belgian endive
> ½ pound Roquefort or Maytag blue cheese, at
>   room temperature
> ¼ cup heavy cream
> Ground black or white pepper
> 18 toasted walnut or pecan halves

Per Serving: Protein: 10.8g   Fat: 21g   Carbohydrate: 2.3g

Cut off the bases of the endive heads and separate them into leaves. Trim the leaves so that they're all more or less the same size. You should have 18 leaves.

In a small bowl, blend the cheese and cream together until they're nearly smooth. Mix in a grinding of pepper. Put a teaspoonful of the cheese on each leaf at the base and press in a walnut half on top. Arrange the leaves sunflower style on a round platter, with a mound of toasted nuts in the middle.

Endive Salad

Core and slice the endive and add other sharp lettuces like radicchio and watercress. Thin out the creamy cheese with a little apple cider vinegar to make a dressing, break up the nuts, and toss the whole thing into a gorgeous winter salad.

LIPTAUER

This utterly delicious cheese spread came from Hungary
to America, where it was often made with cottage cheese
instead of the traditional sheep's milk cheese. Goat cheese
works well too—try using chèvre, or a mix of chèvre
and cream cheese, or even all cream cheese. Serve the liptauer with vegetable dippers: trimmed radishes, scallions,
celery sticks, and sliced green bell pepper. SERVES 8

> 8 ounces chèvre, or half chèvre, half cream cheese,
>   at room temperature
> 8 tablespoons (1 stick) butter, at room
>   temperature
> 1 teaspoon sweet Hungarian paprika
> ½ teaspoon ground caraway seeds
> ½ teaspoon Dijon mustard
> ½ cup minced scallions
> ½ teaspoon anchovy paste

Per Serving: Protein: 5.4g   Fat: 17.2g   Carbohydrate: .7g

Mash the cheese together with the butter in a bowl,
using a fork. Add the remaining ingredients and mix to
combine well. Put the liptauer in a small crock or a bowl,
cover, and refrigerate for 4 hours or overnight to develop
flavor. Bring to room temperature before serving.

ASPARAGUS WITH ORANGE
AND PROSCIUTTO

Although asparagus is in the markets all year, it's worth
waiting for spring and the real thing to make these delectable spears wrapped in prosciutto. SERVES 8

½ cup whipped cream cheese
Minced zest of 1 orange
16 asparagus spears
8 prosciutto slices, chilled and cut in half
    lengthwise

Per Serving: Protein: 1.2g   Fat: 4g   Carbohydrate: 1.1g

Mix the cheese and the orange zest together in a small
bowl with a fork and set aside to develop flavor.

Snap the butts off the asparagus spears where they
break easily. In a large shallow pan or skillet, boil enough
water to cover the asparagus. Add salt to taste. Cook the
asparagus in the simmering water until just tender—
check every minute after 5 minutes. Using tongs, remove
the asparagus from the heat as soon as it's done and let it
drain on a kitchen towel. Let cool to room temperature.

Spread a thin smear of the orange cream cheese over
each prosciutto slice and wrap each one around an asparagus spear in a spiral fashion. Serve right away or chill
until ready to serve.

FRIED CHEESE ON GREENS

This may sound like the ultimate forbidden diet food, but of course it's fine on our diet. Instead of bread crumbs, we'll be using nuts, which are even more delicious.

SERVES 4

> ½ pound Gruyère, Monterey Jack, or fontina
>   cheese, in ½-inch-thick slices
> 1 large egg
> ½ teaspoon water
> ¾ cup finely chopped nuts—walnuts, almonds, or
>   pecans
> Oil for frying
> 4 cups mesclun or other mixed salad greens
> ⅓ cup lemon vinaigrette

Per Serving: Protein: 23.1g   Fat: 45.5g   Carbohydrate: 5.3g

Have ready a cake rack for drying the cheese slices. Mix the egg and water in a soup plate with a fork, beating well. Have the nuts in another soup plate next to the egg wash. Dip the cheese slices one at a time into the egg wash and then into the nuts, coating them all over. Let the slices dry for 15 minutes on the cake rack and refrigerate for half an hour.

When you're ready to serve, heat oil to a depth of 1¼ inches in a skillet or wok. When the oil is hot but not smoking and sends up a faint blue haze, add the cheese slices and fry until golden and crisp on both sides. Drain on paper towels.

Toss the greens with the vinaigrette and distribute among 4 salad plates. Top with the cheese and serve immediately.

Fried Cheese Log

You can also mix goat cheese with cream cheese and chopped herbs—chives, mint, basil, parsley—and form it into 4 skinny logs. Refrigerate the logs, then dip them into the egg wash and nuts and proceed as above.

SHRIMP WITH BACON AND CHEESE

This tasty dish turned up in a Mexican seafood restaurant in Santa Fe. It's really a first course, but if you serve it over sliced romaine dressed lightly with a garlic vinaigrette and double the number of shrimp packages per person, it's dinner.

SERVES 2 AS AN APPETIZER, 1 AS A MAIN COURSE

> 4 (2-inch-long) slices Monterey Jack cheese (¼ inch thick)
> 8 extra large shrimp, shelled and deveined
> 4 thick slices smoky bacon

Per Serving (for 2): Protein: 34g   Fat: 34g   Carbohydrate: 2g

Sandwich each cheese slice between 2 shrimp and wrap a piece of bacon around the whole package. Secure with toothpicks.

Grill the shrimp on an outdoor grill or under the broiler just until the bacon is done, turning over once. Serve on a plate or over romaine salad.

WALNUT PARMESAN LACE CRISPS

These are great little savory party nibblers: finely chopped walnuts and Parmesan cheese bound by egg white in a lacy network of crunch. The trick is to handle the mixture—you wouldn't call it a dough—very gently, not compacting it, until you put it on the baking sheet. At that point you pat and push it into thin rounds. They'll seem loose, but cooking the cheese and egg white binds them. Serve on a tray with cheese, apple slices dipped in lemon juice, and celery sticks.

SERVES 8

> 1 cup walnut pieces
> 1 tablespoon wheat germ
> 1 teaspoon fine yellow cornmeal
> Pinch of salt
> ½ cup finely grated Parmesan cheese
> 1 large egg white

Per Serving: Protein: 6.3g   Fat: 10.4g   Carbohydrate: 1.8g

Preheat the oven to 375°F and lightly butter a large cookie sheet. Put the walnuts, wheat germ, cornmeal, and salt in the bowl of a food processor and chop the nuts fine—do not overprocess. Add the cheese and pulse once or twice to mix.

In a medium mixing bowl, whisk the egg white until foamy. Add the nut mixture to the egg white and toss with a fork to mix. Switch to your hands, rubbing the mixture gently through your fingers to combine; the mixture should remain crumbly.

Using a tablespoon measure, spoon slightly mounded tablespoons of the mixture onto the baking sheet, leaving a little room between each mound. With your fingers, gently press and shape the mounds into thin crackers. Bake the crackers for 8 to 10 minutes; they should turn a shade or two darker, but they shouldn't get very dark. Cool on the baking sheets for 3 minutes, then carefully transfer the crackers to a cooling rack. Cool completely before serving. Store in a covered dish. To recrisp, warm the crackers in the oven for several minutes.

HOT GARLIC SHRIMP

These Spanish-style shrimp should be served sizzling hot
from the oven with toothpicks for spearing. Use an ovenproof dish just large enough to hold the shrimp and at-
tractive enough to serve them in. SERVES 10

> 1½ pounds medium raw shrimp, shelled, with tails
>   left on
> ¾ cup olive oil
> 6 whole garlic cloves, smashed
> Salt to taste
> Chopped parsley for garnish

Per Serving: Protein: 13.8g   Fat: 2.6g   Carbohydrate: .6g

Put the shrimp in an ovenproof bowl and pour the
olive oil over them. Drop the garlic cloves into the oil and
let the shrimp marinate in the refrigerator for at least 1
hour and up to 5 or 6 hours. Bring to room temperature
before procceding.

Preheat the oven to 450°F. Roast the shrimp just until
they turn pink, about 6 minutes. Remove the shrimp
from the oven, sprinkle the parsley over, and serve immediately with toothpicks.

CHEESE BALLS

Not the giant cheddar balls of fifties holiday parties, these
have a more exotic air. You can roll them in either finely
chopped pecans or finely chopped mint—or both—and
serve them mounded into a little tower on a round or
square plate. If these are cocktail fare, be sure to provide
plates and toothpicks, since the olive oil will drip.

SERVES 8

½ pound mild chèvre
6 ounces feta cheese, drained
½ teaspoon ground cumin
¼ teaspoon ground red pepper (cayenne)
¼ cup finely chopped mint leaves *or* pecans
¼ cup olive oil

Per Serving: Protein: 5.9g   Fat: 10.5g   Carbohydrate: .3g

In a large bowl or in the food processor, combine the
cheeses with the cumin and cayenne. Mix well. Form the
mixture into small balls—about 24 is the right number.
Put the mint or nuts on a plate and roll the balls in it to
cover. Chill on a plate for at least an hour and up to 4
hours.

Remove from the refrigerator and let stand for half an
hour. Arrange the balls into a little tower and pour the
olive oil over. Serve with toothpicks.

MEXICAN SHRIMP COCKTAIL

Serve these zesty shrimp in a tapered glass or a small glass
bowl. SERVES 4

  ½ pound medium or large raw shrimp

  2 diced tomatoes, no seeds

  ½ medium cucumber, peeled and cut in tiny dice

  ¼ cup minced red onion

  ¼ cup chopped cilantro

  1 avocado, diced

  Jolt of hot pepper sauce

  ½ cup Clamato juice

  1 lime, cut into 8 slices

  Cilantro sprigs to garnish

Per Serving: Protein: 6.3g   Fat: 4.2g   Carbohydrate: 5.4g

Have a large pot of boiling water on the stove. Toss in
the shrimp and cook just until they turn pink. Drain in a
colander over the sink. When the shrimp are cool enough
to handle, shell them, removing the vein. Put the shrimp
in a bowl, cover, and refrigerate until ready to serve.

In a large bowl, mix everything else except the lime
and cilantro sprigs. Add the shrimp and divide the cocktail among 4 glasses or bowls. Hang 2 lime slices over
the edge of each glass and decorate with cilantro sprigs.
Serve immediately.

THREE THINGS TO DO WITH
SMOKED SALMON

SUSHI WITHOUT RICE

SERVES 6

4 ounces smoked salmon, presliced
1 Hass avocado
12 sprigs cilantro
¼ cup cream cheese mixed with horseradish

Per Serving: Protein: 4.5g   Fat: 8.2g   Carbohydrate: 1.3g

Separate the salmon slices into 12—if there aren't 12
slices, cut the slices you have into 12 equal parts. Halve
the avocado; remove the pit and peel off the skin. Cut
each avocado half into 6 slices. Lay the salmon slices flat
on a work surface. Tuck an avocado slice and a sprig of
cilantro close to one end of each salmon slice, folding
the edges over as necessary to make a little package the
size of the avocado slice. At the other end, spread a teaspoon of the cream cheese. Roll the slices up toward the
cream cheese end and press together to seal.

SMOKED SALMON PINWHEELS

SERVES 6

4 ounces smoked salmon, presliced
¾ cup cream cheese with chives

Per Serving: Protein: 4.9g   Fat: 8g   Carbohydrate: .6g

Separate the salmon slices into 12—if there aren't 12 slices, cut the slices you have into 12 equal parts. Spread each slice with 1 tablespoon cream cheese and roll lengthwise. Cut each log into 4 pinwheels.

SMOKED SALMON CANAPÉS

SERVES 8

1 ounce smoked salmon
1 long hothouse cucumber
½ cup cream cheese with chives
Sprigs of dill from 1 bunch

Per Serving: Protein: 1.2g   Fat: 3.9g   Carbohydrate: 1.3g

Cut the salmon into pieces the width of the cucumber. Score the cucumber skin lengthwise with a fork to make stripes or peel large stripes with a vegetable peeler. Slice the cucumber about ¼ inch thick. Spread a dab of cream cheese on each slice, top with a piece of salmon, and put a sprig of dill on top.

SMOKED SALMON WITH CAVIAR

This fancy restaurant dish is so easy to make—and so impressive—that it's a good thing to have in your repertoire. Serve it with champagne and crackers for a big occasion. SERVES 8

½ pound smoked salmon
1 cup heavy cream, whipped to soft peaks
2 handfuls of delicate greens—mâche or mesclun
½ ounce caviar, black or red

Per Serving: Protein: 6.2g   Fat: 2.6g   Carbohydrate: 1.2g

In the workbowl of a food processor, purée the salmon—it should be as smooth as possible. Put the salmon in a mixing bowl and fold the whipped cream into it. Force the mixture through a food mill.

Arrange the greens over a serving plate and mound the smoked salmon mixture on top. Spread the caviar over the salmon mound and serve with crackers.

SALMON TARTARE

Yes, this is raw salmon, and while I wouldn't recommend beef tartare, salmon is quite safe to eat raw—and entirely delicious. If you're nervous about it, try using half raw salmon and half smoked salmon the first time. Feel the salmon all over for stray bones before you chop it.

SERVES 4

½ pound raw salmon fillet, chopped coarse

¼ cup minced scallions, including some green

½ teaspoon sea salt

Freshly ground black pepper to taste

2 tablespoons olive oil

2 drops hot pepper sauce

½ teaspoon minced lemon zest

2 tablespoons chopped chives

Per Serving: Protein: 11.3g   Fat: 13.1g   Carbohydrate: trace

Mix all the ingredients together in a bowl and cover with plastic wrap. Refrigerate at least 1 hour until ready to serve. Serve on Wasa crackers spread with butter or horseradish cream cheese.

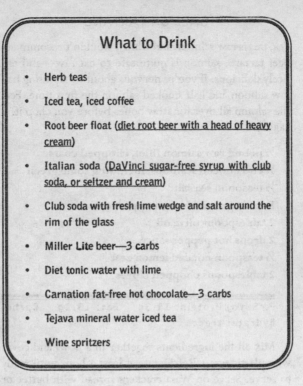

What to Drink

- Herb teas

- Iced tea, iced coffee

- Root beer float (<u>diet root beer with a head of heavy cream</u>)

- Italian soda (<u>DaVinci sugar-free syrup with club soda, or seltzer and cream</u>)

- Club soda with fresh lime wedge and salt around the rim of the glass

- Miller Lite beer—3 carbs

- Diet tonic water with lime

- Carnation fat-free hot chocolate—3 carbs

- Tejava mineral water iced tea

- Wine spritzers

SMOKED TROUT ON WATERCRESS

This is an ideal starter for a holiday meal, the bright idea
of my friend Barbara Witt. The trout will break naturally
into little chevrons, which perch on top of a zesty salad
dressed with a creamy lemon vinaigrette. SERVES 6

  2 smoked trout
  2 bunches watercress, washed, spun dry, and
      heavy stems removed

Per Serving: Protein: 3.9g   Fat: 15.4g   Carbohydrate: .7g

DRESSING
1 shallot, minced
½ teaspoon salt
2 tablespoons fresh lemon juice
Minced zest of half a lemon
6 tablespoons light olive oil
1 teaspoon Dijon mustard
2 teaspoons heavy cream
Salt and pepper to taste

Take the trout flesh off the bony frame and pull it into
chevron shapes where it breaks naturally. Set aside. Tear
the watercress into bite-size sprigs and set aside in a large
bowl.

Make the dressing: In a screw-top jar, mix the shallot with the salt and lemon juice and set aside for 15 minutes to half an hour.

When ready to serve, add the remaining dressing ingredients to the jar and shake well. Taste for seasoning, then pour over the watercress. Toss well and arrange the salad on serving plates. Arrange the trout pieces on top and serve immediately.

CHICKEN SATAY

This works as an appetizer or a main course—it's so good and so easy that you might want to make it dinner. The chicken is threaded on 6-inch wooden skewers, about 14 of them. Soak the skewers first in cold water for half an hour so they don't burn in the oven, or use metal shish kebab skewers. SERVES 6 FOR DINNER, 18 AS AN APPETIZER

  3 whole boneless chicken breasts, skin removed
  ½ cup roasted peanuts
  1 teaspoon mild curry powder
  ¼ cup soy sauce
  2 tablespoons dark sesame oil
  Pinch of chili powder
  Garnish: chopped cilantro leaves and a few sprigs,
      optional

Per Serving (for 18): Protein: 10.6g   Fat: 5.3g   Carbohydrate: .5g

Preheat oven to 325°F. Cut the chicken into ½-inch chunks and arrange them on the skewers evenly. Rest the skewers on a baking sheet covered with foil. In a nonstick skillet, roast the peanuts over medium heat until fragrant. Let them cool a little and chop them coarse.

Put the nuts in a bowl and add the remaining ingredients except the cilantro. Stir well and pour the sauce over the chicken skewers. Bake for 10 minutes and serve on a platter, garnished with the cilantro leaves and whole sprigs.

DEVILED EGGS, PLAIN AND FANCY

Eggs have been so vilified for cholesterol reasons for so long that lots of people have just forgotten about deviled eggs—but try offering a plate of them; they disappear almost instantly. The basic recipe is for plain deviled eggs; fancy options follow. SERVES 6

> 1 dozen extra-large eggs, at room temperature
> 6 tablespoons mayonnaise
> ½ teaspoon dry mustard
> Salt and pepper to taste
> Paprika, optional

Per Serving: Protein: 12.2g   Fat: 22.2g   Carbohydrate: 1g

Put the eggs in a large saucepan with cold water to cover. Slowly bring the water to a boil. The minute the water boils, remove the pan from the heat. Cover and let the eggs stand in the hot water for 15 minutes—set the timer.

When the eggs are done, put the pan in the sink and run cold water into it. When the eggs are cool enough to handle, tap them against the side of the pan all over to loosen the shells. Let them sit in the cold water until you're ready to peel them.

Remove the shells and cut the eggs in half crosswise. Remove the yolks to a bowl, mash them well with a fork, and add the mayonnaise, mustard, and salt and pepper. Cut the very ends off the egg-white cases so they'll stand up easily, and stuff them with the egg yolk mixture. Sprinkle paprika over the tops if you like.

Deviled Eggs With Smoked Salmon

Chop 2 slices of smoked salmon and stir into the egg-yolk mixture. Add a tablespoon of drained capers. Top each egg half with a frond of fresh dill.

Per Serving: Protein: 13g Fat: 22.4g Carbohydrate: 1g

Deviled Eggs With Caviar

Top each egg half with a spoonful of red or black caviar.

Per Serving: Protein: 13.3g Fat: 23g Carbohydrate: 1.1g

SALAMI AND EGGS WITH ARUGULA

A sort of antipasto, presented on a big platter. Scatter sprigs of arugula over the platter, then tuck in very thin slices of salami, as many kinds as you can find. In the center, make a mound of hard-cooked eggs or deviled eggs, page 86, allowing 2 whole eggs or 4 deviled egg halves per person. Decorate the eggs with more arugula sprigs. Give each person a small plate and pass the salt and pep-permill.

DILL PICKLED HARD-COOKED EGGS

Instead of pitching out the juice from the emptied dill pickle jar, fill it with hard-cooked eggs—just be sure they're all submerged in the green liquid. After 3 days they're ready to eat, but they'll keep for weeks in the refrigerator. These are great snacks, but they're also delicious as hors d'oeuvres, cut in half lengthwise and spread with a little sour cream, then sprinkled with salt and white pepper. (Zero carbs.)

NACHOS

No tortillas here, but these are a delicious way to have something close to the real thing. SERVES 2

Skins from 2 roasted potatoes, page 293, with as little flesh as possible
⅓ cup grated Monterey Jack cheese
Half a 4-ounce can chopped green chiles

Per Serving: Protein: 2g Fat: 3g Carbohydrate: 12g

Preheat the oven to 400°F. Sprinkle the cheese and chiles over the potato skins and put them on a cookie sheet. Bake for 10 minutes or until the cheese is melted and the potatoes are crispy. Cut each potato skin in half and serve hot.

CUMIN SALT

Delicious with hard-cooked eggs or for dipping crudités into—cucumber spears, kohlrabi, daikon, etc.

ENOUGH FOR 8 SERVINGS

1½ teaspoons ground cumin
½ teaspoon ground black pepper
Pinch of ground red pepper (cayenne)
2 teaspoons salt

Mix everything together and store in a sealed jar.

TEA EGGS

Here's a recipe to astound your friends. The Chinese have figured out some very interesting things to do to eggs, and this is one of the most intriguing. The eggs are hard-cooked once, and then again, for a very long time, in spiced tea; their shells are cracked all over to give the surface of the eggs a beautiful crackled glaze, like old porcelain. Serve the eggs on a little nest of watercress in a basket. SERVES 12

> 12 large eggs, at room temperature
> ¼ cup Chinese tea leaves (tea bags from Chinese takeout are okay)
> 1 quart water
> 1 teaspoon 5-spice powder
> ½ teaspoon salt
> 2 teaspoons soy sauce

Per Serving: Protein: 6.1g   Fat: 5.6g   Carbohydrate: .6g

Put the eggs in a saucepan of water to cover and bring the water slowly to a simmer. Let the eggs simmer, uncovered, for half an hour.

Have ready a bowl of cold water and put the eggs into it when they come off the fire. Crack them all over very gently—the shell should stay intact but be cracked all over in spiderweb fashion.

Bring the quart of water to the boil and add the tea leaves. Let steep for 8 minutes—the tea should be very strong—then strain out the leaves. Return the brewed tea to the saucepan and add the 5-spice powder, the salt, soy, and the cracked eggs. Simmer the eggs gently, uncovered, for one hour, replacing water as necessary. (Don't worry, the eggs will be tender inside.) Let cool before removing shells.

GEORGIAN EGG SALAD

This fascinating Russian take on egg salad comes from Darra Goldstein's prize-winning cookbook, *The Georgian Feast*. It's delicious on Wasa crackers. SERVES 4

    4 large eggs, hard-cooked
    3 tablespoons unsalted butter, softened to room
          temperature
    ¼ cup ground walnuts
    2 tablespoons minced fresh dill
    2 tablespoons minced fresh cilantro
    2 tablespoons minced scallions, white part only
    ⅛ teaspoon salt

Per Serving: Protein: 7.1g   Fat: 17.7g   Carbohydrate: 1.6g

Mash the eggs with the butter in a small bowl. Stir in the remaining ingredients and mix well.

PROVOLETA

This Argentinian classic makes a hearty first course or a delicious lunch—just add a big green salad and a plate of sliced tomatoes. You can also make it with Parmesan cheese, for an expensive treat. Whatever you serve with it, be sure you have red wine.

SERVES 2 AS A MAIN COURSE, 4 AS AN APPETIZER

½ pound provolone cheese
Sage or oregano leaves, chopped fresh or dried
Black pepper

Per Serving (for 4): Protein: 14g   Fat: 16g   Carbohydrate: 2g

Cut the provolone into 2 thick slices. Grill them about 6 inches from the coals until the cheese is golden brown and soft, just starting to run. If you let it go a minute too long, you'll have a puddle of cheese (delicious, however). Put the cheese on small plates, sprinkle with sage or oregano, and grind pepper on top. Serve with a knife and fork.

TRICOLOR PEPPER CRESCENTS

These savory peppers aren't quite soft when they're cooked—they still have a little texture. They're good for a buffet or as part of an antipasto platter. SERVES 6

   3 bell peppers, green, red, and yellow if possible
   3 garlic cloves, sliced thin
   1 large tomato, seeded and cut in dice
   12 anchovy fillets
   12 teaspoons olive oil

Per Serving: Protein: 2g   Fat: 10g   Carbohydrate: 3.5g

Preheat the oven to 350°F. Quarter the peppers and remove the stems, seeds, and ribs. Lay the pepper crescents on a baking sheet and scatter the thin garlic slices over them, about 3 to a crescent. Top with the tomato dice. Lay an anchovy fillet over the tomato and garlic, and add salt and pepper to taste. Drizzle a teaspoon of olive oil over each crescent and bake them for half an hour.

Let cool to room temperature before serving.

BRIE QUICHE

This is wretched excess, but very delicious. You can serve it on a bed of watercress and topped with caviar for an over-the-top appetizer. Also works for dessert with grapes, snappy apples, or pears. SERVES 10

4 large eggs
1½ cups half-and-half
1 pound ripe Brie, including the rind, at room
    temperature
⅛ teaspoon salt

Per Serving: Protein: 14g   Fat: 19g   Carbohydrate: 2.6g

Preheat the oven to 350°F. Separate the eggs. In a mixing bowl, beat the egg yolks with the half-and-half. Chop the cheese in the workbowl of a food processor until you have a paste. Add the creamy yolks and combine thoroughly. Pour the mixture into the mixing bowl and stir in the salt and pepper.

Beat the egg whites with the salt until stiff and stir ⅓ of them into the cheese mixture. Fold in the remainder with a rubber spatula.

Pour the custard into an 8-inch quiche pan and grind a little more pepper on top. Bake for 30 minutes or until set. Serve at room temperature.

CRACKLINGS

Some commercial cracklings, aka pork rinds, are pretty good—McPorkers from Louisiana, for instance—but the vast majority are tasteless at best. The real thing is made when hogs are butchered and lard is rendered outdoors in big iron pots stirred with a shovel. But you can also do it at home, and it's a cinch. If you're a porcophile, these cracklings will be sheer Pig Heaven. You'll probably have to order the fat ahead from your butcher.

2 pounds pork fat, preferably from the loin, in 1-inch cubes

¼ cup water

You want as little flesh on the fat as possible, since any meat will turn hard in the cooking process. Cut out any bits of meat that escape the butcher.

Preheat the oven to 250°F.

In a cast-iron skillet, heat the pork fat cubes with the water over medium heat until the fat begins to melt. Stir the cubes gently a couple of times.

Put the skillet in the oven and give the contents a stir every 20 minutes or so. The temperature of the fat shouldn't go above 255°. The cracklings will be done when bubbles form and the cubes start to float to the surface, after 1½ to 2 hours. Skim them off and drain well in a colander—you want all the fat to be cooked out, and they'll continue to drain after they're cooked.

When the cracklings have finished draining, roll them in paper towels and salt them. They're delicious hot, but also good at room temperature. Try them on salads. You can even bag and freeze them to use later. Save the lard for cooking. As a variation, try dusting the finished cracklings with chili powder.

Soups

〽

A hearty soup can of course be a meal in itself, and that's a very satisfying way to eat—just add a salad and cheese. It's easy enough to improvise soups by simply sautéing the basic seasoning elements—onions, garlic, celery, etc.—in a little butter or oil and adding cubes of leftover meat or sausage slices, then cut-up vegetables. Once all these basic elements are sautéed, you can just add broth or water and let it all simmer together for a while, then taste for seasoning. Finish the soup with garnishes—croutons sizzled in a little butter, tiny cubes of cheese, a spoonful of cream, olivada, roasted red pepper dice, minced herbs, a sprinkle of grated Parmesan, etc. Simple enough, and yet there's one big problem: most soups benefit from a thickening agent, which is almost always starch. Since we won't be using potatoes or pasta or rice or beans or barley, except in the tiniest amounts, we need an alternative. Possibilities include a tablespoon or two of instant flour blended into the soup shortly before serving or a big dollop of vegetable purée. The purées can include leftovers; likely candidates are broccoli, cauliflower, zucchini, spinach, etc. But consider the other flavors in the soup—if the elements would be good together on a plate, they'll work in the soup. The ultimate thickener is cream, of course, but there are more interesting possibilities. One that also adds protein to the mix is beating a couple of eggs together well, then stirring them into the hot soup with a fork just before serving to make egg strands.

CREAM OF TOMATO SOUP,
WITH OR WITHOUT CRAB

When too many tomatoes are around in Indian summer, this is the soup to make. Or you can make it with canned tomatoes, which work perfectly well. Either way, it's luxurious. SERVES 6

    3 tablespoons clarified butter or Plugra, page 48
    3 shallots, chopped
    3 pounds ripe tomatoes or 2 (14½-ounce) cans
        Muir Glen diced tomatoes
    ¼ teaspoon dried thyme
    2 cups chicken broth
    ¼ teaspoon baking soda
    ½ cup heavy cream
    Pinch of ground red pepper (cayenne)
    Salt and ground black pepper
    1 tablespoon grated horseradish, optional
    ½ pound picked crabmeat, optional

Per Serving: Protein: 1.2g   Fat: 13.1g   Carbohydrate: 7.2g

In a large saucepan, melt the butter and add the shallots. Cook slowly for 10 minutes or until soft. Cut the fresh tomatoes in cubes and discard the seeds. Add the tomatoes to the saucepan along with the thyme and chicken broth. Bring to a simmer and cover. Cook slowly for 20 minutes.

Turn off the heat and purée the soup in the blender or right in the saucepan with a hand-held blender. Add the baking soda, cream, and cayenne. Heat the soup for serving but don't let it boil. Stir in the horseradish just before you ladle it into warm soup bowls. Scatter the crab on top or just finish the soup with a grind of black pepper and a feathering of cream on top.

CREAM OF MUSHROOM SOUP

This is Mexican maestra Diana Kennedy's way of cooking
mushroom soup—it's unusual and unusually good. Not
too many soups begin with the instruction to turn on the
oven. SERVES 6

1 pound cremini or wild mushrooms
1 tablespoon fresh lemon juice
4 small garlic cloves, chopped
2 tablespoons butter
1 tablespoon safflower oil
Salt and pepper to taste
2½ cups chicken broth
½ cup crème fraîche, page 161, or heavy cream
6 tablespoons Madeira
Croutons and snipped chives for garnish, optional

Per Serving: Protein: 3.1g   Fat: 9.8g   Carbohydrate: 5.7g

Preheat the oven to 300°F. Wipe the mushrooms clean
with a damp cloth and slice thin. Spread them out in a shallow, ovenproof dish in a double layer. Add the lemon juice,
garlic, butter, and oil to the mushrooms and season lightly
with salt and pepper. Bake the mushrooms for about an hour
or until they are completely cooked and the juice is thick and
dark. Set aside a few mushrooms for garnish and put the rest
in the blender jar. Add the broth and blend smooth.

In a heavy saucepan, heat the chicken broth for about
5 minutes. Add the cream, stir it in, and cook for 5 more
minutes, but don't let it boil.

Put a tablespoon of Madeira in the bottom of each
soup cup and add the hot soup. Garnish with the optional
croutons and chives and the reserved mushrooms.

SAUERKRAUT SOUP

This is great comfort food on a winter's day, and it's a meal in itself. And dinner's ready in less than half an hour. You might want to stir in a spoonful of Dijon mustard at the table to punch up the flavors. Wasa crackers with horseradish cream cheese and a salad of sharp greens would be good with this pungent soup. SERVES 4

½ cup chopped leeks
2 cups sauerkraut, well rinsed and chopped
4 cups chicken broth
2 cups chopped kale, about 4 large-stemmed
    leaves
1 pound sliced kielbasa, sautéed until golden and
    drained
Salt and pepper to taste
Garnishes: a spoonful of sour cream per person, a
    sprinkle of fresh snipped dill, a spoonful of
    mustard

Per Serving: Protein: 17g   Fat: 23g   Carbohydrate: 8g

In the same skillet you used to sauté the kielbasa, cook the leeks in a tablespoon of the drippings until they begin to color.

In a large saucepan, combine the leeks, sauerkraut, and broth. Bring to a simmer and add the kale. Cook until the kale is tender, about 10 minutes. Add the kielbasa and simmer 10 more minutes. Taste for salt and pepper. Ladle the soup into 4 deep bowls and pass the garnishes on the side.

ESCAROLE SOUP WITH MEATBALLS

This old Italian favorite is a meal in itself. You can make the meatballs ahead and freeze them, so you can put the soup together quickly once they're defrosted. Escarole is especially low-carb—if you substitute other greens, such as kale, you'll need to up the ante. SERVES 3

½ pound ground sirloin
½ cup grated Parmesan cheese
¼ cup crumbled garlic croutons
2 tablespoons minced parsley
¼ teaspoon salt
Pepper to taste
1 large egg, lightly beaten
½ cup plus ¼ cup minced onion
3 tablespoons olive oil
2 garlic cloves, minced
5 cups shredded escarole, rinsed and dried
4 cups chicken broth
Hot red pepper flakes, optional

Per Serving: Protein: 30g   Fat: 23g   Carbohydrate: 9g

Make the meatballs: In a mixing bowl combine the meat, half the cheese, the croutons, parsley, salt, pepper, egg, and ½ cup of minced onion. Mix well with your hands and divide into 24 little meatballs.

In a dutch oven or other large, heavy pot, heat 1 tablespoon of the olive oil over medium-high heat. When it's hot, add the meatballs—half at a time—and sauté until they're golden brown all over. Remove the meatballs to a plate.

Add the remaining olive oil to the pot along with the additional ¼ cup of onion and cook over low heat, stirring frequently, until the onion is soft. Add the garlic and cook for another couple of minutes. Stir in the escarole, cover, and cook until it's wilted, about 3 minutes. Add the broth and the meatballs, bring to a boil, then simmer uncovered for about 3 minutes. Serve in warm soup plates, sprinkled with the remaining Parmesan and pepper flakes.

COLD CUCUMBER SOUP WITH MINT
AND LEMON

A good soup to make when the dog days arrive and it's so
hot you don't want to cook—or for that matter, eat too
much. The soup goes together in minutes and can be
made in the morning. Add shrimp and you have a complete meal. If you're serving the soup for company, you
might dice the cucumber fine instead of grating it; remove the seeds first.

SERVES 4 AS A MAIN COURSE WITH SHRIMP, 6 AS A FIRST
COURSE

    1½ Knorr chicken bouillon cubes
    2 cups hot water
    1 cup yogurt (not low-fat or nonfat)
    1 cup sour cream
    1½ medium cucumbers, peeled and grated (about
        1½ cups)
    Grated zest of 1 lemon
    Juice of 1 lemon (2 tablespoons)
    2 tablespoons chopped fresh mint leaves
    2 tablespoons snipped chives or minced scallions
    Dash of white pepper, optional
    1 pound cooked shelled shrimp, optional

Per Serving as first course: Protein: 2.7g Fat: 9.3g Carbohydrate: 5.8g

---

Per Serving with shrimp: Protein: 29g Fat: 16g Carbohydrate:
10.5g

Dissolve the bouillon cubes in the hot water and let cool. In a large bowl, whisk the broth with the yogurt and sour cream until smooth. Add the cucumber and everything else but the pepper and shrimp, if using. Cover the soup and refrigerate for at least 2 hours. Whisk again before serving and taste for seasoning. Serve the soup with a grinding of white pepper on top and divide the shrimp among the bowls.

BLT SOUP

Yes, you can make BLTs wrapped in a big romaine leaf or a tortilla and they're very good if messy—but this interesting soup from Deer Meadow Vineyards in Virginia is a whole different take on the subject. SERVES 4

4 slices smoked bacon
1 tablespoon butter
½ cup chopped onion
½ cup chopped green bell pepper
½ cup chopped celery
2 garlic cloves, minced
1 quart chicken broth
1 medium tomato, diced
Chopped or shredded romaine or arugula
½ cup cream
Salt, pepper, and hot pepper sauce to taste
¼ cup croutons for garnish, optional

Per Serving: Protein: 7.7g   Fat: 17.4g   Carbohydrate: 6.8g

Fry the bacon crisp and crumble it when cool; set aside. In a soup pot, melt the butter and sauté the onion, green pepper, celery, and garlic over medium heat until tender. Add the chicken broth and bring to a boil. Lower heat and simmer for 10 minutes.

Just before serving, add the tomato, romaine, crumbled bacon, and cream. Mix well and season to taste. Heat gently and serve, topped with croutons if you like.

VICHYSSOISE

No, it's not potato vichyssoise, but it tastes amazingly like it—and has all the richness, the smooth texture, and the satisfying quality we love about vichyssoise. If you serve this to company, they won't guess it's not made with potatoes. Try adding 2 teaspoons of curry powder with the onion for a lively version. SERVES 6

> 2 tablespoons olive oil
> 1 medium onion, chopped, about 1 cup
> 4 cups chicken broth
> ½ large head cauliflower
> ½ cup heavy cream
> 1 cup half-and-half
> White pepper
> Snipped chives
> Snipped dill

Per Serving: Protein: .5g   Fat: 17.6g   Carbohydrate: 3.6g

Heat the oil in a large soup pot and add the chopped onion. Cook, stirring from time to time, until the onion is soft, about 5 minutes. Add the chicken broth and bring to a simmer.

Meanwhile, chop the cauliflower into small pieces—the food processor is fine for this—about the size of croutons. Add the cauliflower to the broth, cover, and cook until tender, from 5 to 10 minutes.

Purée the soup in the blender in 2 batches. Let cool for ½ hour, then add the cream and half-and-half, whisking in. Add white pepper to taste.

Chill for at least 2 hours, blend again before serving, and add a grind of white pepper and a scatter of herbs to each bowl.

MEXICAN CHICKEN SOUP

This earthy soup is the one to make when you want a fast, comforting one-dish meal on a cold or blustery day. Of course it's better with homemade chicken broth, but canned works fine here. The secret ingredient is the chipotle chile, see page 38. SERVES 4

1½ tablespoons olive oil
½ medium onion, chopped
2 large garlic cloves, minced
1 small carrot, minced
2 medium zucchini, diced
1 bunch Swiss chard leaves, cut into ribbons and
    chopped
1 quart homemade chicken broth or 3 (13-ounce)
    cans low-sodium chicken broth
2 large boneless whole chicken breasts, cut into
    bite-size pieces
2 canned chipotle peppers, rinsed, seeded, and
    minced
Salt and pepper to taste
1 cup Monterey Jack cheese cubes
½ cup chopped cilantro leaves
½ avocado, diced
1 lime, cut into wedges

Per Serving: Protein: 46g   Fat: 39g   Carbohydrate: 14g

In a large saucepan or dutch oven over medium-high heat, warm the oil and when it's hot add the onion. Cook, stirring frequently, until it's soft, about 4 minutes. Add the garlic and stir for 1 minute.

Add the carrot, zucchini, and chard, and cook, stirring, for another minute. Add the broth and bring the soup to a boil, then lower the heat and simmer for 8 minutes, or until the carrots are tender.

Add the chicken pieces and the minced chile peppers and cook for another 5 minutes or until the chicken is cooked through. Season to taste with salt and pepper.

To serve, divide the cheese cubes among four deep soup bowls, ladle the soup over, and garnish with cilantro and avocado dice. Pass a dish of lime wedges to squeeze over the soup at the table.

ROASTED PEPPER SOUP
WITH FETA CHEESE

You can make this soup with either the pan-roasted peppers on page 298 or jarred peppers or your own oven-roasted peppers. SERVES 2

12 ounces (about ¾ cup) roasted red bell peppers
1 cup chicken broth
1 garlic clove, pressed
½ teaspoon oregano
1 cup heavy cream
Salt to taste and lots of black pepper
⅓ cup crumbled feta cheese
Additional oregano to garnish

Per Serving: Protein: 5.9g   Fat: 50.5g   Carbohydrate: 6.7g

Blend the peppers with the chicken broth in a blender or food processor. Put the mixture in a heavy saucepan and heat gently with the garlic and oregano until it comes to a boil. Reduce the heat and simmer, uncovered, for 5 minutes. Add the cream and bring to a simmer. Taste for seasoning. Pour into deep soup bowls, crumble feta cheese on top, and sprinkle with pepper and additional oregano.

SWISS CHARD AND ZUCCHINI SOUP

A delicious soup made of two of our vegetable heroes.
The recipe comes from Diana Kennedy; the chile garnish
is the only hint of its Mexican origin. SERVES 6

2 tablespoons butter
¼ pound Swiss chard, leaves roughly chopped,
    stems chopped fine
3 tablespoons finely chopped white onion
2 garlic cloves, chopped
½ pound zucchini, in very small cubes
3 cups chicken broth
Salt and pepper to taste
Optional: ¼ cup heavy cream; finely chopped, hot,
    skinny, green chile, to taste

Per Serving: Protein: 1.1g   Fat: 4g   Carbohydrate: 3.6g

Melt the butter in a heavy saucepan over medium heat
and add the chard stems, onion, and garlic. Cook, stirring
constantly, over a high flame for about 5 minutes. Add
the zucchini and the chard leaves along with 1 cup of the
broth. Cover and cook over a medium flame until the
vegetables are just tender—about 10 minutes.

Put half the vegetables and half a cup of broth in a
blender jar and blend until almost smooth. Repeat with
the remaining vegetables and another half cup of broth.
Heat the purée in the saucepan with the remaining broth;
add salt and pepper to taste. Bring to a simmer and cook
gently over a low flame for about 5 more minutes. Add
the cream if desired, blend thoroughly, and pour the soup
into warm bowls. Garnish with the optional chile.

NAPA CABBAGE SOUP WITH TOFU

This fast, clean-tasting soup is the creation of Martha
Rose Shulman, who's famous for her low-fat recipes. This
one can be vegetarian if you make it with vegetable stock
instead of chicken broth. SERVES 6

1 quart chicken broth (canned low-sodium is fine)
1 quart water
1 pound (½ medium-size head) napa or savoy
        cabbage, shredded
6 scallions, including the firm green, sliced thin
1 garlic clove, minced
2 tablespoons soy sauce
2 tablespoons dry sherry
2 teaspoons grated fresh ginger
½ pound firm tofu, cut into thin slivers
1 tablespoon cornstarch, dissolved in 2
        tablespoons water
2 large eggs, beaten
Salt and pepper to taste
⅓ cup chopped cilantro, for garnish

Per Serving: Protein: 10.2g   Fat: 5.7g   Carbohydrate: 6.4g

Combine the broth, water, cabbage, scallions, garlic, soy, sherry, ginger, and tofu in a large soup pot. Bring to a boil. Reduce the heat and simmer 10 minutes, or until the cabbage is cooked through but still has some texture. Stir in the dissolved cornstarch and stir the soup until it's slightly thickened.

Beat the eggs in a small bowl and slowly stir them into the simmering soup with a fork or a chopstick so that they form little strands. Add pepper, taste the soup, and add salt if necessary. Serve immediately in warm bowls and garnish with the cilantro.

COMFORTING BROCCOLI SOUP

This is quick, nourishing, and satisfying, a good soup to
have in your repertoire for a fast meal. SERVES 4

  1 tablespoon olive oil
  1 pound kielbasa or smoked ham, in small chunks
  4 fat garlic cloves, chopped
  1 (14½-ounce) can Muir Glen diced tomatoes,
        including juice
  1 quart hot chicken broth
  Salt and pepper to taste
  1 large bunch broccoli, about 1¼ pounds, stems
        peeled and chopped fine, florets chopped
  1 teaspoon red pepper flakes, optional
  ¼ cup chopped Italian parsley
  ½ cup grated Parmesan cheese

Per Serving: Protein: 17g   Fat: 24g   Carbohydrate: 7.1g

In a dutch oven or a heavy soup pot, heat the olive oil
over medium heat and add the meat chunks. Sauté until
lightly golden. Add the garlic and cook for 1 minute. Add
the tomatoes and chicken broth, cover, and bring to a boil.

Add the broccoli pieces and return to the boil, then
lower to a simmer and cook, uncovered, 10 minutes or
until the broccoli stems are tender. Ladle the soup into
warm bowls and add a big pinch of hot pepper flakes if
you like. Sprinkle parsley and Parmesan over each bowl
and serve immediately.

Salads

〽

Whether they're first-course salads or main-dish hearty salads, you'll find yourself eating salads every day. It's easiest to just grab some expensive baby mesclun greens that are all washed and ready to go, but that gets boring after a while. The greens possibilities are almost endless: watercress, arugula, endive, cabbage ribbons, Asian greens like tat soi, parsley, endive, and even—if you have an herb garden—all herbs, a particularly intriguing salad. You'll make a lot more salads with a lot less grief if the greens are cleaned and waiting in your crisper in the refrigerator, so it's worth being organized about it, at least some of the time.

A bed of greens makes the perfect foil for protein picked up at the market or leftovers in the refrigerator—everything from takeout chicken cut into strips to smoked salmon or turkey, leftover steak, shrimp and crab and lobster to plain old ham and cheese. A salad is also the perfect place to play with higher-carb foods that can be offered in small amounts, such as fruit: orange slices, pear or apple wedges, chunks of mango. Additional protein can come from hard-cooked eggs, cheese (salty cheeses like feta and ricotta salata are particularly good in salad), and bacon bits.

Dressings can be rich and creamy, light and zesty, whatever suits the ingredients. Herbs such as mint,

tarragon, dill, and basil are wonderful snipped into salads.
Garnish salads with toasted nuts, cheese dice, strips of
bell pepper, pitted Greek olives, slivers of sun-dried
tomato, a scattering of croutons, and Parmesan cheese.
Something crisp—a frico (page 130) or the gouda crisps
on page 132 or a few little fried pappadums—finishes
the plate and adds a lot to a salad's appeal.

BASIC EARLY SUMMER CHOPPED
VEGETABLE SALAD

Before the tomatoes arrive, there are other joys of summer to make salad out of. This one is classic. It's refreshing and almost instant. SERVES 4

  1 bunch radishes, chopped
  1 medium cucumber, chopped
  6 scallions, chopped
  2 green bell peppers, seeded and chopped
  ½ cup sour cream
  Salt and pepper, lots of pepper, to taste
  1 tablespoon cider vinegar, optional
  1 tablespoon chopped dill, optional

Per Serving: Protein: .9g   Fat: 6g   Carbohydrate: 6.4g

Put the vegetables in a salad bowl and mix the remaining ingredients together in a small bowl. Stir the
dressing into the vegetables and mix well.

MUSHROOM, CHEESE, AND PROSCIUTTO SALAD

This is really an appetizer salad, but it also works for a light lunch or supper. SERVES 4

½ pound cremini mushrooms, caps only
1 tablespoon fresh lemon juice
⅓ pound Swiss cheese, cut into matchsticks
3 tablespoons olive oil
Salt and lots of pepper to taste
4 thin slices prosciutto, cut into little squares
1 bunch arugula, heavy stems removed

Per Serving: Protein: 12.7g   Fat: 21.5g   Carbohydrate: 2.7g

Wipe the mushroom caps clean with a slightly damp paper towel and cut into thin slices; put them in a serving bowl. Sprinkle the lemon juice over the mushroom slices. (You can do this half an hour ahead of serving.)

When ready to serve, add the cheese, oil, salt and pepper, and prosciutto to the mushrooms and toss well. Serve on a bed of arugula on salad plates.

PARSLEY SALAD

Refreshing, unusual, and so good you'll make it often.
You can use curly parsley or Italian flat-leaf, but remember that some people find curly parsley tends to stick in
their throats. SERVES 4

> Plucked leaves from 2 bunches parsley, about 4
>   cups
> 4 oil-packed sun-dried tomatoes, drained and
>   sliced thin
> ¼ cup grated Parmesan cheese
>
> DRESSING
> ¼ cup olive oil
> 2 tablespoons fresh lemon juice
> 2 garlic cloves, pressed
> Salt and pepper to taste

Per Serving: Protein: 2.1g   Fat: 16g   Carbohydrate: 2.5g

Be sure the parsley is completely dry, then put it in a
serving bowl. Add the sun-dried tomatoes and Parmesan
and toss together.

In a screw-top jar, shake the dressing ingredients together until well combined, then pour over the salad.
Toss thoroughly and serve immediately.

GREEK SALAD

This is such a mainstay of the low-carb life, and it's usually so badly made in America, that it's worth having a recipe just to remind ourselves to make it. SERVES 4

1 pound tomatoes (3 medium), in quarters
1 medium cucumber, peeled if necessary and
      sliced
½ cup coarsely chopped flat-leaf parsley
1 medium green bell pepper, sliced thin
4 scallions, including the firm green, sliced thin
¼ cup extra virgin olive oil
Salt and pepper to taste
½ cup crumbled feta cheese
12 kalamata olives, pitted
Pinch of oregano

Per Serving: Protein: 1.5g　Fat: 18g　Carbohydrate: 7g

Place the vegetables in a serving bowl. Pour the olive oil over and sprinkle with salt and pepper. Mix well. Crumble the feta cheese on top and dot with the olives. Sprinkle oregano over the dish and serve.

GREEK SALAD, NO TOMATOES

This is more like tossed salad than regular Greek salad,
but it's equally good. SERVES 4

4 cups torn romaine leaves
3 scallions, sliced, including the firm green
1 large cucumber, peeled if necessary, sliced thin
4 ounces feta cheese
¼ cup olive oil
2 tablespoons red wine vinegar
Dash of cinnamon
Pepper to taste
8 kalamata olives, pitted

Per Serving: Protein: 1g   Fat: 13g   Carbohydrate: 2g

Put the romaine, scallions, and cucumber in a salad
bowl and toss. Crumble the feta cheese on top. In a
screw-top jar, mix the oil, vinegar, cinnamon, and pepper
and shake well. Pour the dressing over the salad and toss
well to combine. Tuck in the olives and serve immediately.

POTATO SALAD

Just kidding. Actually this is cauliflower salad, but it tastes almost exactly like potato salad and the texture isn't wildly different. You'll probably have leftover dressing, depending on the size of the cauliflower. SERVES 6

    1 cauliflower, cut into florets
    ½ cup sliced scallions, including the firm green
    3 celery ribs, chopped fine, including some inner
        leaves
    ½ green bell pepper, chopped fine
    ¼ cup chopped parsley
    Salt and pepper to taste

    DRESSING
    2 teaspoons Colman's dry mustard
    2 tablespoons cider vinegar
    1 cup mayonnaise, Hellmann's or Best Foods

    3 hard-cooked eggs, chopped
    ½ to 1 teaspoon celery seeds, to taste
    Paprika for garnish

Per Serving: Protein: 3g   Fat: 32.1g   Carbohydrate: 4.8g

Steam the cauliflower florets until tender but not soft. Set aside to cool.

Put the scallions, celery, bell pepper, and parsley in a large salad bowl. Add salt and pepper.

Make the dressing: mix the mustard, vinegar, and mayonnaise together in a small bowl until smooth.

When the cauliflower is cool, chop and add it to the vegetables and mix with enough dressing to just coat the vegetables. Stir in the eggs and celery seeds and mix well. Sprinkle paprika on top and cover with plastic wrap. Let sit in the refrigerator for at least 2 hours for flavors to develop.

MEXICAN CAULIFLOWER SALAD

This salad takes cauliflower in an unusual direction. If you have Mexican oregano, so much the better.

SERVES 6

3 cups cooked cauliflower florets, page 122

⅓ cup vinaigrette, page 119

½ teaspoon oregano, preferably Mexican

1 avocado, cubed

3 ounces ricotta salata or cream cheese, cubed

Per Serving: Protein: 1.7g   Fat: 19g   Carbohydrate: 2.8g

Mix the cauliflower with the vinaigrette and oregano. Toss lightly with the avocado and cheese and serve on a platter.

PEPPERY COLESLAW

This is *New York Times* food writer Suzanne Hamlin's famous coleslaw, which has been widely copied and attributed. That's because it's so delicious that everyone claims it as their own. You will too. The recipe makes a lot, but it just gets better as it ages, which is why you start a day ahead. SERVES 10

SLAW

2 pounds green cabbage, cored and shredded

1 small turnip, peeled and shredded

2 carrots, peeled and shredded

4 radishes, chopped

⅔ cup finely chopped red onion

¼ cup finely chopped Italian parsley

3 tablespoons minced fresh dill

DRESSING

1 cup mayonnaise

½ cup cider vinegar

1 teaspoon sugar

¼ teaspoon ground black pepper

⅛ teaspoon ground white pepper

¼ teaspoon hot red pepper flakes, optional

½ teaspoon salt

Per Serving: Protein: .7g   Fat: 17.6g   Carbohydrate: 5.2g

In a large bowl toss together the slaw ingredients. In a small bowl, whisk together the dressing ingredients. Add the dressing to the slaw and toss, mixing thoroughly. Taste for salt and toss again. Cover and refrigerate for 24 to 48 hours, stirring from time to time. Just before serving, taste for seasoning and stir thoroughly.

TEX-MEX COLESLAW

This is a mellow coleslaw but you can add fire in the form of more spices, minced hot peppers, or hot pepper sauce.
SERVES 6

> 3 cups shredded cabbage
> ½ cup sour cream
> 1 tablespoon mayonnaise
> 1 tablespoon cider vinegar
> Salt and pepper to taste
> ½ teaspoon chili powder
> ½ teaspoon ground cumin
> 1 teaspoon Mango Vignette (page 40), optional
> 1 tablespoon chopped cilantro

Per Serving: Protein: .6g   Fat: 5.8g   Carbohydrate: 2.6g

Put the cabbage in a mixing bowl. In a small bowl, combine all the remaining ingredients except the cilantro. Mix the dressing into the cabbage thoroughly, then stir in the cilantro. Refrigerate for at least half an hour to develop flavor.

ASIAN COLESLAW

You don't have to make this with napa cabbage, the most commonly available Chinese cabbage, but it makes a subtle difference in both flavor and texture that seems right with the Asian seasonings. Taste the dressing to be sure you need the Equal. You may want a sweet taste and you may want some fire, in which case use the hot pepper flakes. SERVES 6

1 head napa cabbage
¼ cup minced scallions, including some green
1 tablespoon minced fresh ginger

DRESSING
⅓ cup rice wine vinegar
1 tablespoon soy sauce
2 tablespoons dark sesame oil
2 tablespoons safflower oil
1 packet Equal or 1 teaspoon sugar, optional
½ teaspoon hot red pepper flakes, optional

1 tablespoon minced cilantro
⅓ cup chopped roasted peanuts, optional

Per Serving: Protein: 3.3g   Fat: 14g   Carbohydrate: 2.7g

Remove and discard the outer leaves of the cabbage and shred the rest of the head—you should have about 6 cups of shredded cabbage. Mix the cabbage with the scallions and ginger in a bowl and set aside.

Make the dressing: just mix everything together, tasting to see if you need the Equal or the pepper flakes.

Stir the dressing into the vegetables and toss well to mix. Serve in a salad bowl with the cilantro and peanuts sprinkled over the top.

FENNEL AND ORANGE SALAD

This very refreshing salad gives you the exhilarating taste of orange—but not a lot of it. SERVES 8

    1 head Boston lettuce, in bite-size pieces
    2 medium fennel bulbs, trimmed and sliced thin
        crosswise
    Salt and pepper
    Extra virgin olive oil
    1 navel or Valencia orange, peel and white pith
        removed
    16 black olives, pitted

Per Serving: Protein: trace   Fat: 5.5g   Carbohydrate: 3.5g

Mix the lettuce with the fennel slices. Add salt and pepper to taste and toss with just enough olive oil to barely coat the greens. Mix well.

Slice the orange crosswise as thin as possible, removing any seeds. Quarter the slices and lay them over the top of the salad; trickle a little more olive oil on top. Decorate the oranges with the olives; salt and pepper lightly and serve immediately.

Three Crispy Crunches

FRICO

This crisp little wafer of cheese hails from Friuli in Italy, where it's made with Montasio cheese—not usually available here, but you can use Parmesan. It may take a try or two to get this technique down, but you'll be very glad you did. These are delectable, with a wonderful crunch.

SERVES 3

½ pound coarsely grated Parmesan cheese
1 tablespoon melted butter or olive oil
Optional: 1 teaspoon cumin seed or caraway
        seed

Per Serving: Protein: 20g   Fat: 18g   Carbohydrate: 2g

Measure out ⅔ cup of the cheese. Brush a 7-inch non-stick skillet with a teaspoon of the butter or oil. Add the cheese, spreading it out evenly. Add a third of the optional seeds, scattering them over the top of the frico. Cook over medium-low heat for 3 to 4 minutes or until the cheese melts and gets crusty (but don't let it brown). Press down on the top of the frico with a spatula and pour off any oil that accumulates. Turn and cook 1 more minute, until the edges are crisp.

Remove the frico to a baking sheet covered with paper towels. Blot any extra oil and let cool to room temperature. Remove any crumbs in the skillet and make the other 2 fricos in the same manner.

FRICO BOWL

To make a little frico bowl to serve a salad, drape the hot frico over an upside-down bowl and let it cool and dry in place.

CORN CRISPS

This is an old-time recipe from the heartland that's truly delicious. You can instantly update it by adding lots of pepper and Parmesan or a small spoonful of cumin seeds just before it goes into the oven.

SERVES 12

¾ cup white or yellow stone–ground
      cornmeal
1 cup boiling water
½ teaspoon salt
3 tablespoons melted butter

Per Serving: Protein: .5g   Fat: 3g   Carbohydrate: 4.5g

Preheat the oven to 400°F. Stir the cornmeal and boiling water together in a large glass measuring cup. Add the salt and melted butter. Mix well and pour onto a cookie sheet. Using a spatula, spread the batter out as thin as you possibly can—the thinner, the crisper.

Bake the cornmeal for half an hour or until crisp and golden brown. Break into 12 roughly even pieces.

GOUDA CRISPS

These have their origin in Patricia Wells's recipe for Cheese Crisps in her <u>Patricia Wells at Home in Provence</u> (Scribner)—she makes them with a local sheep cheese. This version uses Gouda and spicy seeds, cumin or caraway. The cumin has an exotic taste that goes with Indian or Mexican flavors; the caraway is much more familiar, and would be very good with a glass of vodka. If you have a toaster oven, it's perfect for making these.

For each wafer:

SERVES 1

1 tablespoon coarsely grated Gouda cheese
    (chilled cheese is easier to grate)
Pinch of cumin seeds or caraway seeds

Per Serving: Protein: 1g   Fat: 2g   Carbohydrate: 0g

Using a nonstick cookie sheet, make little mounds of the cheese spaced at least 2 inches apart. Spread the cheese out a bit in a free-form circle so it will melt evenly. The mounds may stay round or they may spread into cheese oysters. Sprinkle the seeds over the top.

Slide the pan under a preheated broiler, 3 or 4 inches below the heat. You'll have to turn the sheet several times so that the wafers cook evenly; they're done in just a couple of minutes, when they're bubbly and golden brown at the edges. Remove the pan from the oven, let sit another minute or two, and remove with a spatula to a cake rack to cool. Blot any oil with paper towels. Let the cookie sheet cool before making another batch.

The wafers will keep for a week tightly covered.

RED AND GREEN COLESLAW

You don't have to add the Mango, of course, but it makes
an intriguing difference. If you leave it out, add ½ teaspoon more vinegar. SERVES 4

2 cups finely shredded green cabbage
1 cup finely shredded red cabbage
2 scallions, including the firm green, in thin
        rounds
1½ teaspoons cider vinegar
1 tablespoon Mango Fat-free Dressing &
        Marinade, page 40
1 tablespoon Dijon mustard
1 tablespoon mayonnaise
¼ cup sour cream
Salt and pepper to taste
2 teaspoons caraway seeds

Per Serving: Protein: .4g   Fat: 5.2g   Carbohydrate: 4.3g

Mix the two cabbages and scallions together in a large
bowl. Mix the remaining ingredients—except the caraway seeds—together in a screwtop jar and shake well.
Pour over the cabbage and toss well to combine. Add the
caraway seeds and mix well. Taste for seasoning and let sit
in the refrigerator for 30 minutes to develop flavor.

OLD-FASHIONED CUCUMBER SALAD

Good with fish, good on a buffet table, pretty good in general. And made in moments. You could make this more substantial by adding crumbled feta cheese.

SERVES 4

- 1½ pounds cucumbers
- ¼ cup sour cream
- 2 tablespoons white vinegar
- ¼ teaspoon salt
- ⅛ teaspoon white pepper
- 1 tablespoon snipped chives
- 1 tablespoon snipped fresh dill

Per Serving: Protein: .3g   Fat: 2.5g   Carbohydrate: 2.7g

Peel the cucumbers and remove the seeds. Slice them thin and put them in a bowl. In a mixing bowl, combine the remaining ingredients and pour over the cucumbers. Toss lightly and transfer to a serving bowl. Garnish the bowl with sprigs of fresh dill and serve within half an hour.

SPANISH CAULIFLOWER SALAD

This is a carnivore's variation on *Greens* author Deborah
Madison's exuberant way with cauliflower. It has strong,
lively tastes that take our familiar vegetables to a new
level. The secret is to slice the cauliflower as thin as possible. SERVES 4

1 small cauliflower
2 cups watercress
2 scallions, sliced fine
1 cup diced celery heart and leaves
1 small green bell pepper, sliced thin
1 small cucumber, peeled, seeded, and chopped
12 green Spanish pimiento-stuffed olives, halved
1 tablespoon capers, rinsed
8 ounces smoked ham, diced
½ cup parsley leaves
Sherry Vinaigrette, page 136

Per Serving: Protein: 10.4g   Fat: 3.1g   Carbohydrate: 7.5g

Remove the green leaves from the cauliflower and cut
off the heavy stem near the base. Separate the head into
florets and peel the stalks. Lay each floret on a work surface and slice it lengthwise as thin as you can. Slice the
stalks the same way. Put the slices into a mixing bowl.

Remove the large stems from the watercress and
roughly chop the rest. Put in the mixing bowl along with
the remaining ingredients except the vinaigrette. Toss
everything together, then add the vinaigrette and toss
again.

SHERRY VINAIGRETTE

MAKES ABOUT ½ CUP, TO SERVE 4

2 garlic cloves, coarsely chopped
Salt to taste
1 hard-cooked egg
1½ tablespoons sherry vinegar or aged red wine
        vinegar
1 teaspoon Dijon mustard, optional
6 tablespoons extra-virgin olive oil
Pepper to taste

Per Serving: Protein: 1.5g   Fat: 22.4g   Carbohydrate: .9g

Pound the garlic with ¼ teaspoon of salt in a mortar
until it breaks down into a purée, then add the egg yolk
and mash it in well. (Discard the white or dice it and add
to the salad.) Combine the garlic, vinegar, and mustard in
a small bowl, then whisk in the oil and season with pepper. Taste and correct the balance; the dressing should
be a little on the tart side.

TABBOULEH

This Middle Eastern classic is such a favorite that it seems
a pity we can't have it. Well, we can't have the gummy
American version jammed with cracked wheat, but
there's another tradition in the Middle East, where the
tabbouleh is often more of a parsley salad with just a little grain and all the same zesty flavors. The ¼ cup of grain
may seem miserly, but it will swell to about ⅔ cup once
it soaks in water. This salad keeps well, so you can make
a lot and serve it for several days. SERVES 4

¼ cup medium-grain bulgur (cracked wheat)
½ cucumber
Salt
1 large bunch Italian flat-leaf parsley (1 ⅓ cups
    chopped)
4 scallions, including an inch of the greens
1 teaspoon coarse sea salt
2 tablespoons olive oil mixed with 1 drop pure
    lemon oil, page 41
1 tablespoon fresh lemon juice
¼ cup chopped mint leaves
¾ cup chopped tomato, no seeds
Pinch of ground cumin

Per Serving: Protein: 1g   Fat: 7.1g   Carbohydrate: 10g

Put the bulgur in a bowl and cover with water; let sit
for 30 minutes. Peel the cucumber and cut it in half
lengthwise. Scoop out the seeds. Chop it into small dice,
toss with a sprinkle of salt, and set it to drain in a colander in the sink while the bulgur is soaking.

Meanwhile, wash and completely dry the parsley. You can use stems and all; chop the whole bunch. Chop the scallions.

When the bulgur is finished soaking, drain it through a sieve into the sink, then roll it in a towel to dry—it should be as dry as possible. Put the bulgur in a bowl with the scallions and sea salt; with your hands, work the scallions and salt into the grains for several minutes.

Mix in the olive oil, lemon juice, mint, and tomatoes. Dry the cucumber dice with a kitchen towel and add that too. Mix everything together well to combine, add the cumin, and taste for seasoning. Let sit for at least half an hour to develop flavor.

MAUDE SALAD

This famous salad was invented at the much-missed
Chasen's restaurant in Beverly Hills and named for owner
Maude Chasen. It speaks of a happier era, when a rich and
delectable salad wasn't politically incorrect. Cut the chili
sauce in half and you'll reduce the carbs to 6.2 per serving. SERVES 8

> 8 cups shredded mixed lettuces—iceberg,
>   romaine, chicory
> 4 cups seeded diced tomatoes
> 4 hard-cooked eggs, chopped
> 2 bunches chopped chives (about ½ cup)
> 1 cup crumbled Roquefort cheese

Per Serving: Protein: 21g   Fat: 78g   Carbohydrate: 8.2g

DRESSING
1 cup mayonnaise
¾ cup sour cream
2 garlic cloves, minced
½ cup chili sauce
¼ cup red wine vinegar
Salt and pepper to taste
¾ cup crumbled Roquefort cheese

Combine the lettuces, tomatoes, eggs, and chives in a salad bowl. Toss and chill until ready to serve.

Make the dressing: Blend everything but the salt and pepper and Roquefort in a bowl. Add salt and pepper to taste. Stir in the Roquefort and mix well.

When ready to serve, remove the salad from the refrigerator and toss with the dressing. Sprinkle the salad with the remaining cup of Roquefort.

SALMON AND GREEN BEAN SALAD
WITH DILL

This combination of tastes is simply winning—perfect low-carb fare that everyone else will love too. SERVES 4

  Olive oil for the salmon
  Salt and pepper
  1½ pounds salmon fillet
  1 pound steamed green beans
  4 scallions, chopped, including some of the firm
      green
  1 tablespoon chopped fresh dill
  2 tablespoons fresh lemon juice
  ¼ cup extra-virgin olive oil
  1 teaspoon lemon thyme leaves or 1 tablespoon
      chopped parsley

Per Serving: Protein: 34g   Fat: 32g   Carbohydrate: 7.4g

Rub the salmon all over with olive oil and sprinkle with salt and pepper. Set aside on a baking sheet to season for at least 5 minutes or up to half an hour.

Preheat the broiler. Broil the salmon for 8 to 12 minutes, or until it's done all the way through but still juicy. Remove from the oven and let cool.

Put the beans in a large serving bowl. Add the scallions and dill; mix well. In a small screwtop jar, shake up the lemon juice, oil, and salt and pepper to taste. Pour the dressing over the beans. Flake the salmon over the beans and toss everything together well. Sprinkle the herbs over the top and serve.

Tuna and Green Bean Salad with Dill

You can make the same dish with three 3½-ounce cans of tuna in place of the cooked and cooled salmon, preferably Genova tuna imported from Italy. With the tuna, use a red wine vinaigrette.

WATERMELON SALAD WITH PECANS AND FETA

This wonderful salad sometimes appears on breakfast tables in the Middle East. For low-carb cooks, it's probably best considered a relish, since we can't eat a huge amount of it—but it's much too good to leave out of the repertoire. SERVES 4

2 cups watermelon cubes, seeds removed
½ cup feta cheese cubes
8 toasted pecan halves, chopped
8 slivered mint leaves
1 tablespoon fresh lime juice
Grinding of fresh pepper

Per Serving: Protein: 1.2g   Fat: 2.7g   Carbohydrate: 6.5g

Mix everything together and toss well. Serve right away.

THAI-STYLE SHRIMP SALAD

This quick salad depends on a couple of condiments: Thai spices and Mango Fat-free Dressing & Marinade. But you could also use shrimp boil for Thai spices and cider vinegar with orange zest and a drop of vanilla for the dressing. SERVES 2

1 tablespoon Thai spices
2 garlic cloves, chopped
¼ pound medium raw shrimp
1 hard-cooked egg, chopped
1 celery rib plus some of the inner leaves, chopped fine
2 scallions, chopped, including the firm greens
½ medium cucumber, seeded and chopped
2 tablespoons chopped cilantro

Per Serving: Protein: 45g   Fat: 50.1g   Carbohydrate: 9.1g

DRESSING
⅓ cup mayonnaise
1 tablespoon Mango Fat-free Dressing & Marinade, page 40
Salt and white pepper to taste

¼ cup chopped roasted peanuts

In a large saucepan heat 3 cups of water with the Thai spices and garlic. When it's boiling, toss in the shrimp and cook just until they turn pink and curl. Drain in a colander in the sink. Remove shells when the shrimp are cool enough to handle and chop roughly.

Meanwhile, assemble everything else in a medium-size salad bowl and make the dressing by whisking together the mayonnaise, the dressing, and salt and pepper to taste.

When the shrimp are ready, mix everything together and top with a scattering of peanuts. Or serve the salad on a bed of greens and top with the peanuts.

COBB SALAD

If you have hard-cooked eggs hanging around—as you should—and you bring home a rotisserie chicken, you can have this classic Hollywood salad ready in about 10 minutes. SERVES 4

1 head iceberg lettuce, chopped
1 small head romaine, chopped
1 bunch watercress, chopped
4 inner celery ribs, sliced diagonally
1 avocado, diced
2 large tomatoes, chopped
1 whole roast chicken breast, chopped, about 1½
      cups
2 hard-cooked eggs, chopped
¼ pound blue cheese, crumbled
8 bacon slices, fried crisp and crumbled
⅓ cup olive oil
2 tablespoons white wine vinegar
Salt and pepper to taste
1 garlic clove, smashed

Per Serving: Protein: 28.9g   Fat: 65g   Carbohydrate: 7.9g

Mix the greens, avocado, tomatoes, and chicken in a large salad bowl. Scatter the eggs, cheese, and bacon over the top. In a screw-top jar, mix the remaining ingredients and shake well. Remove the garlic and drizzle the dressing over the salad. Toss at the table just before serving.

MIDDLE EASTERN LAMB SALAD

You can serve the salad without the lamb, of course, but it's a particularly delicious, zesty combination of flavors.

SERVES 4

½ leg of lamb, butterflied
1 tablespoon olive oil
Salt and pepper to taste
1 teaspoon ground cumin
2 garlic cloves, pressed

Per Serving: Protein: 65.9g   Fat: 41.7g   Carbohydrate: 4.4g

SALAD
½ cup pecan pieces
4 ounces feta cheese, crumbled
¼ cup olive oil
1½ tablespoons fresh lemon juice
2 cups baby spinach leaves
1 cup mint leaves, chopped coarse
Salt and pepper to taste

Rub the lamb all over with the oil and then with the salt and pepper, cumin, and garlic. Grill the lamb, turning once, until it reaches an internal temperature of 135°F for medium-rare. This will take about 40 minutes on a charcoal or gas-fired grill.

While the lamb is cooking, make the salad. Toast the pecan pieces on a baking sheet in a 325° oven for about 10 minutes or until they smell toasty. Mix the remaining ingredients together in a salad bowl and toss well. Scatter the pecans over the top. Serve thin slices of the warm grilled lamb over the salad.

TUNISIAN ROASTED VEGETABLES
WITH TUNA

In Tunisia this traditional salad is grilled and served as an
appetizer. But it's easy to oven-roast the vegetables, and
the salad is so good that it's worth adding an extra can of
tuna and serving it as a main course.

SERVES 4 AS A MAIN COURSE

    4 bell peppers—red, green, yellow, or a
        combination
    1 medium onion, unpeeled
    4 medium tomatoes
    1 small green chile—jalapeño or serrano—seeded
        and minced
    3 tablespoons olive oil
    1½ tablespoons fresh lemon juice
    Salt and pepper to taste
    2 (3½-ounce) cans light tuna packed in oil,
        drained
    2 hard-cooked eggs, cut into wedges
    6 anchovy fillets, page 40, optional

Per Serving: Protein: 14.7g   Fat: 6.2g   Carbohydrate: 10.3g

---

Preheat the oven to 475°F. Put the peppers and onion
on a baking sheet on the top shelf of the oven for 30 minutes. Add the tomatoes for the last 5 minutes. The vegetables should be soft and very well browned.

Peel and seed the peppers (page 297), then dice them.
Peel and dice the onion. Peel the tomatoes, take out as
many seeds as you can, and dice the flesh. Save any juices
for the salad.

Put the vegetables in a serving bowl and stir in the chile. Whisk the oil and lemon juice together in a small bowl and add salt and pepper to taste. Pour the dressing over the vegetables and toss gently. Crumble the tuna over the top of the salad and arrange the egg slices over the tuna. Sprinkle the chopped anchovies over the salad and serve.

Sauces, Marinades, and Salsas

/\\\

A diet that allows butter, cream, olive oil, eggs, olives, nuts, and cheese clearly offers the cook a cornucopia of ingredients to make food sing. Though we've tended to think of sauces as French, and therefore rich and expendable, in fact they're endlessly versatile and delicious, and not even necessarily rich.

If you can take a few extra minutes to make real mayonnaise—in a blender or a food processor or by hand—you'll be endlessly rewarded. All sorts of flavorings go into the real thing, from the classic garlicky aioli of Provence to smoky chipotle chiles from Mexico. You can add herbs and spices almost ad infinitum. But real mayonnaise is so good it stands alone—and good store-bought mayonnaise isn't too far behind.

A butter sauce is almost instant: just melted butter and the pan juices plus a jolt of whatever seems missing (something hot, something spicy, something smoky, something tart, a particular herb or spice). It can be just butter and a little sherry vinegar or balsamic vinegar, or just butter and chopped toasted nuts. Or just ghee (page 48), heated into a nutty-tasting sauce.

Marinades are more familiar from the low-fat era. Here's a good place to use citrus, lots of garlic, and other elements that are a little too high-carb to use in any quantity—you get the flavor in the marinade without the carbs.

Salsa is one of those crossover foods from the high-carb diets—fresh and delicious and wonderfully useful, it goes on almost everything. Make your own or find a good commercial product that doesn't use sweeteners.

The most important thing is to remember to use these great flavor enhancers. If you're not used to making something extra to serve with the main course, try to make it a habit. Plain grilled food, however delicious, can get boring, and these tasty elements hold the secret to making it new and fresh every time.

ROMESCO SAUCE

One of the classic sauces from Catalonia in Spain, this one is hot and addictive. It goes with meat, fish, shellfish, chicken, salad, almost anything you can think of.

MAKES 1 CUP, 16 SERVINGS

> 2 ounces blanched almonds, about ⅓ cup
> 3 garlic cloves, unpeeled
> 2 medium tomatoes
> 1 dried hot chili pepper
> 3 tablespoons red wine vinegar
> Salt to taste
> ½ cup olive oil

Per Serving: Protein: .5g   Fat: 8.4g   Carbohydrate: .9g

Preheat the oven to 350°F. Put the almonds, garlic, tomatoes, and chili pepper on a baking sheet and roast them for 10 to 15 minutes. The almonds should be lightly browned and the vegetables and garlic should be soft. Peel the tomatoes and remove the seeds. Slip the peel off the garlic.

Put the almonds, tomatoes, garlic, and chili pepper in a blender jar and grind thoroughly. Add the vinegar and salt, then gradually trickle in the oil until the sauce thickens. The sauce will keep for several days tightly covered in the refrigerator.

ANCHOVY BUTTER

Very good on Wasa crackers and with smoked fish or sardines. Just spread some on a cracker, add the fish, and top with a couple of sweet onion rings and a few watercress leaves. MAKES 12 TEASPOONS, 6 SERVINGS

½ teaspoon anchovy paste or ½ anchovy, soaked in
    milk for 15 minutes and minced
½ teaspoon minced parsley
Several drops of fresh lemon juice
4 tablespoons (½ stick) unsalted butter, at room
    temperature

Per Serving: Protein: trace   Fat: 7.3g   Carbohydrate: trace

With the back of a fork, mix the ingredients together until smoothly combined. Put the anchovy butter in a little crock to serve or store it in the refrigerator, tightly sealed.

TARATOR

There's a soup called tarator in Yugoslavia—made with cucumbers and yogurt—but there's also this sauce by that name in the Middle East. Tarator sauce is very good over steamed vegetables, especially beets and cauliflower.

SERVES 8

> ½ cup hazelnuts, walnuts, or pine nuts, toasted
>   (page 51)
> 2 garlic cloves, crushed
> ¼ cup olive oil
> 3 tablespoons fresh lemon juice
> ½ cup yogurt
> Chili powder to taste
> Salt to taste

Per Serving: Protein: 2.4g   Fat: 11.9g   Carbohydrate: 2.1g

Put everything but the chili powder and salt in the workbowl of a food processor and blend smooth. Pour the sauce into a bowl and add the chili powder, stirring it in well. Add salt to taste.

CHIMICHURRI SAUCE

Argentina is the homeland of this addictive sauce, which is served with the incomparable Argentine mixed grill—chicken, ribs, and sausages. Just remember to make it a few hours ahead for best flavor. SERVES 12

½ cup olive oil
¼ cup red wine vinegar
1 large onion, chopped
1 garlic clove, crushed
1 cup finely chopped parsley
1 cup finely chopped cilantro
1 teaspoon dried oregano
¼ teaspoon ground red pepper (cayenne)
1½ teaspoons salt
1 teaspoon ground black pepper

Per Serving: Protein: 0g   Fat: 9.3g   Carbohydrate: .7g

Whisk together the oil and vinegar, then add the other ingredients. Let stand for several hours to develop flavors.

TABLE SALSA

This fresh salsa adds zest to anything it touches—
everything from eggs to broiled or grilled meat to pork
rinds to carnitas. Don't make it more than half an hour
before you serve it or it will lose some of its sparkle. If
you want the salsa really hot, leave the chile seeds in—
extra fiber, after all. MAKES ABOUT 18 TABLESPOONS

> 1 medium tomato, chopped
> ¼ cup chopped scallions
> 2 tablespoons roughly chopped cilantro
> 2 serrano chiles or jalapeños, chopped fine
> ½ teaspoon salt
> 1 tablespoon fresh lime juice

Per Serving: Protein: 0g   Fat: 0g   Carbohydrate: .5g

Mix everything together. After about 3 hours, the salsa
will begin to seriously deteriorate and lose flavor.

HORSERADISH CREAM

This could hardly be easier to make, and it's especially delicious with roast beef. Fresh horseradish is best but hard
to find; if you're using bottled horseradish, drain it well
and squeeze dry first. MAKES 1 CUP, SERVES 8

> 1 cup heavy cream
> 1 tablespoon grated horseradish, or to taste

Per Serving: Protein: .6g   Fat: 10g   Carbohydrate: .9g

Whip the cream until you have soft peaks. Stir in the
horseradish and serve at once.

ORANGE MAYONNAISE

Good for dipping and also for using as the base for a
chicken salad. Add a little curry powder to take it in a different direction. Instead of the juice, you could use a couple of drops of citrus oil, page 41, and thin the
mayonnaise with a little mild vinegar, such as champagne
vinegar, or rice vinegar. MAKES 1 CUP, 8 SERVINGS

>   1 cup mayonnaise
>   2 teaspoons grated orange zest
>   2 tablespoons fresh orange juice
>   1 teaspoon mild curry powder, optional

Per Serving: Protein: trace   Fat: 22g   Carbohydrate: .3g

Mix everything together in a bowl and let sit for half
an hour to develop flavor.

CHIPOTLE MAYONNAISE

Making this mayonnaise depends on having the chipotle paste, page 38. Once you've made this, though, you'll keep it on hand willingly. It seems created to eat with shrimp, but it's also delicious with other fish, chicken, and vegetables. MAKES 1½ CUPS, 12 SERVINGS

> 2 garlic cloves, pressed
> 2 tablespoons chipotle paste, page 38, or 2 canned
>   chipotle peppers in adobo, rinsed, seeded,
>   and minced
> 1½ cups mayonnaise

Per Serving: Protein: trace   Fat: 22g   Carbohydrate: .5g

Mix everything together in a food processor and serve in a bowl to dip into.

CURRIED MAYONNAISE

This won't be a lot better if you make it from scratch, so
you may as well use a good brand of prepared mayonnaise, like Hellmann's or Best Foods. A nice mild curry
powder is the right thing here—if you can't find one you
like, use garam masala, an Indian spice mix that's widely
available. If you can't find the Mango Vignette, use apple
cider vinegar. MAKES ¼ CUP, 2 SERVINGS

  ¼ cup mayonnaise
  ½ teaspoon mild curry powder
  1 teaspoon Mango Fat-free Dressing & Marinade,
      page 40

Per Serving: Protein: 0g   Fat: 11g   Carbohydrate: trace

Mix everything together in a small bowl and keep refrigerated.

GARLIC MAYONNAISE

This is a useful item to have on hand, and it will keep several days in the refrigerator. It's the essential element for the aioli platter on page 209 (see Two Great Feasts), but also good for dipping vegetables and spooning into certain soups. Try adding a teaspoon of Dijon mustard along with the egg. Leave out the garlic and you have regular mayonnaise. MAKES 1 CUP, 8 SERVINGS

> 3 garlic cloves
> ½ teaspoon sea salt
> 1 egg yolk
> 1 whole egg
> 1 cup mild extra-virgin olive oil
> 1 teaspoon fresh lemon juice or more to taste

Per Serving: Protein: .5g   Fat: 14g   Carbohydrate: trace

Cut the garlic cloves lengthwise and then mince them. Using a mortar and pestle, work the salt into the garlic until you have a paste (or do this on a plate with the back of a fork if you have no mortar). Scrape the garlic paste into the workbowl of a food processor. Add the egg yolk and whole egg and pulse briefly to blend. With the feed tube open and the machine running, pour the oil in a slow but steady stream into the workbowl until it begins to come together to form the mayonnaise. Add the lemon juice. Serve immediately or refrigerate for several days, tightly sealed.

BASIL MAYONNAISE

Delicious with raw vegetables. **MAKES 1 CUP, 8 SERVINGS**

> **1 cup mayonnaise: Hellmann's or Best Foods**
> **¼ cup snipped fresh basil leaves**
> **Several grinds of fresh pepper**

Per Serving: Protein: trace   Fat: 22g   Carbohydrate: trace

Mix everything together by hand in a small bowl. Keeps refrigerated, tightly covered, for a week.

CRÈME FRAÎCHE

This much milder form of sour cream is delicious with berries, or just about any place you'd use sour cream.
MAKES 2 CUPS

> **1 cup heavy cream**
> **1 cup sour cream**

Per Serving: Protein: 12.2g   Fat: 136g   Carbohydrate: 16.4g

Mix the two creams together well and let stand 24 hours at room temperature. Place in a tightly sealed jar in the refrigerator. Keeps 1 week.

BLUE CHEESE DRESSING

You can just throw everything but the chives together in the food processor to make this dressing, then stir in the chives—or if you'd like a little texture, you can make it by hand. MAKES 1½ CUPS, 12 SERVINGS

4 ounces blue cheese, such as Roquefort
½ cup sour cream
½ cup mayonnaise
¼ teaspoon pepper
dash of hot pepper sauce
¼ cup minced chives

Per Serving: Protein: 2.3g   Fat: 11.9g   Carbohydrate: .5g

In a small bowl, break up the cheese with a fork and mash it lightly, leaving some small chunks. Add everything else but the chives and mix together thoroughly. Stir in the chives. Cover the bowl tightly and store in the refrigerator up to 1 week.

PESTO

You may wish you had pasta for pesto, but that's no reason to forgo the pesto, which can go on fish, vegetables such as tomatoes and green beans, spaghetti squash, and cheese—mozzarella and goat cheese come to mind. The easiest way to make it is in a blender.

MAKES 1½ CUPS, 12 SERVINGS

    1 cup olive oil
    1 garlic clove, minced
    2 cups lightly packed basil leaves, preferably small
    3 tablespoons pine nuts or walnuts
    ½ cup grated Parmesan cheese

Per Serving: Protein: 1.8g   Fat: 20.7g   Carbohydrate: .3g

Put the olive oil in the blender jar and add everything but the cheese. Blend until smooth, scraping down the jar if necessary. Transfer the pesto to a bowl and stir in the cheese. It will keep a couple of days in the refrigerator.

To Freeze Pesto

To freeze pesto, make it without the cheese and the garlic; add those when you defrost it.

TAPENADE

You can buy jarred tapenade in specialty markets, but this is so easy and so much more delicious that it's worth making just to have it around. It will keep, tightly covered in the refrigerator, for several weeks. You can also add little chunks of tuna to tapenade. MAKES 1 CUP, 8 SERVINGS

> 1 cup imported black olives, such as kalamatas,
>   pitted (see instructions page 165)
> 4 anchovy fillets
> 2 tablespoons drained capers
> 1 teaspoon Dijon mustard
> 1 tablespoon white wine vinegar
> Optional: 2 or 3 drops pure orange oil, page 41

Per Serving: Protein: .8g   Fat: 3.7g   Carbohydrate: .8g

Combine everything in the workbowl of a food processor and blend briefly to combine.

OLIVADA (OLIVE PASTE)

You can of course buy this already prepared—for a price—but it's much more delicious if it's homemade. And it's so easy and so useful that it's worth doing.

What do you do with olivada once you've got it? It's terrific spread on salmon to be broiled (page 216), as the base for tapenade, spread on grilled eggplant, or dolloped on deviled eggs. MAKES 1 CUP, 8 SERVINGS

> 1 cup imported black olives, such as kalamatas
> ¼ cup drained capers
> 2 small garlic cloves, minced
> ½ teaspoon dried thyme
> 1 or 2 tablespoons olive oil, as needed
> 1 or 2 drops pure lemon oil, page 41

Per Serving: Protein: .2g   Fat: 5.2g   Carbohydrate: 1.1g

To pit the olives, put them on a cutting board and cover several at a time with the flat side of a large chef's knife or cleaver. With your fist, press down on the surface of the knife to open the olives. Once they're all open, just pull the pits out with your fingers.

Mix everything but the two oils together in the workbowl of a food processor and process until you have a rough paste. Mix the olive oil with the lemon oil and add slowly with the motor running until you have a loose paste.

Cover the olivada tightly and store in the refrigerator, where it will keep for weeks.

Olivada With Tuna

Add a can of drained flaked tuna and mix well. Serve spread inside red pepper boats, page 310, as an hors d'oeuvre.

PEANUT BUTTER

Making your own can be as easy as dumping a can of roasted peanuts in the food processor and processing away. But the best peanut butter, like the best coffee, is freshly roasted, and it's a snap to make. Just find the freshest raw peanuts you can—you may have to mail-order them; see Sources—and you're in business. You can make them without salt (not as good in my opinion) and without extra oil (it'll be more like peanut paste than peanut butter). You can leave the skins on if you like their slight bitterness. And of course you can roast them as much as you like, anywhere from lightly golden to dark gold—beyond that, they tend to taste a little bitter. Stop roasting a little before you think the nuts are ready; according to the peanut wizards at Nuts D'Vine (see Sources), peanuts cook from the inside out, so they continue to cook a bit after they come out of the oven. Like commercial peanut butter, a 2-tablespoon serving of homemade has 7.7g protein, 16g fat, and 4.8g carbs.
MAKES ABOUT 1 CUP

> 1 pound raw peanuts, skinned
> 1 teaspoon salt
> 1 tablespoon peanut oil

Preheat the oven to 325°F. Spread the peanuts out on a roasting pan or a baking sheet with shallow sides. Roast them for 20 minutes, stirring occasionally. You may want to roast them another 5 or 10 minutes; taste a peanut and see what you think. Once they're roasted, let the peanuts cool before proceeding.

Put half the peanuts and half the remaining ingredients in the workbowl of a food processor. Process until creamy; remove the peanut butter to a storage jar and process the remaining batch.

Keep the peanut butter covered and in the refrigerator, where it will keep for at least 1 month.

Chunky Peanut Butter

Process a third of the peanuts first, just until they're roughly chopped. Set them aside and proceed with the rest of the peanuts. Mix the chopped peanuts into the finished peanut butter.

Nut Butters

Make almond, cashew, and hazelnut butter the same way. Try mixing almonds and hazelnuts together.

CRANBERRY SAUCE

There's no turkey at Thanksgiving without cranberry
sauce—and this is a perfect place to use stevia (page 34),
since the cranberry taste will overpower the back-taste of
the stevia. Of course, you can also dump many little packets of Equal into this sauce, too. SERVES 12

> 1 pound cranberries
> Zest of 1 orange, grated
> Stevia or Equal to taste

Per Serving: Protein: .1g   Fat: trace   Carbohydrate: 2g

Put the cranberries in a heavy saucepan with ½ cup of
water. Cook over medium heat until the cranberries pop
and deflate into a sauce. Add the orange zest and the
sweetener to taste. Cool to room temperature before
serving.

Main Dishes

〽️

Main dishes are the easiest category of all to work with—protein, whether it's grilled, broiled, roasted, fried, sautéed, simmered, or braised. Dinner may just be a burger and salad when you're rushed, but there are almost no limits on what you can improvise within the guidelines.

If you have an outdoor grill, summer turns out to be a series of great quick meals from the grill, punched up with sauces and salsas and served over salads, cooked greens, or sliced tomatoes. To make life even easier, grill extras, both protein and vegetables, to make instant left-over dishes—steak salad, chicken salad, marinated roasted vegetables, etc.

Cold-weather dishes such as stews and pot roasts are perfect for low-carb cooks, both for entertaining and home cooking. Favorite dishes like chili and brisket turn up over and over on the list of what people would really like to eat. In traditional cooking, a lot of these dishes require potatoes or flour, but they're really not necessary—meat will brown perfectly well without flour as long as it's dry and you've salted it just before browning. For potatoes, try substituting turnips in a stew (old wrinkled ones will be bitter, so avoid those).

You may notice that contemporary recipes often use a lot of sugar for main dishes—a little sugar will most likely accomplish the same thing, and may be a good way to incorporate some sweetness into your meal without completely blowing it. A touch of brown sugar in a spice rub for meat, for instance, or a teaspoon of marmalade in a marinade may bring up new dimensions of flavor with minimal carb impact. But know your own limits: if a little sweetness will send you looking for more, just stick with the savory dishes, which are entirely satisfying on their own.

CRISPY CHICKEN CUTLETS

A great way to cook boring chicken cutlets—this is a
lower-carb adaptation of the way Eileen Weinberg makes
them at her Times Square takeout shop, Good & Plenty
To Go. Just remember to let the chicken sit for a couple
of hours before baking to develop flavor. SERVES 6

> 6 chicken cutlets
> Salt
> Pepper to taste
> 1 cup mayonnaise
> ½ teaspoon pure lemon oil, page 41, or ¼ cup fresh
>   lemon juice
> 2 garlic cloves, minced
> 2 scallions, chopped, including the firm green
> Several sprigs fresh thyme, leaves only

Per Serving: Protein: 14.6g   Fat: 31.3g   Carbohydrate: .6g

Salt the cutlets lightly and rub the salt in on both sides.
In a small bowl mix together the remaining ingredients.
Spread the flavored mayonnaise over the chicken, coating
both sides, and let it marinate for 2 hours.

Preheat the oven to 350°F. Put the cutlets on a foil-
lined baking sheet and bake for 20 to 30 minutes or until
the outside is golden brown and crispy. If they're not
crispy, run them under the broiler.

ONE-POT CHICKEN WITH RED PEPPERS

Make this dish when red bell peppers are plentiful and cheap in the market, at the end of summer. You can use all chicken thighs—eight—if you'd rather. SERVES 4

    3 tablespoons olive oil
    4 chicken thighs
    2 boneless chicken breasts, cut in half crosswise
    Salt and pepper to taste
    6 garlic cloves, chopped
    1 medium onion, chopped
    1 thick slice bacon, diced
    2 red bell peppers, seeded and chopped
    1 bay leaf
    1 teaspoon dried thyme
    1 (14-ounce) can Muir Glen diced tomatoes,
          including juice, or 1 pound skinned, seeded,
          and chopped tomatoes
    Chopped parsley

Per Serving: Protein: 23.3g   Fat: 24.3g   Carbohydrate: 8.4g

Heat the oil in a heavy pot, such as a dutch oven. When it's hot, add half the chicken pieces and fry over medium heat until they begin to color. Remove the cooked chicken and brown the remaining pieces. Add salt and pepper. Add the garlic and onion and cook until they begin to color. Add the cooked chicken to the pot along with the bacon, peppers, bay leaf, and thyme. Fry until the bacon begins to color, then add the tomatoes and let it all bubble. Stir everything together, turn the heat down to low, cover, and simmer for an hour or longer, until the juices are reduced to a sauce. If this hasn't happened after an hour and a half, remove the chicken and turn the heat up to thicken the sauce. Check the seasoning, remove the bay leaf, and serve hot, sprinkled with parsley.

CHICKEN IN THE POT

This old French classic couldn't be easier or more comforting. Prep time is about five minutes, cooking time
about an hour. You'll have lots of delicious chicken broth
left over for making soup. This is basic; add mushrooms
if you like. SERVES 4

    1 (3½- to 4-pound) roasting chicken
    1 (13½-ounce) can chicken broth
    1 chicken bouillon cube
    1 fat leek, well washed and chopped
    1 carrot, scraped, in large chunks
    3 medium turnips, peeled and cut into large
        chunks
    2 celery ribs, chopped, plus a sprig of leaves
    Salt and pepper

Per Serving: Protein: 41.8g   Fat: 20.8g   Carbohydrate: 5.7g

Rinse the chicken inside and out and put it in a dutch
oven or another heavy pot—about 6 quarts is the right
size. Add the chicken broth, the bouillon cube, crumbled, and enough water to cover the chicken. Bring to a
simmer and skim off the foam that rises to the surface.

Add the vegetables, tucking them in around the
chicken. Cover the pot but leave the lid slightly askew.
Cook at just below a simmer for 30 minutes, then turn
the chicken so it will cook evenly. Cover again and cook
30 more minutes.

Remove the chicken to a platter and keep warm under
a loose covering of foil. Remove the vegetables to a bowl.

Skim the fat from the surface of the broth and strain the broth. Taste for seasoning.

Slice the chicken and place it in warm soup plates. Add salt and pepper to taste. Arrange the vegetables around the chicken and ladle about ½ cup of broth over the top.

GARLICKY BAKED CHICKEN

Throw this simple chicken dish together the night before
you plan to serve it, then just bring it to room temperature and tuck it in the oven when you're ready to eat.
You'll cut the carbs even lower if you use the lemon oil
instead of the fresh lemon juice. SERVES 4

> 1 tablespoon paprika
> Salt and pepper to taste
> 8 chicken thighs
> 3 garlic cloves, pressed
> ¼ cup olive oil
> 3 tablespoons fresh lemon juice or ½ teaspoon
>   pure lemon oil
> Pinch of oregano

Per Serving: Protein: 31g   Fat: 26.2g   Carbohydrate: 1.7g

Rub the paprika, salt, and pepper well into the chicken
pieces. In a small bowl, mix together the garlic, oil, and
lemon juice. Put the chicken in a glass or ceramic roasting pan and pour the marinade over it. Turn the chicken
with tongs to coat it completely, then cover and refrigerate overnight.

Bring to room temperature before baking. Preheat the
oven to 400°F. Sprinkle the chicken with oregano. Put the
uncovered roasting pan with the chicken in the oven and
roast for 40 minutes, turning the pieces once. Serve on a
bed of watercress.

FRIED CHICKEN

There are several ways to go here: you can use regular flour to dredge the chicken before it goes in the pot (which will cost you about 5 carbs per serving, not bad), you can use nut flour (about 3 carbs per serving, and a little expensive), or you can use . . . pork rinds! This sounds bizarre, but it's delicious—the chicken is incredibly crispy and you'll probably find everyone begging you for the recipe.

To make the pork rinds stick, the secret is dipping the chicken first in a formula developed by San Francisco restaurateur Nancy Oakes: egg white and cream—another bizarre idea, but it works perfectly. SERVES 4

8 chicken thighs

1 tablespoon paprika

Salt and pepper to taste

Peanut oil or lard for frying, about 1 quart

3 large egg whites

⅓ cup heavy cream

1 teaspoon Durkee's Red Hot Sauce

1½ cups crumbled pork rinds, page 45

Per Serving: Protein: 38.9g   Fat: 33.6g   Carbohydrate: .8g

Several hours before you want to cook the chicken, rinse it well, trim off any odd bits, pat it dry, and rub it with the paprika, salt, and pepper. Set aside to season for 2 hours or refrigerate if it will be longer.

Heat the oil in a dutch oven over medium heat. Meanwhile, whisk the egg whites in a bowl with the cream and the hot sauce. Put the crumbled pork rinds in a soup plate. Using tongs, dip the chicken pieces first in the egg white mixture, then in the pork rinds, coating well. When the oil reaches 370°F, it's ready for the chicken.

Fry the chicken pieces in two batches, cooking them 10 minutes on each side or turning them frequently, as you prefer. Don't let the temperature go over 375°. When the chicken pieces are done, remove them to a platter lined with paper towels and immediately salt and pepper them. Cook the second batch of chicken. Filter the oil through a coffee filter and refrigerate to use a second time.

The Bird

The contemporary turkey is unstuffed, as our government wishes, and therefore can be cooked at a higher temperature (which makes for a juicier bird). Try this method, which is favored by several prominent Manhattan restaurateurs. Cooking time will be 2½ to 3 hours.

SERVES 8

1 (12- to 14-pound) turkey, preferably fresh
1 pound sliced smoked bacon
4 cups turkey broth (made from giblets) or
        chicken broth
Salt and pepper to taste

Per Serving: Protein: 33.2g   Fat: 5.6g   Carbohydrate: 0g

Rinse the turkey inside and out and place on a rack in a heavy roasting pan. Let the bird sit for several hours, covered with a kitchen towel, to come to room temperature.

Preheat the oven to 450°F. Arrange the bacon slices over the turkey breast. Put the bird in the oven and roast for half an hour. Turn the heat down to 375° and remove the bacon to use for another purpose. Don't baste the turkey; just let it cook until done. (Use an instant-read thermometer to check: the inner fold of the thigh should be 165°.) If it begins to look perfectly brown too soon, cover the breast loosely with foil. When the turkey's done, remove it to a serving platter to rest for 10 minutes, tented with foil.

To make pan gravy, pour off all but ¼ cup of the fat.

Add 4 cups of turkey broth or chicken broth to the pan and scrape up all the little bits. Put the roasting pan over medium heat and boil to reduce the juices by half, stirring frequently. Add salt and pepper to taste.

SAUSAGE STUFFING WITH NUTS

This stuffing seems less like a side dish than the main course. It harks back to the forcemeat stuffings of classic French cuisine that moistened the dry interiors of wild game birds. It's rich, dense, and savory—a little goes a long way, notes Suzanne Hamlin, who created it.

SERVES 4

½ cup pecan halves
½ cup pine nuts
2 tablespoons olive oil
1 cup minced onion
8 ounces bulk pork sausage (such as Jimmy
        Dean)
1 green bell pepper, seeded and diced
¼ cup minced parsley
2 tablespoons chopped fresh sage or thyme
        leaves, optional
¼ teaspoon freshly grated nutmeg
Ground black pepper to taste
2 large eggs

Per Serving: Protein: 14g   Fat: 37g   Carbohydrate: 7.6g

Preheat the oven to 350°F. Spread the pecans out on a baking sheet. Spread the pine nuts out on another baking sheet. Toast each batch of nuts 5 to 8 minutes, until they begin to smell nutty and take on color. Check the pine nuts frequently, since they can easily burn. Cool the nuts and break the pecans into large pieces.

In a large skillet, heat the olive oil and add the onion. Cook for 2 minutes over medium heat. Add the sausage, breaking it up with the side of a spoon. Cook slowly until the sausage is browned.

Stir in the nuts and the remaining ingredients except the eggs. Whisk the eggs together lightly and combine with the sausage mixture. Transfer the stuffing to a greased 9-inch baking dish. Cover with foil and bake on the middle rack of the oven for 25 minutes.

What's Inside the Turkey?

Probably nothing, now that the USDA begs us not to stuff turkeys. You can disobey or just cook the stuffing separately. Stuffing seems virtually synonymous with bread crumbs, so what's the alternative for the low-carb Thanksgiving? Here are three options, all variations on real recipes that never had any bread in them to begin with. And they're both delicious.

SAUERKRAUT STUFFING

MAKES 6 CUPS, 8 SERVINGS, ENOUGH FOR A 12-POUND TURKEY

4 bacon strips, diced
1 large onion, sliced thin
1 pound sauerkraut, well rinsed and drained
1 teaspoon caraway seeds
1 tart apple, chopped
1 cup dry white wine
Pepper to taste

Per Serving: Protein: 1g   Fat: 6.5g   Carbohydrate: 13g

In a large skillet over medium heat, cook the diced bacon until it's golden. Add the onion and cook 4 minutes longer. Add the sauerkraut, caraway, and apple. Toss well and cook for 5 minutes. Add the wine and simmer 5 more minutes. Drain off any extra liquid and stuff the turkey with the sauerkraut mixture. Roast as usual.

GINGERED WILD RICE STUFFING

Exotic and luxurious, this variation of a James Beard stuffing can be even more festive if you add ½ pound of chopped wild mushrooms, sautéed in butter until the liquid they release is reabsorbed.

MAKES 7 CUPS, ENOUGH FOR A 12-POUND TURKEY; SERVES 9

1½ cups wild rice
1 rounded teaspoon salt
4 tablespoons (½ stick) butter
Turkey liver, chopped very fine
1 large onion, chopped very fine
¾ cup very finely chopped celery and inner
        celery leaves
1 garlic clove, chopped very fine
½ cup chopped parsley
½ teaspoon dried thyme
½ teaspoon dried rosemary
½ teaspoon dried marjoram
Big pinch of ground ginger
Ground black pepper to taste
½ cup chopped walnuts

Per Serving: Protein: 1.6g   Fat: 8.8g   Carbohydrate: 12g

Cook the wild rice: Rinse the rice in a strainer in the sink. Pour 4½ cups of cold water into a heavy saucepan, add the salt, cover, and bring to a boil over medium heat.

Uncover and simmer for about 35 minutes or until the rice is just tender but still has lots of texture. Drain in a strainer over the sink and set aside.

Melt the butter in a wide skillet and gently sauté the turkey liver until brown, about 4 minutes. Add the onion and celery and sauté 4 more minutes, until the onion softens. Add the garlic, parsley, thyme, rosemary, marjoram, and ginger. Stir well to combine.

In a mixing bowl, combine the rice and the seasonings. Mix in the nuts. Stuff the turkey right before roasting and close the cavity with a skewer.

ROAST CHICKEN WITH EGG STUFFING

This mother-and-child reunion dish is certainly unusual, but before you pass it by, try it; the stuffing is amazingly good, and you can play with the ingredients almost endlessly. Basically it's glorified egg salad, using one hard-cooked egg per pound of roast chicken. The recipe is Suzanne Hamlin's inspired response to the challenge of no-bread stuffing.

You can make the stuffing several hours ahead; just cover and refrigerate it until you're ready to cook the bird. For a 6-pound roasting chicken (cut recipe in half for a 3-pounder): SERVES 6

> 6 large hard-cooked eggs, chopped
> 1 cup finely chopped fennel or celery, plus a few
>   minced leaves
> 3 scallions, including the firm green, in thin
>   rounds
> ¼ cup mayonnaise
> Salt and lots of pepper to taste
> Optional: the chicken liver, cut in small pieces
>
> 1 6-pound roasting chicken
> 1 tablespoon extra-virgin olive oil

Per Serving: Protein: 35.3g   Fat: 23.8g   Carbohydrate: 1.5g

In a mixing bowl, combine the eggs, fennel, minced leaves, and scallions. Stir in the mayonnaise and combine. Add salt and pepper and the optional liver and stir again to blend.

Stuff the chicken right before roasting. Rinse out the cavity and dry it well. Spoon in the stuffing and secure the opening to the cavity with a skewer.

Preheat the oven to 450°F. Put the stuffed bird in a heavy roasting pan, breast up, and rub all over with olive oil. Slide the pan into the oven on the middle rack. After 10 minutes, run a spatula under the chicken and move it around a little so it doesn't stick. Roast until the leg wiggles easily and the juices run clear when you poke a cooking fork into the breast where it meets the leg. A 6-pound chicken will be done in about 70 minutes; a 3-pound bird takes 35 to 40 minutes. Let the cooked chicken rest for 10 minutes on a serving platter before slicing. To serve, spoon the stuffing onto plates and moisten with some of the cooking juices.

ASIAN ROAST DUCK

Duck always seems like a hassle, but this one is simplicity itself. Just remember to let it sit with its seasonings in the refrigerator for a couple of days so it will be crispy.
SERVES 2

> 1 (5-pound) duckling, neck and giblets removed
> Coarse salt and pepper to taste
> 3 garlic cloves, pressed
> 1 tablespoon 5-spice powder
> 1 orange, quartered
> 2 scallions
> 2 tablespoons sherry
> Garnish: chopped scallions

Per Serving: Protein: 21.5g   Fat: 32.1g   Carbohydrate: .5g

Wash and dry the duck two days before you plan to cook it. Sprinkle the duck with salt and pepper, and rub it with garlic and 5-spice powder, all over and inside. Leave the duck unwrapped on a refrigerator shelf to dry out and season—this will make the skin crispy. Let come to room temperature before cooking.

Preheat the oven to 375°F. Prick the duck all over with a wire brush—but just the fat; don't pierce the flesh. Put the quartered orange and scallions (bent) in the cavity. Put the duck on a rack in a shallow roasting pan and roast for 1 hour and 15 minutes. About halfway through the cooking, pierce the skin at the joint where the leg and breast meet on each side. Let the duck rest under tented foil for 20 minutes before carving.

Pour off almost all of the fat from the drippings and add 2 tablespoons of sherry to the drippings in the pan. Scrape them up over medium heat until you have a little sauce; season to taste. Quarter the duck and serve with the pan sauce, with scallions scattered over.

Tofu Tips

This best of all the vegetable protein sources is a useful item to have on hand, even if you're not fond of tofu.

- To bring out its best, use extra-firm tofu and freeze it first, right in the package, for at least 24 hours. Defrost, drain off the liquid, and either slice and squeeze out as much liquid as you can or crumble and squeeze. This extra step will give it a better texture and make it easier to work with. It will also save you the extra work of the elaborate pressing routine you'd need to use otherwise.

- Tofu can be added to soups and stews but it's much better if you sauté it in a little oil to crisp it first.

- Fried tofu is especially delicious—it gives the best texture and has a lovely golden color. Take this additional step before you add tofu to a stir-fry.

JERK TOFU

Keep jerk tofu around for a snack (let it marinate overnight) or serve it hot for dinner over a bed of stewed Southern greens or stir-fried collard greens. This zesty tofu is based on an idea of soy queen Dana Jacobi.

SERVES 8 AS A SNACK, 4 AS A MEAL

> 1 pound extra-firm tofu, frozen, defrosted, sliced lengthwise in quarters, and squeezed dry (page 188)
> 2 teaspoons Busha Browne's jerk seasoning
> Olive oil for the skillet

Per main-course serving: Protein: 12.1g   Fat: 1g   Carbohydrate: 2.6g

In a glass dish large enough to hold the tofu slices, smear half the jerk seasoning over the bottom. Add the tofu slices and cover them with the remaining jerk seasoning. Cover with plastic wrap and set aside to marinate overnight.

When you're ready to cook, scrape off the paste. Heat a heavy skillet and add a spoonful of olive oil. When it's hot, drop in the seasoned tofu slices and cook them 4 minutes on each side. Serve over Southern-style greens or refrigerate to use as a snack.

CURRIED TOFU

This light, zesty curry can be made in just a few minutes if you have the tofu ready—i.e., frozen, defrosted, drained, and pressed (see instructions on page 188). It's another good reason to keep tofu in the freezer.

SERVES 2

½ pound firm tofu, in 1-inch cubes
1 tablespoon peanut oil
1 small onion, sliced thin
1 small green bell pepper, sliced thin
2 serrano chiles, seeded and minced
2 teaspoons curry powder
½ cup canned coconut milk
½ cup chicken broth
Salt to taste
⅓ cup chopped cilantro leaves
3 tablespoons chopped roasted peanuts

Per Serving: Protein: 15.9g   Fat: 26.5g   Carbohydrate: 6.5g

Press the tofu dry on paper towels. Heat the peanut oil in a large skillet, and when it's hot add the tofu cubes. Sauté, turning frequently, until the tofu is golden brown. Add the onion and peppers and cook until they're wilted a little. Add the curry powder, the coconut milk, and the chicken broth. Stir well to combine and add salt to taste.

Bring to a simmer and let the tofu cook for several minutes, until the sauce begins to thicken. Serve in soup plates garnished with the cilantro and peanuts.

EGGPLANT PIZZA

This dish lies somewhere between eggplant parmigiana and pizza. It's a layer of golden brown eggplant crust topped with pizza sauce and little bits of topping, so that every bite is a little different. You can get fancy and use bits of goat cheese, drizzled with a little pesto, or just use cheese all by itself. SERVES 4

    1 pound eggplant, peeled and cut into ⅓-inch
        slices
    2 tablespoons olive oil
    Oregano
    Pepper
    Salt to taste
    ¼ cup pizza or pasta sauce, page 194
    4 slices Genoa salami, quartered, or 8 slices
        pepperoni
    1 thick slice fresh mozzarella, diced
    2 pieces oil-packed sun-dried tomato, in bits
    2 tablespoons grated Parmesan cheese

Per Serving: Protein: 2.8g   Fat: 10g   Carbohydrate: 6.1g

Preheat the oven to 425°F. Brush the eggplant slices lightly with olive oil on both sides and place them on a baking sheet in the oven. Bake 10 minutes, turn and bake 15 more minutes. The slices should be golden brown on both sides—if they're not, turn the lighter side down and bake a few more minutes.

Fit the eggplant slices into a 10-inch pie plate with shallow sides. Cut extra pieces to fill in the blanks. Sprinkle the eggplant with oregano, pepper, and a little salt, then spread the sauce thinly over the top. Scatter the salami, cheese, and tomato bits evenly over the top and finish with a drift of the Parmesan cheese.

Broil the pie until the cheese is bubbly and beginning to brown.

A LOT LIKE PIZZA

Next to pasta and bread, pizza is probably the most missed food on the low-carb diet. This ersatz pizza is built on a raft of tofu, which doesn't sound very appetizing, but actually you could get to love it. Vegetarians will obviously want to skip the pepperoni. SERVES 5

1 pound extra-firm tofu, frozen and thawed, page 199
Olive oil
Oregano
Salt and pepper
Pizza sauce (recipe follows)
Fresh basil leaves, optional
1 cup shredded mozzarella, or more to taste
Pepperoni slices, optional

Per Serving: Protein: 18.2g Fat: 18g Carbohydrate: 3g

Carefully slice the tofu lengthwise into 5 slices. Place the slices on a double layer of paper towels and cover with another double layer. Gently press down on the tofu with your palms, trying to press out as much liquid as you can without breaking or crumbling the tofu.

Heat a tablespoon or two of olive oil in a nonstick skillet over medium-high heat. Add the tofu slices and sauté for several minutes on each side until crisp. Remove the tofu to a baking sheet with a rim, spaced well apart. Sprinkle with oregano and salt and pepper to taste. Spread a couple of tablespoons of pizza sauce over the slices, add the basil leaves if using, and top with the cheese and pepperoni.

Run the tofu pizza under the broiler just until the cheese is melted and golden.

Note that leftover pizza slices make a good snack—reheat them in a toaster oven.

PIZZA SAUCE

SERVES 8

1 tablespoon olive oil
1 (14½-ounce) can Muir Glen diced tomatoes
2 garlic cloves, pressed
Sprinkle of oregano
Sprinkle of ground red pepper (cayenne)
Salt and pepper to taste
Squirt of tomato concentrate from a tube (or 1 to 2
     tablespoons tomato paste)

Per ¼ cup Serving: Protein: .8g   Fat: 3.5g   Carbohydrate: 3.6g

Heat the oil in a small skillet over medium heat. Add the tomatoes and garlic, sautéing until the tomatoes begin to lose a little of their liquid. Add the remaining ingredients and let the sauce cook down until almost all the liquid is gone and the mixture is thick, about 5 minutes. If it's chunkier than you'd like, purée it in the food processor.

The sauce will keep for several days in the refrigerator. To use after storing, drain off any liquid that's accumulated and heat briefly in the microwave.

The Stir-Fry

If you can manage to live without the rice, stir-fries offer the low-carb cook convenience, great taste, and a chance to play in the kitchen. There are only a few rules. You don't even need a wok; you can use a large skillet and just add a little more oil because the surface is wider.

Many stir-fry recipes use relatively high-carb ingredients—cornstarch, sugar, oyster sauce, hoisin sauce. Skip the cornstarch but go ahead and use a pinch of sugar; use just a little of the high-carb sauces or get Kikkoman's Stir-Fry Sauce, which runs 1 carb per teaspoon—enough for a serving. This sauce contains a number of seasonings such as oyster sauce and sherry and will give you that authentic take-out Chinese taste. Use snow peas sparingly (pick up a few from the salad bar). Here are the basic points:

1. Cut the ingredients roughly the same size—diced, shredded, or sliced—and make sure they're dry.

2. Have everything ready at the edge of the stove. Stir-frying goes like lightning, so have your cooking shovel in hand, ready to stir and scoop.

3. Use the highest possible heat.

4. Heat the wok for ½ minute before adding peanut oil.

5. Add the oil in a circle around the edge of the wok.

6. The oil is ready when tiny bubbles form, wisps of smoke rise, and a piece of scallion floats and sizzles when dropped in.

7. Add the meat, chicken, or seafood and cook while stirring for a minute or two.

8. Add the vegetables and minced garlic, ginger, and scallions. Cook and stir for several more minutes—fewer for delicate things like asparagus, more for broccoli (steam it briefly in the microwave to speed things along, but be sure it's dry before you add it to the wok).

9. Add the seasonings: Stir-fry Sauce, or soy sauce and chili oil, or five-spice powder, hot pepper flakes, mushroom soy sauce, rice wine vinegar, oyster sauce, hoisin sauce, pinch of sugar, etc. Mix well and cook for another minute.

10. Nuts should be crisped in the hot oil first, before you add any of the other ingredients, then set aside. Fold them into the stir-fry just before serving.

Using these basic ideas, play with ingredients you have on hand. It's almost impossible to come up with a combination that doesn't taste pretty good.

FIVE-MINUTE CLAM STEW

This homey recipe is the invention of the late gastronome Roy Andries de Groot, who claimed to serve it several times a month. And why not? It's fast, it's made from staples, and it's delicious. The canned baby clams from Thailand are particularly good. SERVES 4

8 tablespoons (1 stick) butter

3 (10-ounce) cans minced clams

1 teaspoon thyme

4 drops hot pepper sauce

Dash of Worcestershire sauce

Salt to taste

2 pints light cream or half-and-half

½ lemon

Paprika

Finely snipped fresh dill

Finely snipped watercress leaves

Per Serving: Protein: 24.7g   Fat: 49.8g   Carbohydrate: 20g

In a 2-quart saucepan, melt all but 2 tablespoons of the butter over medium heat, but don't let it brown. Strain the clams through a sieve and reserve the clam broth. When the butter is melted, stir in the thyme, hot sauce, Worcestershire, and salt. Cook for a minute, then add the clam broth and turn the heat to high, stirring occasionally until the mixture reaches a boil. Lower the heat and add the cream, stirring—be careful not to let the cream boil. When the cream is hot, add the clams, stir again, and cook for 2 minutes.

Ladle the stew into 4 heated bowls. Squeeze a little lemon juice into each bowl. Divide the remaining butter in quarters and drop a piece in the center of each portion. Sprinkle a ring of paprika around the butter and add an outer ring of the snipped greens. Serve immediately.

Two Great Feasts

Here are two informal but delectable meals to set out on great platters. They're both based on the traditional French grand <u>aioli monstre</u> of Provence—which features salt cod and a bevy of steamed vegetables to be consumed with generous amounts of intensely garlicky mayonnaise. Here, poached cod or snapper substitutes for the salt cod in the French version. There's also a Mexican version based on shrimp, with a smoky chipotle pepper mayonnaise that's also very garlicky. Both versions can be served hot or at room temperature. Serve something refreshing—grapes, melon—for dessert.

THE FRENCH VERSION

Choose any or all of the vegetables listed below as well as some hard-cooked eggs. Steam the vegetables (except for the cherry tomatoes and peppers) earlier in the day and serve them at room temperature—or, if you prefer, reheat them for half a minute in simmering water.

Young turnips, peeled and quartered
Asparagus stalks, tough ends snapped off
Green beans, tailed
Cauliflower, cut into florets
Cherry tomatoes
Small zucchini, cut in half lengthwise
Red bell peppers, thickly sliced
Small fennel bulbs, trimmed and quartered
The Garlic Mayonnaise, page 160

THE FISH

Have one fillet per person of cod or red snapper. Bring 1 quart of water to a boil with 1 garlic clove, a bay leaf, and ¼ teaspoon salt. Reduce the heat to a simmer and add the fish. Turn off the heat and cover the pot; let stand for 10 minutes or until the fish flakes. Remove fish from the pot with a slotted spoon and place on a platter. Surround with the vegetables and eggs and serve with a big bowl of aioli.

THE MEXICAN VERSION

Use the same vegetables as above, but instead of the white fish, use shrimp. Add to the cooking stock a few peppercorns and some mustard seeds. Cook the shelled shrimp just until they turn pink and begin to curl. Drain and set aside.

CHIPOTLE MAYONNAISE

2 garlic cloves, pressed
2 canned *chipotle chiles en adobo*, rinsed,
        seeded, and minced, or 2 tablespoons
        chipotle purée, page 38
1½ cups mayonnaise

Mix everything together in the food processor and serve in a bowl with the shrimp, vegetables, and eggs.

TUNA WITH MINT, GARLIC, AND SOY

Easy, unusual, and versatile—you can either grill this tuna
or broil it. The key thing is to salt it first for half an hour
to bring out the flavor. SERVES 2

  2 tuna steaks, 1 inch thick
  Salt
  Olive oil
  1 garlic clove, minced
  1 tablespoon soy sauce
  1 tablespoon chopped mint
  Lemon wedges

Per Serving: Protein: 34g   Fat: 1.4g   Carbohydrate: trace

Half an hour before cooking, rub the tuna steaks
lightly with salt and olive oil and let stand. Mix together
the garlic, soy, and mint. Just before cooking, rub the
seasoning into the steaks and either grill or broil 2 minutes per side—the tuna should be rare. Serve immediately with lemon wedges.

OYSTER STEW WITH MUSHROOMS

You can buy the oysters already shucked; be sure to save the liquor that comes with them. If they don't feel smooth, they may still have some sand on them, so give them a quick rinse.

If you have wild mushrooms, so much the better—chanterelles, morels, they'd all be delicious with the oysters. And a big pinch of saffron added with the cream will make the dish even better. SERVES 4

1 pound brown or white market mushrooms
3 tablespoons butter
1 shallot, minced
3 dozen shucked oysters, with their liquor
1 cup heavy cream
Salt and pepper
Chopped parsley to garnish

Per Serving: Protein: 10g   Fat: 33g   Carbohydrate: 9.7g

Wipe the mushrooms clean with slightly damp paper towels and chop them coarse. Warm the butter in a wide skillet and when it's starting to sizzle, add the shallot and mushrooms. Cook them over medium-low heat, stirring several times, until the mushrooms begin to reabsorb their juices, about 10 minutes. Set aside.

In a large saucepan, warm the oysters and their liquor over medium heat uncovered for about 3 minutes or until they just begin to curl—the edges will look like they're starting to grin. Take out the oysters and set aside; let the liquor continue to cook down until it's just a few tablespoonfuls. Add the cream and cook 5 minutes more, then add the mushrooms and oysters. Heat for 2 more minutes, add salt and pepper to taste, and serve immediately in soup plates with parsley scattered over.

BAKED SEA BASS

Start the sea bass a couple of hours before you plan to cook it. It works equally well as a hot or a cold dish, served with one of the seasoned mayonnaises in the Sauces chapter (pages 150-168). SERVES 4

1 whole sea bass, about 4 pounds

MARINADE
1 garlic clove, minced
½ teaspoon salt
Pepper to taste
2 tablespoons fresh lemon juice
½ cup olive oil
2 teaspoons dried oregano

Per Serving: Protein: 26.8g   Fat: 9.9g   Carbohydrate: 1.3g

Put the fish on a piece of foil large enough to wrap around it.

Make the marinade: In a small bowl, mash the garlic with the salt and pepper. Add the lemon juice and whisk in the olive oil and oregano.

Pour half the marinade over the fish and rub it in on both sides. Wrap the foil closely around the fish and put in the refrigerator to season for a couple of hours.

Preheat the oven to 350°F. Open the foil, pour the remaining marinade over the fish, and seal the package again.

Set the fish package on a baking sheet and bake for 40 to 50 minutes, or until the flesh is opaque when tested with the point of a knife.

Remove the foil and serve the fish on a platter, hot or cold, or at room temperature, with a seasoned mayonnaise sauce.

Plain Green Wrapper

LETTUCE PACKAGES

Sometimes you just want something a little like a sandwich that's not just stuck on a cracker. It could be a tortilla, or it could be a leaf wrapper. If you remember the great little lettuce packages they serve in Vietnamese restaurants, it may not seem so strange to do just that: tuck your salad or sandwich filling into a lettuce leaf. This can be anything from tomato, mayonnaise, and bits of bacon (BLT) to curried egg salad to chicken shreds with an Asian sauce. This idea comes from Martin and Sally Stone, who fill their leaves with bean concoctions— not on our diet, alas.

Here's how:

SERVES 1

Large romaine leaves, iceberg lettuce leaves,
     or Savoy cabbage

Per Serving: Protein: 0g   Fat: 0g   Carbohydrate: trace

Fill a large skillet with water and bring it to a boil. Have a bowl of ice water ready to dunk the leaves as soon as they come out of the skillet, with paper towels nearby to dry them. Drop a few leaves at a time into the skillet and let them cook for just half a minute, then pull them out with tongs and send them to the ice water. Leave them there a minute and then dry them well.

Have your filling ready. Put the leaf rib side down on a work surface and press down gently with your hand—

but you don't want the leaves to break. Put a mound of
the filling on the bottom half of the leaf and fold in the
two sides of the leaf. Roll up the leaf into a little package and put it on a plate seam side down. Repeat with remaining leaves and filling.

GRAPE LEAVES

These are now available in jars in most supermarkets.
You don't have to be traditional and stuff grape leaves
with a rice mixture. You can just give them a good rinse,
pull off the stems, and tuck something interesting inside,
such as a finger of feta cheese. Add a little pepper and a
couple of drops of olive oil and wrap up the package.
You can either grill these or sauté them in a little olive
oil in a skillet until the cheese starts to melt.

SALMON IN GRAPE LEAVES

This is New York chef Rozanne Gold's idea for baking
salmon fillets—delicious, and even better with a little
tapenade spread over the salmon before it's wrapped.
For each serving, use a 6-ounce salmon fillet and spread
it with 1 tablespoon of tapenade. Set aside to season for
2 hours. Wrap the fish in 2 rinsed and stemmed grape
leaves, tucking in the ends to make a tidy package. Preheat the oven to 450°F. Put the salmon packages in a
baking dish filmed with olive oil. Paint the tops of the
grape leaves with a little more oil and send them to the
oven for 8 minutes.

NUT-CRUSTED SWORDFISH

You can use almost any kind of nuts here: almonds, walnuts, pecans, or macadamia nuts. SERVES 4

4 (6-ounce) skinless, boneless swordfish pieces
Olive oil
Salt and pepper
½ cup chopped nuts, with their skins
½ teaspoon dried thyme
5⅓ tablespoons butter, melted (⅓ cup)

Per Serving: Protein: 32.6g   Fat: 29.6g   Carbohydrate: 1.1g

Preheat the oven to 450°F.

Rub the fish all over with olive oil and sprinkle with salt and pepper. Set aside for 5 minutes to season.

Mix the nuts with the thyme and put on a plate. Put the melted butter on another plate. Dip the fish in the butter and then in the nut mixture, patting to be sure it sticks.

Put the crusted fish on a baking sheet and roast for about 6 minutes or until done.

ROASTED SWORDFISH WITH HERBS

The fish roasts in the broiler on a bed of herbs: rosemary,
sage, thyme—just one or all three if you have them.
SERVES 4

    4 (6-ounce) pieces boneless, skinless swordfish
    Olive oil
    Salt and pepper
    4 sprigs rosemary
    4 sprigs sage
    4 sprigs thyme
    4 sprigs lemon thyme

Per Serving: Protein: 28.8g   Fat:9.3g   Carbohydrate: 0g

Rub the fish all over with olive oil and sprinkle with
salt and pepper; set aside for 5 minutes to season.

Make 4 little beds of herbs for the fish on a baking
sheet, saving the lemon thyme to put on top. Arrange the
fish on top of the herbs and preheat the broiler. Strip the
leaves of lemon thyme from the branches and distribute
the leaves equally over the swordfish pieces. Set under the
broiler and roast until the fish is cooked; about 6 minutes.
It should be opaque when you test it with the point of a
knife.

NEW ORLEANS SPICY SHRIMP

This delectable shrimp, served at Upperline restaurant in
New Orleans, works as a first course or a small meal on
its own. You can leave out the white pepper if you don't
have any—or buy some; it has a distinct taste all its own
that works together with, not instead of, black pepper.

SERVES 2 AS A MAIN DISH, 4 AS A FIRST COURSE

1 pound medium shrimp, shelled and deveined

MARINADE:
¼ cup olive oil
1 teaspoon ground red pepper (cayenne)
1 teaspoon chili powder
1 teaspoon ground cumin
½ teaspoon ground white pepper
Several grinds of black pepper

SPICY MAYONNAISE
1 cup Hellmann's mayonnaise
2 teaspoons chili powder
1 garlic clove, minced

2 tablespoons butter
½ red onion, sliced
Salt to taste
Romaine lettuce to make a bed for the shrimp

Per Serving: Protein: 46g   Fat: 110g   Carbohydrate: 3.9g

Mix the shrimp with the marinade ingredients in a bowl and let sit for ½ hour. Meanwhile, stir the spicy mayonnaise ingredients together.

In a skillet large enough to hold the shrimp, melt the butter over high heat. When it's sizzling, toss in the shrimp and the onion. Shake the pan and toss the shrimp; they're ready when they're pink and they start to curl, in just a couple of minutes. Salt them and remove from the heat.

Arrange romaine leaves on individual plates and divide the shrimp among them on top of the greens. Serve the mayonnaise on the side.

HOT PEEL-IT-YOURSELF
SHRIMP TWO WAYS

One of these recipes is genteel, the other gutsy—but both are to be eaten outdoors, on tables spread with newspaper or oilcloth. It's a good idea to serve small hot towels (wring them out in hot water and steam them in the microwave).

SHRIMP WITH DILL BUTTER
SERVES 1

1 chopped garlic clove per person
Several peppercorns per person
⅓ pound medium shrimp per person
¼ cup (½ stick) butter per person
1 teaspoon minced fresh dill per person
½ teaspoon fresh lemon juice per person

Per Serving: Protein: 30.6g   Fat: 46.6g   Carbohydrate: 2g

Bring a pot of water to the boil and add the garlic and peppercorns. Drop in the shrimp and cook them just until they turn pink and curl. Remove immediately and drain.

Melt the butter and add the dill and lemon juice. Give each person a plate with shrimp and a small bowl for the dill butter and let them peel their own.

NEW ORLEANS SHRIMP
SERVES 1

**2 teaspoons shrimp boil or Old Bay Seasoning per
    person**
¼ lemon per person
⅓ pound medium shrimp per person
Hot pepper sauce

Per Serving: Protein: 30.6g   Fat: 2.6g   Carbohydrate: 2.2g

Heat a pot of water to the boil and add the spices and
the lemon. Add the shrimp and cook just until they turn
pink and curl. Remove immediately and drain. Serve with
more lemon wedges and pass a bottle of hot pepper
sauce.

MARGARITA SHRIMP

This has all those great margarita flavors, plus shrimp and avocado and cilantro. It takes almost no time to make; shelling the shrimp is the only real work here. SERVES 4

1 pound large shrimp, shelled and deveined
2 tablespoons fresh lime juice
2 tablespoons butter
1 jalapeño pepper, seeded and minced
3 garlic cloves, chopped
1 teaspoon ground red pepper (cayenne), optional
Salt and ground black pepper
¼ cup tequila
4 cups romaine lettuce sliced in ribbons
1 avocado, pitted, peeled, and diced
2 tablespoons chopped cilantro leaves

Per Serving: Protein: 23.9g   Fat: 15g   Carbohydrate: 5.5g

Put the shrimp in a bowl and pour the lime juice over; mix well. In a wide nonstick skillet, melt the butter. When it's foaming, add the minced pepper and garlic and cook for 2 minutes over medium heat. Add the shrimp and lime juice and the cayenne and cook about 4 more minutes, or until the shrimp are pink and start to curl. Add salt and pepper to taste, then pour in the tequila. Cook for 3 minutes more or until the liquid is reduced to a little sauce.

Serve the shrimp on a bed of romaine ribbons, decorated with the avocado and sprinkled with cilantro.

Bringing up Flavor

When you're making very simple grilled or roasted meats and poultry and fish, it helps to bring out the natural flavors as much as you can. The best way to do this is with good old sea salt and its frequent companion, olive oil. Time is the secret ingredient.

- Fish steaks and fillets: Rub fish all over with olive oil and sprinkle with salt. Let sit at least 5 minutes to develop flavor.

- Steaks: Mediterranean cook Paula Wolfert films steak with olive oil, sprinkles it with coarse salt, and refrigerates it uncovered overnight.

- Meat in general: Presalting and letting the meat sit to develop flavor doesn't, as some cookbooks warn, make it less juicy—it just makes it more flavorful.

- Pork: Today's extra-lean pork often leaves a lot to be desired in the taste and juiciness department. Brining is San Francisco restaurateur Nancy Oakes's way around that problem. This is her formula: Dissolve ½ cup of salt in 9 cups of hot water. Let the brine cool in the refrigerator and then add the pork, weighing it down so it stays submerged. Eight hours will do it. You can add flavoring ingredients like garlic, thyme, bay leaf, chilies, citrus zest, mustard, etc. Some pork comes already brined; check the label to be sure.

LIME SCALLOPS

Simplicity itself—and you can either grill or broil these zesty skewered scallops. Be sure to let them marinate for at least a couple of hours to develop flavor. The recipe comes from Eileen Weinberg of Good and Plenty to Go in Manhattan. SERVES 6

2 pounds sea scallops
½ cup fresh lime juice
3 tablespoons olive oil
Dash of salt and pepper to taste
2 limes, in wedges, for skewering
Garnish: 2 tablespoons chopped cilantro

Per Serving: Protein: 25.3g   Fat: 8.2g   Carbohydrate: 4.2g

Mix the scallops, lime juice, oil, and seasonings together in a glass bowl and let marinate for at least 2 hours. When you're ready to cook, thread the lime wedges and scallops on skewers—1 lime wedge, then 3 scallops, etc. Cook under the broiler or over a charcoal grill for 5 or 6 minutes, turning once. Serve the skewers sprinkled with the cilantro.

WHOLE POACHED SALMON

For a summer dinner party, there are few dishes so elegant as the whole salmon—and you make it completely ahead. The only catch is that you need a fish poacher, bought or borrowed. The classic accompaniment is green mayonnaise (add ⅓ cup each finely chopped parsley, watercress, and spinach to a cup of mayonnaise. Snip in a few chives and add lemon juice and zest to taste). Serve the salmon on a bed of greens, simply decorated with lemon slices and sprigs of dill—or make a dramatic presentation by layering unpeeled cucumber slices like scales (or tiles) over the fish. SERVES 10

> 1 whole salmon, about 10 pounds, gutted
> 3 celery ribs, cut up
> 3 carrots, cut up
> 1 medium onion, cut up
> 2 tablespoons salt
> 1 teaspoon pepper
> ¼ cup chopped parsley
> 2 cups dry white wine
> Garnishes: lemon slices, dill sprigs, cucumber
>   slices

Per Serving: Protein: 45.2g   Fat: 24.6g   Carbohydrate: trace

Place the salmon on the rack in the fish poacher. Arrange the vegetables around it, add salt and pepper and parsley, and pour over the wine. Add cold water to cover the fish. Put the lid on the poacher and set it over 2 burners on medium heat. Once the liquid comes to a boil, turn the heat down to a gentle simmer. Set the timer for 25 minutes.

Check the fish with a fork next to the backbone; probably it won't be done for another 15 minutes or more, but you want to catch it when it comes away from the bone and is an opaque pink, not red. Remove it from the poacher while still on the rack. Once it's cool, remove the skin on the top side—or you can cover and refrigerate it, then remove the skin before serving, even the next day. Garnish as desired (see above) and serve with green mayonnaise.

CITRUSY SALMON PAVED WITH
POPPY SEEDS

Oven-roasting fillets of salmon is a deliciously quick way
to deal with them. You can ask the fishmonger to remove
the skin from the fillet if you like. Give each fillet a quick
feel before you begin the recipe to be sure there are no
lurking tiny bones. SERVES 4

    4 salmon fillets, about 6 ounces each
    Juice of ½ Valencia orange
    Juice of ½ lemon
    Salt and pepper to taste
    3 tablespoons melted butter
    1½ teaspoons poppy seeds

Per Serving: Protein: 33.8g   Fat: 26.8g   Carbohydrate: 4g

In a shallow glass dish large enough to hold the fillets
in one layer, mix the juices and the salt and pepper. Lay
the salmon over the mixture, then turn to coat both sides.
Let the fillets season for 20 minutes at room temperature,
turning once.

Line a shallow baking dish with aluminum foil and
brush it with 1 tablespoon of the butter.

Preheat the oven to 425°F. Arrange the fillets in the
foil-lined dish, then press the poppy seeds into the top
sides. Roast the salmon for 8 to 12 minutes, depending on
thickness. When it's done, heat the remaining butter and
drizzle over the fish.

SALMON WITH GARLIC CREAMED SPINACH AND CHANTERELLES

This is a variation of a very simple but very delicious meal that appears on the spring menu at Gramercy Tavern in New York City. It's the perfect solution to the entertaining problem—both elegant and easy, and no one would ever guess that it's diet food. If you can't find chanterelles, other wild mushrooms work well here.

SERVES 4

4 salmon steaks, about 1 inch thick
Olive oil for grilling the salmon
Salt and pepper to taste

GARLIC CREAMED SPINACH
3 pounds fresh spinach, cleaned and stemmed
¼ cup heavy cream
1 garlic clove, chopped
2 tablespoons butter
Salt and pepper to taste

½ pound chanterelles or other wild mushrooms,
       trimmed and cleaned
2 tablespoons butter

Per Serving: Protein: 34g   Fat: 29.4g   Carbohydrate: 5g

Rub the salmon all over with olive oil and salt and pepper it generously. Set aside to season on a grill for broiling.

Make the spinach: In a large pot over medium heat, wilt the spinach in just the water that clings to it after rinsing. Meanwhile, put the cream and garlic in a small saucepan and heat gently for a few minutes, then turn off the heat and let the garlic steep in the cream. When the spinach is done, still bright green but entirely wilted, drain it well in a colander and squeeze the moisture out of it.

Now cook the chanterelles: Melt the butter in a skillet over medium heat and add the mushrooms when it's sizzling. Cook the mushrooms until they have a golden brown edge, about 5 minutes.

Meantime, slide the salmon about 4 inches under the broiler—turn the steaks after 5 minutes; they will be done in about 5 more minutes. Test with the point of a knife. Heat the spinach and add the butter, salt, and pepper. Just before serving, heat the cream and add it to the spinach, mixing in well until it almost disappears. Reheat the mushrooms and serve at once.

Crusty Coating for Roast Beef, Lamb, or Pork

This extremely simple, extremely flavorful crust from Sally and Martin Stone has—amazingly—no bread crumbs. First rubbing the meat with salt and dry mustard dramatically improves the flavor.

SERVES 6

Beef, lamb, or pork roast
Salt
2 teaspoons Colman's dry mustard

CRUST

¼ cup Dijon mustard
2 garlic cloves, crushed
1 tablespoon soy sauce
1 tablespoon olive oil
1 tablespoon crumbled dried rosemary (for
        pork or lamb) or thyme (beef)

Per Serving: Protein: 0g   Fat: 2.2g   Carbohydrate: .3g

Salt the roast all over and rub with the dry mustard.

Mix the crust ingredients together and cover the roast with it. Let stand for 2 hours to develop flavor.

Cook the roast on a rack in a roasting pan as explained below.

BEEF AND LAMB

SERVES 6

For a 3-pound roast of top sirloin or a 4-pound half leg of lamb, preheat the oven to 500°F. Roast the meat for 15 minutes, then lower the heat to 350° and roast 45 minutes more, or until the internal temperature is 130° for medium rare. Let the meat rest on a serving platter for 20 minutes under tented foil before carving.

PORK

Per Serving: Protein: 104g   Fat: 49.5g   Carbohydrate: 0g

For a 5-pound boneless pork loin, preheat the oven to 400°F. Roast the pork for 15 minutes, then lower the heat to 350° and cook for about 1 hour or until the internal temperature is 145°. Let roast rest on a serving platter for 20 minutes under tented foil before carving.

BOWL OF RED

Yes, chili is on this regimen, as long as you don't toss in
beans or a lot of tomatoes. That means Texas-style chili,
which is probably the best anyway. You can add chopped
canned chile peppers to the brew or toss in cubes of plain
old green bell pepper. But here's the basic chili.

SERVES 8

    2 tablespoons olive oil (or lard, if you have it)
    1 large onion, chopped
    3 garlic cloves, smashed
    4 pounds boneless chuck, in dice or ground for
        chili
    ½ cup ground mild red chile, preferably New
        Mexican
    2 tablespoons ground cumin
    2 teaspoons dried oregano
    1 tablespoon sweet paprika
    1 teaspoon cider vinegar
    ½ cup strong brewed coffee or 1 tablespoon
        instant coffee powder
    3 cups water as needed
    1 tablespoon salt
    ½ teaspoon ground red pepper (cayenne),
        optional
    2 tablespoons cornmeal
    Optional garnishes: sour cream, chopped cilantro,
        grated cheese

Per Serving: Protein: 38.6g   Fat: 64.5g   Carbohydrate: 6.6g

In a large dutch oven, heat the oil and cook the onion over medium heat until it's soft. Add the garlic and cook until it's transparent. Add the meat in several batches along with the chile, cumin, oregano, and paprika. Remove each batch to a large bowl as it's cooked. Stir and cook until the meat is browned, then put all the meat back in the pot and add the vinegar, coffee, and enough water just to cover the meat. Add the salt and cayenne and stir well.

Cover the pot and cook over low heat for 2 hours, stirring from time to time. Remove the lid and simmer for a final hour. Skim off any fat on the surface. Add the cornmeal and stir in well. Cook for 15 more minutes and serve hot in deep bowls. Garnish with sour cream, chopped cilantro, and grated cheese.

The One and Only Tortilla

One of the frustrations of low-carb eating is all the great Mexican food you can have—guacamole, salsa, carnitas—without being able to eat the high-carb tortillas that make it so satisfying. But the La Tortilla Company has come to our rescue with a whole-wheat, oat-fiber tortilla that costs just 3 carbs. It's a little chewy, especially if you fry it, but this tortilla works for everything from chips to wrap-up sandwiches to quesadillas (just slice some cheese and put it between two of these tortillas, grill on both sides in a dry skillet, and you've got a terrific snack). A few leaves of cilantro strewn over the cheese will taste even better.

I like this tortilla so much I use it for breakfast toast as well—I just throw it over a gas burner until it begins to puff up, then turn it briefly so it has a few toasty marks. You can also heat the tortillas in a microwave or a skillet.

For a store near you that carries the tortillas, or to order a bunch for yourself (you can freeze them), see Sources. Be sure you get the Fat-Free tortillas; there are several others with higher carb counts.

MEAT LOAF

This is more or less Mom's meat loaf, with a couple of twists. To save carbs on ketchup, you can spread a little salsa over the meat loaf before you add the bacon strips. Drain it in a strainer first to get rid of extra liquid.

SERVES 6

> 2 Wasa sesame rye crackers, crushed in a food
>   processor
> ⅓ cup milk
> 3 pounds meat loaf mix (veal, pork, and beef), at
>   room temperature
> 2 tablespoons butter
> 1 large green bell pepper, minced
> ½ cup chopped onion
> 6 large garlic cloves, pressed
> 1 teaspoon dried thyme
> 2 large eggs, lightly beaten
> 1 tablespoon Worcestershire sauce
> 1 teaspoon paprika
> 1 teaspoon salt
> 1 teaspoon ground black pepper
> 2 tablespoons ketchup or strained salsa
> 4 bacon strips

Per Serving: Protein: 41.8g   Fat: 74.7g   Carbohydrate: 5.9g

Preheat the oven to 350°F. Put the Wasa crumbs in a small bowl and pour the milk over them. Set aside.

Put the meat in a large bowl. Melt the butter in a skillet and add the green pepper and onions. Cook gently for about 3 minutes or until soft, stirring often. Add the sautéed pepper and everything else but the ketchup and bacon to the meat and mix it lightly with your hands.

Put the meat loaf into a glass loaf pan and spread the ketchup over the top. Lay the bacon over the ketchup and bake the loaf for 1 hour and 15 minutes. Remove from the oven and let rest for 10 minutes before slicing.

ITALIAN MEAT LOAF

No Italian would recognize this gussied-up meat loaf, but it's a good choice for a dinner party, since it's sort of festive—for meat loaf. You could make one long skinny meat loaf, but you risk having the center undercooked, so it's safer to form two loaves and bake them in a roasting pan. SERVES 10

1 tablespoon olive oil

1 medium onion, chopped

3 pounds meat loaf mix—pork, beef, and veal

1 teaspoon salt

½ green bell pepper, chopped fine

½ red bell pepper, chopped fine

½ cup smashed garlic croutons

2 teaspoons Italian mixed herbs (oregano, basil, rosemary, thyme)

½ teaspoon ground black pepper

½ teaspoon paprika

2 large eggs, lightly beaten

½ cup half-and-half

3 ounces prosciutto, diced

1 cup diced fresh mozzarella

1 cup grated Swiss cheese
¾ cup grated Parmesan cheese

Per Serving: Protein: 34.7g   Fat: 39g   Carbohydrate: 4.2g

Preheat the oven to 350°F. In a small skillet over medium heat, warm the olive oil and add the onion. Sauté the onion until it's soft.

In a large mixing bowl, mix all the remaining ingredients (saving out a handful of the cheeses) together with your hands, including the onions. Mold the mixture into two loaves and place them in a roasting pan or another pan large enough to hold them with no crowding—there should be a couple of inches between the meat loaves and the edge of the pan so that they'll brown all over.

Bake the meat loaves for 45 minutes, then scatter the remaining cheese over the tops. Return to the oven until an instant-read thermometer registers 155° at the center of the loaves, anywhere from 15 to 45 minutes more. Let the meat loaves rest for 10 minutes before serving.

Meat Loaf With Tomato Sauce

You can serve the meat loaves with a fresh tomato sauce like the one on page 194.

BEEF STROGANOFF

This dish is so seldom served anymore that it's hard to remember how delicious it is. Instead of the classic noodles,
serve the stroganoff on a nest of cauliflower purée, page
303. SERVES 4

> 1½ pounds boneless sirloin or fillet of beef
> Salt and pepper
> 4 tablespoons (½ stick) butter
> 1 tablespoon safflower oil
> 1 medium onion, sliced thin
> ½ pound portobello mushrooms, sliced
> 1 tablespoon instant flour
> 1 cup beef broth
> 2 tablespoons Dijon mustard
> 1 cup sour cream
> Garnish: 1 tablespoon each chopped dill and
>   chives

Per Serving: Protein: 80.8g   Fat: 73.3g   Carbohydrate: 7.7g

Slice the meat across the grain into thin (⅓-inch)
strips. Season the meat with salt and pepper and let stand
for 2 hours to develop flavor.

In a wide nonstick skillet, melt the butter and oil together; when they stop foaming, sear the beef over high
heat, a few strips at a time, till browned on both sides but
still rare. Remove the meat to a platter as it browns. Add
the onion and sauté over medium heat until browned,
about 5 minutes. Add the mushrooms and sauté until the
liquid they give off disappears. Remove all the vegetables
to the platter with the meat.

In the same skillet, melt the remaining 2 tablespoons of butter over medium heat. When it starts to bubble, add the flour, stirring it with a wooden spoon until it foams. Keep stirring for a minute or two, then add the broth and keep stirring until the sauce thickens. Add the mustard and stir until smooth.

Return the meat and vegetables to the skillet, toss well, and simmer in the sauce for several minutes to heat through. Add the sour cream and heat it but don't let it boil. Serve the stroganoff with fresh dill scattered over the top.

THAI-STYLE BEEF CURRY

This spicy dish is Thai convenience food—all you need is a little 4-ounce can of red curry paste (at Asian food stores) and canned coconut milk, and you're set. Especially good served over a bed of buttered spinach. If the beef cubes are larger than 1 inch, the cooking time will be much longer. SERVES 6

    2 tablespoons peanut or olive oil
    3 tablespoons Thai red curry paste, see page 40
    2½ cups canned coconut milk
    2½ pounds beef chuck, cut into 1-inch cubes
    Salt and pepper to taste
    Garnish: ¼ cup chopped cilantro

Per Serving: Protein: 61g   Fat: 35g   Carbohydrate: 3g

In a dutch oven, warm the oil over low heat and add the curry paste. Stir and cook over low heat for about 5 minutes, then add the coconut milk. Cook and stir for another 3 minutes. Add the beef, bring to a boil, and lower the heat to a gentle simmer. Cook covered for 1½ to 2 hours, stirring from time to time. By now the meat should be soft; if it's not, continue cooking until it is. Raise the heat and cook uncovered another 10 minutes or until the sauce is thick. Taste for seasoning and serve garnished with the cilantro.

OVEN BARBECUED BRISKET

This is one of the few nonsweet barbecue sauces in the
world, teamed with brisket to make a no-mess, deeply
flavorful dish to feed a crowd. Although this is a snap to
make, it's better if you start a day ahead. The deckle, or
front-cut brisket, is especially delicious. SERVES 12

SAUCE
½ (10-ounce) bottle Worcestershire sauce
⅛ cup hot pepper sauce
4 tablespoons (½ stick) butter
1 scant cup cider vinegar
½ tablespoon ground black pepper
1 teaspoon salt
1 teaspoon red pepper flakes, optional

4 garlic cloves, pressed
1 large beef brisket, about 4 pounds

Per Serving: Protein: 45g   Fat: 19.3g   Carbohydrate: 4.7g

Combine all the sauce ingredients in a saucepan over
medium heat and bring to a boil. Stir well, lower the
heat, and simmer for 10 minutes, stirring frequently. Let
cool and refrigerate until ready to use—the sauce will
keep for several days.

The day before you plan to serve the brisket, rub it
with additional salt and the garlic paste, put it in a foil-
lined roasting pan, and cover it generously with sauce.
Pull the foil up over the meat to make a tightly sealed
package. Let sit overnight in the refrigerator to develop
flavor.

In the morning, let the brisket come to room temperature, about 2 hours. Preheat the oven to 325°F. Roast the brisket, still in its package, for 5 hours, then remove it from the oven. Pull the foil down around the meat and return it to the oven to brown. It should absorb most of the sauce and be perfectly done in another half hour.

BEEF BURGOYNE

This American version of Boeuf Bourgogne is a good oven stew that requires minimal effort. You may need more wine and consommé, so have them ready in case the stew begins to dry out. It will take about 3 hours altogether.

SERVES 6

> 2½ pounds round steak or London broil, in 2-inch cubes
> 2 tablespoons olive oil
> 3 garlic cloves, chopped
> ½ teaspoon dried thyme
> 3 bay leaves
> Salt and pepper to taste
> ½ cup canned consommé, or more as needed
> ½ cup burgundy, or more as needed
> 6 whole shallots, peeled
> 1 pound market mushrooms, trimmed and quartered
> 1 tablespoon instant flour, if needed

Per Serving: Protein: 61g   Fat: 22.7g   Carbohydrate: 5.6g

Preheat the oven to 350°. Trim off any extra fat and pat the meat dry with paper towels. Heat the oil in a dutch oven and, when it's hot, brown the meat all over. Add the garlic, thyme, and bay leaves. Add salt and pepper and the liquids. Bring to a boil on top of the stove, cover the stew, and bake in the oven for 1 hour.

Check for moisture; if the stew seems to be getting dry, add another ½ cup of each of the liquids. Add the shallots. Bake another 1½ hours.

Half an hour before serving, add the mushrooms and stir in well. If, when the stew is ready, the sauce seems thin, remove the solids and sprinkle 1 tablespoon of instant flour over the sauce. Cook the sauce down a bit over high heat and add the meat and shallots back in to reheat before serving.

A DIFFERENT HAM

Instead of the usual overly sweet ham glazed with more sugar, try this winey, orangey one. It's hard to say how much of the marinade penetrates the meat, but even if all of it did, you wouldn't have a lot of carbs here.

A partially cooked ham will be tastiest, if you can find one. Remember to start the ham 4 days ahead. SERVES 25

1 large ham, about 12 pounds
1 bottle sauterne
2 large Valencia oranges, quartered
6 dried hot red chile peppers
20 peppercorns
1 cup chopped celery leaves
½ cup chopped parsley
Cloves to decorate the ham

Per Serving: Protein: 40g   Fat: 76g   Carbohydrate: 4g

Four days ahead, marinate the ham: stab it all over many times with the tines of a cooking fork or a skewer, then put it in a large plastic bag. Add the wine, which should completely cover the ham when the bag is closed; if it doesn't, add water to the right level. Squeeze the juice from the oranges over the ham and add in the orange shells. Add everything else except the cloves. Seal the bag tightly with a rubber band and refrigerate until ready to bake.

Four days later, remove the ham from the bag and place it on a rack in a roasting pan. Let come to room temperature, about 4 hours. Preheat the oven to 300°F. Strain the marinade to use for basting the ham. Score the ham and decorate with the cloves. Put the ham in the oven and bake until it reaches a temperature of 150° for an uncooked ham, 130° for precooked, basting frequently with the wine sauce.

CARNITAS

This is a wonderful idea for a casual dinner party. If you haven't had these succulent little morsels of pork tucked into tortillas with guacamole, pickled onions, salsa, sour cream, etc., you'll find them addictive. In Mexico they're cooked in giant cauldrons of lard. Here there are two ways of cooking them: California gardener/cook Sylvia Thompson's oven-roasted carnitas are juicy and delicately flavored; Chicago restaurateur Rick Bayless fries his in lard, which is truer to the Mexican style, and ends up with a crunchy exterior. Either recipe can be made with pork shoulder or country-style ribs, which are actually butterflied chops from the blade end of the pork loin. For a crowd, use the oven-roasted ones.

If you're dieting, you may want to tuck your carnitas into large romaine leaves instead of tortillas. Or slice some ribbons of romaine as a bed for a carnitas salad, add the other elements and toss them together lightly with your fork.

However you cook them, serve the carnitas with bowls of:

Guacamole, page 62
Table salsa, page 156
Chunks of tomato
Pickled onions, page 241
Sprigs of cilantro
Tortillas and/or large romaine leaves
Lime wedges to squeeze over the meat

FRIED CARNITAS

This pork-fried-in-lard is still politically incorrect in America, but it's certainly delicious and it's definitely low-carb. Ideally you'll use a good brand of lard or render it yourself—but in the real world all we can usually get is the supermarket standard, and it will be fine. You can filter the used lard through a coffee filter and save it to use several times again. SERVES 4

> 2 pounds pork shoulder or country-style ribs
> 1 pound lard
> ¼ cup water
> Salt to taste

Per Serving: Protein: 62g   Fat: 30g   Carbohydrate: 0g

Cut the meat into ½-inch-thick strips, 4 inches long and 2 inches wide. In a dutch oven or kettle, melt the lard over a low flame. Add the pork and the water. Simmer the meat gently, uncovered, for about 40 minutes, until it's tender, turning from time to time. Raise the heat to medium-high and fry the pork for about 10 minutes, until it's golden brown and crunchy all over. Drain on paper towels and salt well; serve immediately.

OVEN-ROASTED CARNITAS

This slow-cooking recipe takes about 5 hours to cook, although it's simplicity itself. Just be sure to start early.
SERVES 8

> 4 pounds bone-in pork shoulder or country-style
>   ribs
> Beef broth and water, mixed half and half, to
>   barely cover meat (about ¾ cup broth)
> 1 tablespoon peppercorns
> 1 bay leaf
> 1 teaspoon thyme
> 1 teaspoon oregano, preferably Mexican oregano
> 3 garlic cloves, chopped

Per Serving: Protein: 63g   Fat: 30g   Carbohydrate: 4g

Preheat the oven to 350°F. In a dutch oven (or a Mexican cazuela, if you have one), cover the meat with the mixed broth and water and add the other ingredients. Roast the meat uncovered for 2½ hours, adding more liquid if necessary. Drain off the stock and reserve.

Lower the heat to 275° and cook another 2 hours or more, moistening with stock from time to time. The meat is done when it's just about falling off the bone. When ready to serve, chop the meat roughly and reserve the rib bones for some private nibbling—just reheat them in a 350° oven.

PICKLED ONIONS

Start these at least half an hour before you plan to use them. SERVES 8

2 red onions, thinly sliced
¼ cup mild vinegar
1 bay leaf
Several peppercorns
½ teaspoon oregano, preferably Mexican

Per Serving: Protein: .4g   Fat: trace   Carbohydrate: 2.4g

Place the onion rings in a colander in the sink. Heat a kettle of water to a boil and pour it over the onions. Put the onion in a glass bowl and add cold water just to cover them. Add the remaining ingredients and stir gently to mix. Cover and refrigerate until ready to serve.

ROAST LEG OF PORK WITH SAGE AND GARLIC

This is a great alternative to smoked ham for a party and it's one of the simplest things in the world to cook. Meat guys Bruce Aidells and Denis Kelly came up with the sage-wrapped garlic clove idea. If you like the crispy pork skin—cracklings right on the meat—get the leg a day or two ahead and let the skin dry out while the pork rests uncovered in the refrigerator. If you don't want the skin, just strip it off and rub the pork all over with mashed garlic, sage, salt, and pepper. Whole legs of pork (also called fresh hams) aren't always available, so you may have to order yours ahead. The roast will be easier to slice if you have the butcher remove all but the shank bone and tie the roast. Plan on about 5 hours cooking time.

SERVES 12

> 1 whole leg of pork (10 to 14 pounds), boned and
>   tied
> 12 garlic cloves
> 36 fresh sage leaves, optional
> Salt and pepper to taste

Per Serving: Protein: 112g   Fat: 94g   Carbohydrate: 1g

Preheat the oven to 450°F.

If you're cooking the pork with the skin on, puncture it lightly all over with the tines of a cooking fork. Make 36 slashes in the skin all over the leg. Cut the garlic cloves lengthwise in thirds. Tuck a sage leaf around each sliver and push the slivers into the slashes in the pork.

If you're cooking the pork without the skin, remove it and rub the roast with a paste made from the garlic, sage, and salt and pepper.

Place the pork on a rack in a roasting pan in the lower third of the oven and roast for 20 minutes. Lower the heat to 325° and roast for 3 more hours, turning the pork from time to time so that it roasts evenly—don't baste it. Check the temperature with an instant-read thermometer. The pork will be ready when it reaches 145°, which will probably take another hour or so. If the skin isn't crispy, roast it at 450°F for another 10 to 20 minutes. Let the pork rest loosely covered with foil for 20 minutes before serving. To serve, cut off the skin, for serving in small pieces, then slice the pork.

SOUTHERN-STYLE SMOTHERED
PORK CHOPS

This is the sort of down-home good cooking that got lost
in the low-fat era. But it's still delicious, a wonderful way
to cook today's extra-lean pork, which otherwise isn't
too flavorful. Collard greens are just right with the chops.

Look for chops that have some fat around the edges;
cut it off, dice it, and sauté over medium heat in a heavy
skillet for about 20 minutes or until the fat has cooked off
and you have just the cracklings left. Drain them well, salt
them, and you have a great cook's treat. SERVES 4

    2 tablespoons flour
    Salt to taste
    ½ teaspoon pepper
    4 shoulder-cut or loin pork chops with bone,
        about 6 ounces each
    2 tablespoons vegetable oil or rendered pork fat,
        see above
    1 medium onion, sliced thin
    1 cup hot chicken broth

Per Serving: Protein: 25g   Fat: 23.7g   Carbohydrate: 5.3g

Preheat the oven to 350°F. On a plate, mix 1 tablespoon of the flour, the salt, and the pepper. Dredge the
chops in it on both sides. In a heavy skillet over medium-
high heat, brown the chops in the oil or fat until they're
golden brown. Put them in a baking dish to fit snugly.

In the same skillet, sauté the onion slices over medium
heat, stirring frequently, until they're soft and golden.
Add the remaining tablespoon of flour and stir in thor-

oughly. Continue stirring and add the hot broth slowly.
Cook about 3 minutes more or until the sauce begins to
thicken. Pour the sauce over the chops, cover tightly with
foil, and bake for 20 minutes.

Remove the foil and bake another 20 minutes.

RUBBED RIBS

These are incredibly easy and incredibly good. Of course it's even easier to cook the ribs rubbed with just salt and pepper—good, too. The recipe calls for a few spice-cabinet items you may not have, but it's worth getting them to make these ribs often. Baby back ribs seem like a nice idea, but they don't have as much flavor as the big guys.

THE RUB
SERVES 4

1 tablespoon paprika
½ teaspoon chili powder, such as Gebhardt
½ teaspoon ground black pepper
1 teaspoon celery salt
1 teaspoon lemon pepper seasoning
¼ teaspoon garlic powder
¼ teaspoon onion powder
¼ teaspoon ground red pepper (cayenne)
½ teaspoon salt

THE RIBS
1 tablespoon dark brown sugar
2 racks meaty spareribs
Olive oil

Per Serving: Protein: 51.4g   Fat: 53.6g   Carbohydrate: 3g

To make the rub, mix everything together in a bowl and store in a screw-top jar. Makes almost 3 tablespoons, enough for 2 racks of ribs.

Make the ribs: Mix the sugar into the spices. Rub the ribs with olive oil, then rub them all over with the spice rub. Preheat the oven to 325°F. Put the ribs in a baking dish and cover loosely with foil. Bake for 2 hours, then remove the foil and continue baking until the meat is just ready to pull away from the bone, about another half hour.

LAMB SHANKS

This is one of those comfort foods that need to be served on a bed of cauliflower purée. SERVES 4

3 tablespoons olive oil
4 lamb shanks
6 garlic cloves, sliced
1 teaspoon dried rosemary
Salt and pepper to taste
1 tablespoon balsamic vinegar
4 leeks, including some of the green, sliced thick
1 cup dry red wine

Per Serving: Protein: 30g   Fat: 24.5g   Carbohydrate: 7g

Preheat the oven to 350°F. Heat the olive oil in a dutch oven over medium-high heat until hot. Add the lamb shanks and brown thoroughly all over—you may have to do this in batches. Add the remaining ingredients and stir to combine, then cover the pot and put it in the oven for 2 hours or until the meat is almost falling off the bone.

LAMB YOU CAN EAT WITH A SPOON

This old French recipe produces incredibly succulent, velvety lamb pieces that literally fall off the bone. It's a wonderful dinner-party dish—by the time your guests arrive, the entire house will be perfumed with amazing fragrance. Because it takes up to seven hours to cook, all the work is done ahead.

For your carb-eating guests, you can include lots more carrots and onions and toss in some potatoes, as Suzanne Hamlin does in her version of this dish. SERVES 8

1 (7-to-9-pound) leg of lamb

Salt and pepper

2 medium onions, quartered, or 4 fat shallots, peeled

2 carrots, cut in large pieces

1 whole head of garlic, cloves peeled and halved

6 bay leaves

1 bunch fresh thyme or 1 tablespoon dried thyme

2 bottles red wine—rioja or Chianti

4 turnips, peeled and quartered

Optional: 4 medium potatoes, peeled and quartered

Per Serving: Protein: 60g   Fat: 37.2g   Carbohydrate: 5.4g

Measure your pan before you buy the lamb; it should be a large heavy-lidded casserole, 14 × 11 inches, or a large roasting pan with a cover. If the lamb won't fit in the pan, have the butcher crack the shin bone and just tuck it up along the side of the lamb.

Preheat the oven to 425°F and put the rack at the lowest level.

With a sharp knife, cut away most of the fat on the lamb. Sprinkle the lamb with salt and pepper and rub it into the meat.

On the bottom of the pan, make a nest of the onions, half the carrots, half the garlic, half the bay leaves, and half the thyme. Put the lamb on top. Put the pan in the oven and roast uncovered for 20 minutes, then lower the heat to 300°. Remove the roasting pan from the oven, pour the wine over the lamb, and add the rest of the ingredients except the turnips.

On the stovetop, bring the ingredients to a boil, then cover and return to the oven. Cook for 2 hours, then turn the lamb over and add the turnips. (Add potatoes at this point if you're using them.) Cook for another 2 hours, checking from time to time to see that the vegetables are cooking evenly—move them around with a spoon.

Check to see how the lamb is cooking—when it's done, it will fall off the bone when you pierce it with a fork. A large leg may take 6 hours or more, however. If the lamb is done and it's nowhere near serving time, just leave it on top of the stove and reheat gently when you're ready for it.

Using two large serving spoons, remove the lamb and vegetables to a serving platter and cover with foil to keep warm. Skim the fat from the cooking liquid. Pour all the liquid into a saucepan and boil it down over medium-high heat for about 20 minutes, until the sauce is thick. Serve the sauce on the side with the lamb and vegetables.

LEG OF LAMB WITH A TAPENADE CRUST

You can make this Provençal-style roast with its heady aromas using either a half leg of lamb—the shank end will be the meatiest—or a whole leg. The tapenade recipe makes enough for a whole leg. Let the lamb come to room temperature for several hours before roasting. The longer it sits under the crust, the more flavorful it will be.

There are two versions of the tapenade: a classic one with real anchovy fillets and pitted olives, and a no-fuss version with olive paste and anchovy paste.

SERVES 10 (WHOLE LEG)

TAPENADE:

½ cup pitted imported black olives or olive paste
1 large garlic clove, pressed
2 teaspoons drained and rinsed capers
2 anchovies or 2 teaspoons anchovy paste
¼ teaspoon dried rosemary, crushed
1 tablespoon fresh lemon juice
½ teaspoon Dijon mustard
Olive oil as needed (for the pitted olives)
Lots of freshly ground pepper

THE LAMB

1 whole leg of lamb or 1 shank half leg, at room
     temperature
Salt

Per Serving: Protein: 61g   Fat: 38.7g   Carbohydrate: .7g

For pitted olives and anchovy fillets: In the food processor, blend the olives, garlic, capers, anchovies, and rosemary until almost smooth. Add the lemon juice, mustard, and a little oil to moisten. Season with lots of pepper.

For olive paste and anchovy paste: Blend all the ingredients together in a small bowl with a fork.

Trim the fat from the lamb. Rub the lamb with salt and cover it with the tapenade paste; place it on a rack in a roasting pan to season for 2 hours.

Preheat the oven to 350°F. Roast the lamb for 20 minutes to the pound, or until it reaches an internal temperature of 130° for medium rare. Remove from the oven and let sit under a tent of foil to reabsorb the juices for 20 minutes before carving.

MIDDLE EASTERN EGGPLANT BAKE

The ground lamb at the supermarket is often very cheap—and loaded with fat. This is a good way to use it, since you can cook the lamb and drain off almost all the fat before adding it to the dish. It's worth making extra oven-roasted eggplant so you can toss this dish together for a week-night meal. Leftovers are delicious. SERVES 4

1 medium eggplant, oven-roasted (page 276)
1 tablespoon olive oil
½ cup diced onion
2 garlic cloves, pressed
¼ pound ground lamb
1 teaspoon ground cumin
¼ teaspoon cinnamon
1 teaspoon sweet paprika
¼ teaspoon chili powder
Salt and pepper to taste
1 (14½-ounce) can Muir Glen diced tomatoes,
     including juice
¼ cup crumbled feta cheese
¼ cup grated Parmesan cheese

Per Serving: Protein: 18.7g   Fat: 27.8g   Carbohydrate: 9.7g

Prepare the eggplant and set aside. Preheat the oven to 375°F. In a large skillet, heat the olive oil and when it's hot, add the onion. Sauté the onion until it's soft, then add the garlic and sauté another minute. Remove the onion mixture to a bowl and return the skillet to the heat.

Crumble the lamb into the hot pan and sauté until it's beginning to brown. Pour off any fat that's accumulated and add the spices and salt and pepper. Stir well and sauté until the lamb is completely brown. Return the onion mixture to the skillet and add the tomatoes. Let simmer until most of the juices have evaporated.

In a large gratin dish, make a layer of eggplant slices. Cover with half the lamb mixture and crumble feta cheese on top. Add another layer of eggplant slices and the remaining lamb mixture. Sprinkle the top with the Parmesan.

Bake for 30 minutes, or until the cheese is melted and golden brown.

BASIC QUICHE

This is about as simple as it gets. All you need is an 8-inch quiche pan and you're in business. SERVES 6

Butter for the quiche pan
6 large eggs
1 cup heavy cream
Salt and pepper to taste
1 cup grated cheese—Swiss, Gruyère, Cheddar, etc.

Per Serving: Protein: 12.9g   Fat: 16.3g   Carbohydrate: 2.4g

Preheat the oven to 350°F. Have ready a buttered quiche pan.

Beat the eggs in a bowl with the cream and salt and pepper. Add the cheese, mix well, and pour into the quiche pan. Bake for 40 minutes or until golden brown on top. Serve hot or warm or at room temperature.

Bacon or Ham Quiche: Add ½ cup of crisp bacon bits or diced ham.

Spinach Quiche: Add 1 cup of cooked, squeezed-dry chopped spinach with a little freshly grated nutmeg.

FRIED EGGS WITH CHEESE

This is instant dinner for four. Use another serious hard cheese if you don't have pecorino or pepato, a delicious peppered sheep cheese. SERVES 4

> 2 tablespoons butter
> 4 thick slices pecorino or pepato cheese
> 4 large eggs
> ½ teaspoon salt mixed with ½ teaspoon ground
>   cumin or chile pepper or a combination

Per Serving: Protein: 10.3g   Fat: 15.7g   Carbohydrate: .6g

Heat the butter in a wide nonstick skillet over medium heat. When it's melted, add the cheese slices and cook them until they begin to bubble, in just a few minutes.

Crack an egg on top of each cheese slice, lower the heat, and partially cover the pan. Cook gently until the whites are set and the yolks are opaque. Carefully lift out the cheese slices with a spatula and dust the tops with the spicy salt.

MIDDLE EASTERN EGGS

These delicious scrambled eggs also taste a little South-western—it's that cumin-chile-cilantro combination which can go either way. SERVES 4

2 tablespoons butter
2 scallions, including the firm green, sliced
1 green chile, seeded and minced
1 teaspoon ground cumin
8 large eggs, beaten with salt and pepper to taste
2 tomatoes, seeded and cut into small cubes
1 tablespoon chopped cilantro
Hot pepper sauce, optional

Per Serving: Protein: 12.2g   Fat: 16.7g   Carbohydrate: 4.2g

Melt the butter in a large skillet over medium-high heat, and when it's foaming add the scallions, chile, and cumin. Sauté until the scallions are soft. Add the eggs and tomato pieces and scramble together with the onions and chile. Just before serving, stir in the cilantro and add the hot pepper sauce. Decorate the platter with more sprigs of cilantro.

GREEN CHILE SOUFFLÉ

A delectable casserole that has the Southwest written all
over it—but you don't have to peel any peppers and it
goes together in just a few minutes. If you want this dish
hotter, add a minced seeded jalapeño in with the cheese.
It's easier to arrange the chiles if the sides of the dish
slope a bit—a Mexican cazuela is perfect. SERVES 6

    2 tablespoons butter for the dish
    4 (4-ounce) cans whole peeled chiles
    8 ounces Muenster or jack cheese or a mixture,
        shredded
    ½ pound ham, diced
    8 large eggs
    1 pint heavy cream
    1 teaspoon salt
    1 teaspoon ground black pepper

Per Serving: Protein: 27.2g   Fat: 59g   Carbohydrate: 4.6g

Preheat the oven to 350°F and butter a casserole with
sloping sides or a soufflé dish. Line the dish, bottom and
sides, with the chiles (these will form a crust when the
soufflé is cooked). Make a layer of the cheese and then of
the ham. Beat the eggs well in a bowl and add the cream,
salt, and pepper. Mix well, then pour into the dish.

Bake the soufflé for 40 minutes or until the top is
golden brown and the center is cooled. Serve immediately.

THE FRITTATA

If you've ever struggled with flipping an omelet or served one that looked hilarious, the frittata's for you. Some people flip frittatas too, but there's an easier way: just cook the eggs in the skillet on top of the stove until they're set on the bottom, then run them under the broiler to cook the top.

You can make a little sauce for the frittata by sizzling some sherry vinegar with butter in a small skillet; you can treat it like pizza and add everything you've been missing in pizza, you can slice a wedge in half horizontally and make a frittata sandwich, or you can just have a frittata snack with leftovers. Frittatas work for breakfast, lunch, and dinner, and they're ready in minutes. You can crumble up tofu and add it, you can make them with Egg Beaters if you're a cholesterol-phobe—they're just about perfect.

All you need is a 10-inch nonstick ovenproof skillet and some vegetable to tuck into the frittata—let's say it's chopped mushrooms. It could also be zucchini (3 small) with some torn basil leaves tossed in. You can also make a larger frittata with 6 eggs. SERVES 4

4 extra-large eggs
Salt and pepper to taste
2 tablespoons olive oil or butter
3 cups chopped mushrooms
½ cup grated Parmesan

Per Serving: Protein: 10.3g   Fat: 15.6g   Carbohydrate: 3g

Using a fork, mix the eggs in a bowl with the salt and pepper. Heat the oil or butter in a 10-inch ovenproof skillet and add the mushrooms. Cook until the mushrooms are soft. Pour the eggs over the mushrooms.

Cook the frittata over medium heat until the bottom is set. Sprinkle the cheese over the top, then run it under the broiler until golden brown. Serve hot, warm, or at room temperature.

Pizza Frittata

Just before the frittata goes under the broiler, add ¼ cup pizza sauce over the top, pepperoni slices, ½ cup shredded mozzarella, and a sprinkle of oregano

---

Per Serving: Protein: 8g   Fat: 12.8g   Carbohydrate: 1.4g

Broccoli Frittata

Dice 1 cup of cooked broccoli and ½ cup of roasted red peppers (from a jar) and scatter them over the eggs in the skillet. Crumble ⅓ cup feta cheese on top.

Per Serving: Protein: 8.3g   Fat: 13.5g   Carbohydrate: 3.4g

Side Dishes

〰

In ordinary cookbooks, the side dishes are often heavy on the starch—potatoes, rice and other grains, beans—but here they're mostly vegetables. Some of the dishes feature ingredients from the hero-vegetable category in the next section, but they're highlighted here because they're so useful. Others are moving in the direction of the starchy dishes—spaghetti squash, for instance, and the turnip gratin, which so closely mimics a luscious potato dish. And there's one lone grain—or rather, grass: wild rice, which has so much fiber that it sneaks in under the wire here.

Dishes from other sections can come in under the side-dish umbrella, too; some first courses can turn into side dishes, and even some main courses can too, such as a skinny sliver of quiche. If you're serving guests or having an extravaganza like Thanksgiving, the easiest way to make it a feast is to increase the number of side dishes. This is a perfect way to include beets, for instance, a relatively low-carb vegetable that not everyone loves (see the recipe on page 295).

Remember that purées of cauliflower and broccoli will go a long way toward reminding you of mashed potatoes, and potato skins will make up for almost everything you're missing about potatoes. And take another look at turnips—sweet-young-thing turnips with purple shoulders are just delectable, cooked and mashed with cream and interesting seasonings like ginger and mace. Turnips need a little sweetness, and the sweet spices fill that role.

Finally, don't be afraid to mix vegetables—broccoli and cauliflower seem made for each other, but try spinach with zucchini, green beans with red peppers, cauliflower with everything. For more ideas, get some great vegetable books: Bert Greene's *Greene on Greens* is a good place to start, as is Marian Morash's *The Victory Garden Cookbook* and, for exotica, Elizabeth Schneider's *Uncommon Fruits and Vegetables*. The happier you are with the vegetables you're eating, the easier it will be to stay on the low-carb regimen long-term.

ASPARAGUS WITH ZESTY HERBS

The intensely green herb sauce in this recipe seems to intensify the fresh spring quality of asparagus. You can make the asparagus ahead and just put the sauce together at the last minute. SERVES 6

3 pounds asparagus

ZESTY HERB SAUCE
10 basil leaves
4 watercress sprigs plus more for garnish
5 large mint leaves
Small handful of parsley
1 tablespoon chopped chives
½ teaspoon coarse salt
¼ teaspoon pepper
2 tablespoons fresh lemon juice
⅓ cup extra-virgin olive oil

Per Serving: Protein: 0g   Fat: 12.3g   Carbohydrate: 4.4g

Snap the butts off the asparagus spears at the point where they break naturally. Rinse them and tie them together loosely in bundles; cook in a saucepan full of boiling salted water with the tips standing above the pot. Test for doneness after 6 minutes; they should be al dente. Have ready a bowl of cold water in the sink and plunge the spears into it to keep their color and stop the cooking. Drain on paper towels and set aside on a serving platter to come to room temperature.

Put the herbs in a blender jar, then add the salt and pepper. Blend for a second, then add the lemon juice. Pour in the oil in a trickle while the blender is running on low speed. Shortly before serving, pour the sauce over the platter of asparagus and garnish with watercress sprigs.

WILD RICE

Wild rice is expensive, both in dollars and carbs—a scant half-cup will cost you 15 grams of carbohydrates. But as grains go, that's almost nothing, and for a dinner party wild rice is a perfect choice, festive and delicious.

You can take the carbs down even further by mixing in 2 cups of chopped mushrooms sautéed with 2 slices of bacon, diced, plus 1 minced garlic clove, 1 teaspoon of Worcestershire sauce, salt and pepper, and ½ teaspoon of grated lemon zest. Stir into the rice just before serving. Wild mushrooms would of course be even better.

For a sweeter take on wild rice, sauté ½ cup of chopped pecans in a tablespoon of melted butter. Remove the nuts when they're golden and add another tablespoon of butter. When the butter foams, add 4 sliced scallions, including the firm green, and sauté until just beginning to wilt. Fold the nuts and scallions into the hot cooked rice along with a teaspoon of minced orange zest.
SERVES 6

   1 cup wild rice
   3 cups water
   1 teaspoon salt
   ½ teaspoon fresh lemon juice
   2 tablespoons melted butter

Per Serving: Protein: trace   Fat: 3.6g   Carbohydrate: 5.1g

Put the wild rice in a strainer and rinse well under cold running water. Meanwhile, heat the 3 cups of water in a saucepan until it boils. Add the salt, the lemon juice, and—slowly, in a steady stream—the wild rice. Let the rice boil gently over moderate heat for 35 to 40 minutes, until it's just tender; test a grain or two to see. When it's done, drain it in a sieve and return it to the hot pan. Cover and let sit for 5 minutes, stirring once or twice, to dry thoroughly. Add the melted butter and serve right away.

ZUCCHINI PASTA

A dish similar to this has been on the menu at New York's
Union Square Café for years—people love it, and not
because they're avoiding pasta. Try the same technique
and top the zucchini with pesto sauce. SERVES 2

    4 small zucchini
    2 tablespoons olive oil
    1 large garlic clove, pressed
    1 (14½-ounce) can diced tomatoes, preferably
        Muir Glen
    1 teaspoon oregano
    ½ pound cooked Italian sausage links, cut up
    Salt and pepper
    Several leaves of fresh basil, torn
    ½ cup grated Parmesan cheese

Per Serving: Protein: 20.7g Fat: 36.8g Carbohydrate: 11g

Slice the unpeeled zucchini into ribbons, using a vegetable peeler and turning the squash as you go. Put 1 tablespoon of the olive oil in a saucepan over medium heat;
when it's warm, add the pressed garlic. Sauté briefly, then
add the tomatoes and oregano. Let the sauce simmer uncovered for a few minutes.

Meanwhile, heat the remaining tablespoon of oil in a
wide skillet; when it's hot, add the zucchini. Stir for several minutes until the zucchini is soft and the edges are
clear. Add salt and pepper to taste, then mix in the sauce.
Add the sausage and stir well. Stir in the basil and transfer to a serving dish. Scatter the Parmesan over the top.

ZUCCHINI PANCAKES

Make these delicious morsels in silver-dollar size and
serve them immediately. SERVES 4

1 cup grated (on the largest hole) zucchini
Salt

BATTER
1 large egg, lightly beaten
1 teaspoon water
2 tablespoons grated Parmesan cheese
1 tablespoon flour
Lots of pepper
4 basil leaves, snipped, optional

1 tablespoon butter
1 tablespoon olive oil

Per Serving: Protein: 2.5g   Fat: 8.4g   Carbohydrate: 2.5g

Put the shredded zucchini in a colander in the sink
and salt it lightly. Mix in the salt with your hands and
leave the zucchini to drain for 30 minutes. Squeeze out all
the juices and blot the squash dry with paper towels.

In a large bowl, combine the batter ingredients and
whisk until smooth. Mix in the zucchini.

In a nonstick skillet (or use a griddle), melt the butter
and oil together over medium heat until foaming. Drop
the batter by tablespoons onto the skillet and cook over
medium-high heat until brown. Turn and brown the other
side. Pile the pancakes on a platter, salt lightly, and serve.

SOUTHWESTERN ZUCCHINI PANCAKES

These make a great little side dish. If you can't find masa
harina (which you should keep in the freezer) you can use
corn flour, which isn't much easier to find. If you can
only find cornmeal, use that and add a beaten egg to the
mixture. SERVES 4

    2 medium zucchini, shredded
    ¼ cup masa harina
    ⅛ teaspoon salt
    ⅛ teaspoon ground cumin
    2 tablespoons olive oil
    ½ cup salsa

Per Serving: Protein: .5g   Fat: 7.2g   Carbohydrate: 7.2g

In a bowl, mix the zucchini with the masa, salt, and
cumin—use your hands.

Heat the olive oil in a nonstick skillet over medium-
high heat. Meanwhile, make 12 little pancakes with the
zucchini mixture. When the oil is hot, add the little cakes,
just a few at a time, and sauté them until they're golden
on both sides. Repeat with the remaining pancakes, and
keep the cooked ones warm on a platter under foil.

Serve the pancakes with the salsa.

SPAGHETTI SQUASH WITH
ROASTED PECANS

The point of this squash isn't its wonderful flavor—it has
hardly any—it's the crisp texture and the novelty of having squash turn into pasta right before your eyes. This
recipe is for a Thanksgiving-type dish, but spaghetti
squash is also good treated like pasta: just add a lot of
butter, cheese, and salt and pepper. SERVES 6

   1 spaghetti squash
   6 tablespoons butter
   1 teaspoon dark brown sugar
   ½ cup roasted pecans, chopped (page 52)
   ½ teaspoon cinnamon
   Salt and pepper to taste

Per Serving: Protein: .7g   Fat: 20.6g   Carbohydrate: 9g

Preheat the oven to 350°F. Prick the squash in several
places so it won't explode and set it on a baking sheet in
the oven for 1 hour. Remove it and let it cool enough to
handle.

Cut the squash in half lengthwise and remove the seeds
and stringy bits. Using a fork, gently pull the strands of
squash apart and lift them out of their shell. You can pile
them into a bowl and refrigerate until ready to assemble
the dish.

In a large skillet, melt the butter and add the brown
sugar and the squash. Cook until heated through, stirring
gently. Add the remaining ingredients and stir well. Serve
immediately.

SUMMER SQUASH

This simple green and yellow dish tastes best when little garden squash are in the market and basil is plentiful. But you can also make it in other seasons and use other seasonings, such as oregano and parsley. SERVES 3

    1 tablespoon butter
    1 tablespoon olive oil
    3 small squash, zucchini and crookneck, grated
        (about 2 cups)
    About 8 basil leaves, snipped
    Salt and pepper to taste

Per Serving: Protein: 0g   Fat: 8.3g   Carbohydrate: 2.6g

Melt the butter with the oil in a wide nonstick skillet. When it's foaming, add the squash and cook slowly, while stirring frequently, over medium heat for about 8 minutes, or until just softened. Stir in the basil and salt and pepper. Serve immediately.

FRIED PEPPERS

These succulent strips of red pepper don't need peeling
and they store well in the refrigerator. Put them on an antipasto platter, serve them with a lunch buffet, or team
them with grilled sausages. SERVES 4

1½ pounds red bell peppers
⅓ cup olive oil
Salt to taste

Per Serving: Protein: 0g   Fat: 18.5g   Carbohydrate: 7.6g

Cut the peppers in half, seed them, and cut them in
long ½-inch strips. Warm the oil in a large heavy skillet
over medium heat and add the peppers, skin side down.
Cook without stirring for 7 minutes, then turn the pepper strips and cook them until they're soft. Remove from
the skillet with a slotted spoon and sprinkle with salt to
taste. Serve hot or at room temperature, or store in a
bowl covered with the oil from frying. Seal tightly and refrigerate. Bring to room temperature before serving.

CAPONATA

This pungent vegetable mélange can become addictive. It's good with grilled chicken or meat and makes a great lunch along with celery, cheese, and hard-cooked eggs. It also keeps for a week in the refrigerator. The recipe comes from Roman cook Jo Bettoja. SERVES 6

2 medium eggplants, unpeeled
Coarse salt
2 canned Italian plum tomatoes, drained and
      seeded
2 large bell peppers, 1 red and 1 yellow
2 medium zucchini
2 medium white onions
1 tablespoon rinsed capers, dried
½ cup pitted green olives
1 bay leaf
Pepper to taste
¼ cup white wine vinegar
1 teaspoon sugar
½ cup plus 1 tablespoon extra-virgin olive oil

Per Serving: Protein: .1g   Fat: 23.3g   Carbohydrate: 9g

Cut the eggplants into 1-inch cubes and place them in a colander. Sprinkle with salt and toss. Weight the eggplant with a heavy can on top of a plate and let drain for 1 hour. Rinse and dry thoroughly with paper towels.

Purée the tomatoes and set aside.

Preheat the oven to 350°F. Oil a small roasting pan.

Halve the peppers, remove the seeds, and cut the peppers into 1-inch squares. Cut the zucchini into ¼-inch rounds. Slice the onions thin.

Put all the vegetables in the roasting pan along with the capers, olives, and bay leaf. Sprinkle with salt and pepper.

Combine the vinegar and sugar in a saucepan; heat until the sugar dissolves. Pour the vinegar over the vegetables, then add the oil and mix thoroughly. Bake uncovered for 1½ hours, turning every 30 minutes. Serve at room temperature.

Roasted Vegetables

The Italians have always loved roasting vegetables, but it took Barbara Kafka, author of <u>Roasting: A Simple Art</u> (Morrow, 1995), to show us the full range of possibilities, from cabbage to—of all things—cucumbers. Kafka roasts almost all vegetables at 500° on the upper rack of the oven. She slicks them with fat—olive oil is the obvious choice—and puts them in a close-fitting pan. Add a pinch of dried herbs to the oil and perhaps a minced clove of garlic. Halfway through the cooking turn the vegetables so they'll cook evenly. When they're browned and done, add salt and pepper and perhaps a splash of balsamic vinegar.

Mixed roasted vegetables is an even better idea. Cut the vegetables in roughly 2-inch pieces and cook them according to the times listed below. To serve 6, use 8 cups of vegetables and put them in one layer in a medium-sized roasting pan with 3 tablespoons of herbed olive oil. Toss well and send to the oven, adding the more tender vegetables later according to the time chart.

30 MINUTES
Leeks, cut in 1-inch lengths

20 MINUTES
Zucchini, cut in 1-inch lengths

Medium-sized shallots

Small eggplant, quartered

15 MINUTES
Portobello mushrooms

Bell peppers, cut in 2-inch chunks

Broccoli florets, including a piece of the peeled stem

Cherry tomatoes

BAKED EGGPLANT

This recipe from Roman cook Jo Bettoja is a delicious way to cook garden-fresh eggplant, which doesn't require salting. If all you have is big-old supermarket eggplant, peel it and salt the slices (leaving them to drip in a colander in the sink) for half an hour before patting dry and baking. Leftovers are equally good—just store them in the refrigerator and bring to room temperature before using. SERVES 6

½ cup extra-virgin olive oil
2 pounds eggplant, in ½-inch slices
Salt to taste
2 tablespoons fresh lemon juice
1 teaspoon oregano
Pepper to taste

Per Serving: Protein: 0g   Fat: 18.6g   Carbohydrate: 6g

Preheat the oven to 425°F. To make the first batch of eggplant: Pour half the oil into a 15 × 12–inch roasting pan and spread it around the bottom. Dip half the eggplant slices in the oil to coat both sides and arrange them in the pan in one layer. Bake for 10 minutes. Turn the slices and bake another 10 minutes, or until the eggplant is golden brown. Remove the eggplant to a serving platter and sprinkle with half the lemon juice. Crumble half the oregano on top and add pepper to taste.

Repeat the procedure with the remaining eggplant slices. The eggplant tastes best at room temperature; if it's been refrigerated, let it come to room temperature before serving. The flavor just improves from day to day, up to about 3 days.

CHOUCROUTE

Choucroute is French for sauerkraut—which you may think you don't like, but try it this way; it's sweet and mild and just right for a winter's evening. It's served surrounded by as many different kinds of sausages as you can get your hands on, grilled or broiled, and a pot of mustard and one of horseradish at the table. The sauerkraut is even better made a day ahead, so it's a good company dish. SERVES 6

> 2 pounds fresh sauerkraut (in the dairy case)
> 2 tablespoons butter
> 1 medium onion, sliced thin
> 1 bay leaf
> Lots of pepper
> 1 cup dry white wine
> ¼ cup gin
> 3 cups low-sodium beef broth

Per Serving: Protein: .3g   Fat: 8.6g   Carbohydrate: 2.2g

Rinse the sauerkraut in a colander under running water, then leave it to soak in cold water for half an hour, changing the water twice, to sweeten it. Drain the sauerkraut and fluff it up a bit.

Preheat the oven to 325°F. In a dutch oven, melt the butter and add the onion. Cook the onion over medium-low heat for about 10 minutes, or until it's soft, stirring from time to time. Add the sauerkraut, bay leaf, and pepper. Cover and cook for 10 minutes. Add the liquids and stir well.

Bake the sauerkraut covered for 5 hours, or until the liquid is absorbed. Remove the bay leaf and taste for seasoning; you may need to add salt.

FRIZZLED CABBAGE

This recipe breaks all the rules for cooking cabbage, yet
brings out an amazing sweetness in the vegetable. It won't
even be clear that this is cabbage you're eating. . . . It
makes a good nest for meatballs and a fast side dish. You
can add seasonings to taste a few minutes before serving:
nutmeg, paprika, cumin, dill, hot pepper sauce, whatever seems appropriate. But try it first plain. SERVES 2

> ¼ medium head of cabbage
> 2 tablespoons butter
> Salt and pepper to taste

Per Serving: Protein: 0g   Fat: 11g   Carbohydrate: 2.7g

Cut out the core of the cabbage and slice the remaining wedge in skinny slivers. Melt the butter in a wide
skillet and when it's foaming add the cabbage—you
should have about 2 cups. Cook the cabbage over medium
heat, turning frequently, until it begins to wilt, about 10
minutes. Lower the heat a little and continue to cook
until the cabbage starts to brown and caramelize a bit, another 10 minutes or so—but don't let it burn. Serve immediately.

GREEN BEAN PACKAGES

Vegetables that come to the table wrapped as presents
are always particularly appealing, and that's definitely the
case here. SERVES 1

> **For each serving:**
> **8 skinny green beans, stemmed**
> **1 teaspoon melted butter**
> **Salt and pepper**
> **1 slice smoky bacon**

Per Serving: Protein: 2g   Fat: 16g   Carbohydrate: 3g

Preheat the oven to 400°F.

Steam the beans for 4 minutes, or drop them into boiling water for the same period of time. Drain them, dry
them, and roll them in the butter. Add salt and pepper to
taste.

Place the bacon slice on a baking sheet lined with foil
and arrange the beans in the middle of it. Fold the ends
around the beans—or make a spiral of bacon running
around the bunch of beans. Bake for 20 minutes and serve
hot.

TURNIP GRATIN WITH BLUE CHEESE

This delectable dish of Los Angeles chef Michael Roberts is luxurious enough for a major holiday meal—and everyone will think they're eating potatoes. SERVES 4

    4 medium white turnips, sliced paper thin
    1 yellow onion, sliced thin
    4 tablespoons (½ stick) unsalted butter, melted
    ½ cup heavy cream
    4 anchovy fillets, chopped fine
    ¼ teaspoon freshly grated nutmeg
    ¼ teaspoon pepper
    ½ cup crumbled Roquefort or other blue cheese

Per Serving: Protein: 6.1G   Fat: 27.4G   Carbohydrate: 5.7G

Preheat the oven to 375°F. Toss together the turnips and onion with the butter in a 9-inch round baking dish. Cover tightly with foil and bake for 30 minutes.

In a small saucepan over medium heat, bring to a boil the cream, anchovies, nutmeg, and pepper and cook for 1 minute. Remove the turnips from the oven and take off the foil. Pour the cream sauce over, toss well, and sprinkle the blue cheese over the top. Return the turnips to the oven for an hour, uncovered. The gratin should be golden brown; if it isn't, run it under the broiler for 3 minutes or until it colors.

GREEN BEAN PIE

The original version of this humble recipe hails from Liguria, on the Italian coast—where they would not be adding any walnuts to it. I learned this dish from Colman Andrews, who I hope won't mind my messing around with it. SERVES 8

> Olive oil for the dish
> 2 pounds green beans, trimmed
> Salt
> ½ onion, chopped fine
> 1 garlic clove, minced
> 1 tablespoon extra-virgin olive oil
> 4 sprigs Italian parsley, chopped
> ½ teaspoon dried oregano
> ½ cup grated Parmesan cheese
> 4 extra-large eggs, lightly beaten
> ½ cup ricotta cheese
> Black pepper
> ⅓ cup chopped walnuts

Per Serving: Protein: 7.4g   Fat: 10.2g   Carbohydrate: 7.5g

Preheat the oven to 300°F. Grease a 9-inch quiche dish with olive oil. Cook the beans for 10 minutes in a large pot of boiling salted water. Meanwhile, cook the onion and garlic in the olive oil in a nonstick skillet for about the same amount of time. Drain the beans in a colander in the sink and let them cool under cold water. Set aside. Add the parsley and oregano to the onions and cook for 10 more minutes.

Cut the beans into 1-inch lengths. Remove the skillet from the heat and stir the beans in with the onions, along with half the Parmesan and the eggs mixed with the ricotta. Transfer the mixture to the prepared quiche dish. Add the walnuts to the remaining Parmesan and scatter over the top.

Bake the pie for 45 minutes or until golden brown on top.

SKILLET WATERCRESS

Good as watercress is raw, it's also delicious cooked—a little pricey, but very interesting. SERVES 6

3 tablespoons butter
1 garlic clove, smashed
4 bunches watercress, tough stems removed
Salt and pepper to taste

Per Serving: Protein: 1g Fat: 5.5g Carbohydrate: .6g

Melt the butter in a large skillet and add the garlic. Cook over medium-high heat until the butter is foaming, then remove the garlic clove and add the watercress. Stir and toss the watercress until it's wilted, just a few minutes. Add salt and pepper to taste and serve hot.

SKILLET RADISHES

Cooked radishes are delicious—and these also look pretty. SERVES 4

2 bunches red radishes, washed and trimmed
3 tablespoons butter
1 teaspoon salt
Pepper to taste

Per Serving: Protein: 0g Fat: 8.2g Carbohydrate: trace

In a nonstick skillet, melt the butter and add the radishes. Cook over medium heat until tender, about 4 to 6 minutes. Season with the salt and pepper and serve hot.

COUNTRY-STYLE GREENS

Some greens are higher in carbs than others—collards,
for instance—but they're all so good for you that it's
worth the extra couple of grams. Old Southern cooks
add just a little flour to the greens to give them a creamy
quality—more carbs again, but not enough to think
about. Your call. SERVES 6

> 4 pounds strongly flavored greens—kale, collards,
>   mustard greens, turnip greens, or a mixture
> 1 pound pork shoulder butt, slashed to the bone
>   in 3 places
> Salt and pepper to taste
> 1 tablespoon flour, optional
> Pepper vinegar or cider vinegar

Per Serving: Protein: 10.4g   Fat: 4.6g   Carbohydrate: 3.9g

Remove the stems from the greens and clean them
thoroughly. Put them in a large pot—enameled cast iron
is perfect—with just enough water to cover. Add the
pork butt. Bring the water to a boil, lower the heat, and
simmer, partially covered, for 2 hours or until the greens
are soft and the meat is falling apart. Add salt and pepper
to taste, then the optional flour, mixing well. Serve in
soup plates with some of the meat mixed in and pass the
pepper vinegar on the side.

SPINACH WITH A WHIFF OF GARLIC

A quick way to cook spinach for a dinner party.
SERVES 6

> 2 pounds spinach, stems removed
> 2 garlic cloves, smashed
> 2 tablespoons butter or olive oil
> Salt and pepper to taste

Per Serving: Protein: 0g   Fat: 3.6g   Carbohydrate: 1.6g

Be sure the spinach is clean; then put it in a large
saucepan with just the water that clings to it. Cover and
cook over medium heat, stirring frequently. When the
spinach begins to crumple, drain it in a colander in the
sink, pressing it to extract as much water as possible,
then return it to the pot. Spear the garlic cloves on the
tines of a cooking fork and stir them thoroughly through
the spinach. Add the butter or olive oil. Season to taste
with salt and pepper and serve hot.

SPINACH CHEESE PIE

This is more or less what's inside the traditional Greek spanikopita, minus the phyllo dough layers. It's best made with fresh spinach that's been plunged briefly into boiling water—but frozen spinach works perfectly well too, so that's what the recipe calls for. SERVES 8

> 2 (10-ounce) packages frozen whole-leaf spinach, defrosted
> 2 tablespoons butter
> 1 bunch scallions, including the firm green, chopped (about ¾ cup)
> ½ medium onion, chopped
> 6 eggs, beaten well
> 1 (15-ounce) container whole-milk ricotta
> ½ pound feta cheese, crumbled
> 1 tablespoon chopped dill
> ¼ cup chopped parsley
> Pinch of grated nutmeg
> Salt and pepper to taste
> Olive oil for the pan

Per Serving: Protein: 9g   Fat: 16.9g   Carbohydrate: 5g

Preheat the oven to 350°F.

Let the spinach drain in a colander in the sink. The easiest way to get all the excess moisture out of it is to line your hand with a double thickness of paper towels and squeeze handfuls of spinach dry. Then chop it and set aside.

Melt the butter in a large skillet; when it's foaming, add the scallions and chopped onion. Cook them over medium heat until they're soft, then add the spinach and a sprinkle of salt and pepper, and cook for 3 minutes, stirring from time to time.

Beat the eggs in a large mixing bowl and whisk in the ricotta. Stir in the remaining ingredients, then oil a 13 × 9–inch baking dish well, including the sides. Mix the spinach with the egg-cheese mixture, taste for seasoning, and pour into the pan.

Bake the pie for 30 to 40 minutes, until the moisture disappears and the top has dappled golden spots. Remove from the oven and let sit for 5 minutes before serving.

CREAMED SPINACH WITH PARMESAN

This is the way they make the unusually good spinach at
Bruno's Pen and Pencil restaurant in Manhattan.

SERVES 2

> 1 tablespoon olive oil
> 1 pound cleaned and stemmed spinach
> ⅓ cup heavy cream
> 1 teaspoon butter
> 1 teaspoon grated Parmesan cheese
> Freshly grated nutmeg to taste

Per Serving: Protein: 1g   Fat: 23.4g   Carbohydrate: 2.1g

Heat the olive oil in a large skillet over medium-high
heat. When it's hot, add the spinach and flip it in the oil,
using tongs, for 2 minutes. Remove the spinach to a nest
of paper towels and squeeze it dry. Chop it.

Add to the skillet the remaining ingredients and cook
them down over high heat for a minute or two, until you
have a little sauce. Add the chopped spinach and mix it
well with the sauce. Serve immediately.

SPINACH WITH A TON OF BUTTER

This famous old recipe is so politically incorrect that we're probably the only people in America who'd even consider eating it. But it's amazing; try it and astound your friends. Just remember that it will be four days before they're astounded; it takes spinach a long time to accommodate so much butter. And who would have guessed our old diet friend spinach could get so greedy?

The recipe is French, but there's also a Russian version in which you sprinkle a teaspoon of vodka over the spinach every day, and 2 teaspoons on the last day. You can add lemon juice and a little grated nutmeg, too.

SERVES 4

> 2 pounds spinach, heavy stems removed
> 1 pound (4 sticks) unsalted butter
> Salt and pepper to taste

Per Serving: Protein: 0g   Fat: 88g   Carbohydrate: 4g

Heat a big pot of salted water to the boil and add the spinach. Turn off the heat and let it stand 2 minutes, then drain and rinse under cold water. Squeeze it gently and chop it roughly.

Melt 1 stick of the butter in a heavy saucepan over low heat. Add the spinach and cook it gently, stirring constantly, until all the butter disappears into the spinach. Put the spinach in a bowl and cover; chill until the next day.

Repeat the process with the next stick of butter and the same spinach for three days running. When you're ready to serve the spinach, warm it through and add salt and pepper to taste. Drain it of any liquid butter.

BROCCOLI WITH TOASTED PINE NUTS

This is a delicious combination that also works with cauliflower—or use half broccoli and half cauliflower.

SERVES 4

> ½ cup pine nuts
> 1 head broccoli, florets only
> ¼ cup olive oil
> 2 tablespoons fresh lemon juice
> Salt and pepper

Per Serving: Protein: 4.8g   Fat: 24.2g   Carbohydrate: 7.4g

Warm a small heavy skillet and toast the pine nuts over a medium flame, stirring frequently to make sure the nuts don't burn. Take them out of the skillet the minute they're golden.

Steam the broccoli florets (or cook in the microwave) until tender. Drain on paper towels.

Warm the olive oil in a large skillet and when it's hot, add the broccoli. Cook just until the broccoli begins to turn golden in places, then add the lemon juice and salt and pepper. Add the pine nuts, stir well, and serve immediately.

BAKED CHARD WITH CHILES

In the same way that spinach is delicious with chiles, so is chard. In this dish they go together with melting cheese, sour cream, and eggs—all you need is protein and salad to round out the meal. I know this recipe comes from a cookbook, but I've lost the source. SERVES 6

3 tablespoons olive oil
1 large bunch Swiss chard, washed, chopped, and
            spun dry in a salad spinner
½ cup chopped leeks
2 garlic cloves, pressed
2 jalapeño peppers, seeds and veins removed,
            sliced thin
4 large eggs
4 or 5 drops hot pepper sauce
½ cup sour cream
½ cup grated Monterey Jack cheese
1 teaspoon salt
Freshly ground black pepper to taste
½ cup grated Parmesan cheese

Per Serving: Protein: 9.6g   Fat: 19g   Carbohydrate: 5g

Preheat the oven to 350°F. Grease a 9-inch-square baking pan with a little of the oil.

In a large skillet or wok, heat the remaining oil over medium heat and cook down the chard while stirring until it starts to wilt. Add the leeks, garlic, and peppers, and continue to cook for about 5 minutes or until all the vegetables are soft.

In a large bowl, beat the eggs and add the pepper sauce, sour cream, Jack cheese, salt, and pepper. Stir in the chard. Mix well and spoon into the baking dish. Sprinkle the Parmesan over the top and bake uncovered for 25 minutes. Let cool for 5 minutes before serving.

POTATO SKINS

This is the only potato recipe I can think of that we can all eat—and it's so delicious that it will probably become one of your favorites. If you haven't eaten carbs for a while, you'll be amazed at the sweetness of the potato flesh.

It's up to you how much white to leave inside the skin—if you want to, you can scrape it all out without much trouble. If you leave, say, ¼ inch, you'll feel as if you ate a whole baked potato, but it will probably be only about 10 to 15 carbs. With steak and salad, that works even for restricted diets. And remember that the skins are full of nutrients.

A nice, big, flattish potato will give you the biggest ratio of skin to flesh. And it's worth going to the trouble of getting organic russet or Idaho potatoes—farmers who want to clear their fields of pesticides plant potatoes because they absorb the poisons so readily.

You can serve the potatoes plain, with just butter and salt and pepper, or with those things plus paprika, or with cheese—any kind that's good with potatoes, such as Swiss, Gruyère, Parmesan, etc. But my favorite is peppercorn cheddar. SERVES 2

2 large baking potatoes
3 tablespoons butter, melted
Salt and pepper
Cheese, optional
Paprika, optional

Per Serving: Protein: 0g   Fat: 17g   Carbohydrate: 10g

Preheat the oven to 400°F. Scrub the potatoes and prick them in a couple of places with a cooking fork so they won't explode. Put them directly on a rack in the hot oven for 1 hour, or until the insides are tender and the skins are crisp. Remove from the oven and let cool slightly.

When the potatoes are cool enough to handle, cut them in half lengthwise. Scoop out the flesh with a big spoon—remove all of it or leave a little, as you like. Put the shells on a cookie sheet with a rim. Using a pastry brush, paint the shells generously with the melted butter, add salt, pepper, and either slices of cheese or grated Parmesan—1 tablespoon is about right. You can also omit the cheese and just shake on a little paprika.

Put the cookie sheet with the shells back into the oven for 10 to 15 minutes, or until the cheese is melted and the potatoes are golden and crispy.

No one's stopping you from serving these with the traditional sour cream and chives.

SAUTÉED BEETS

Beets are wonderfully earthy and sweet, and this simple
way of cooking them gives them a bright new face.
SERVES 4

1 pound beets, trimmed
2 tablespoons butter
2 tablespoons fresh orange juice
Salt and pepper to taste

Per Serving: Protein: 1.4g   Fat: 5.5g   Carbohydrate: 8g

Peel the beets and grate them coarse. Melt the butter
in a sauté pan, stir in the beets, and cook, covered, for
about 15 minutes. Just before serving, add the orange
juice, salt and pepper, and reheat.

Your New Best Friends: The Vegetable Heroes

〿

In the low-carb world, vegetables are king—some vegetables, anyway. These are the ones loaded with vitamins, minerals, and fiber that are naturally low in carbohydrate—though often they taste quite sweet. It's hard to imagine that a sweet red bell pepper fits this profile but it does, and you'll find yourself turning to these powerhouses again and again for everyday meals.

Asparagus

Asparagus is almost the definition of spring, though of course it's available all year long now, imported from the ends of the earth without too much success. Try to buy asparagus out of the bundle and choose stalks the same size, whether they're thin or thick. Store it as if it were a bunch of flowers: pour an inch of cold water in a jar and add the asparagus—keep it refrigerated. Asparagus is a good source of potassium and folic acid, and also has some vitamins A, B, and C. You can eat really fresh asparagus raw—try it—but you can also boil, roast, or grill it. Snap off the butt ends at the point where they snap easily and you'll have the tender part. Six asparagus spears are 2.4 carb grams.

Boiled or Steamed Asparagus

FOR BOILED: Snap off tough ends where they break naturally. Rinse the spears. Lay the spears in a wide skillet of salted water. Bring to a boil, then lower heat to a simmer. Test the asparagus after 4 minutes. When barely done, drain and dry on kitchen towels.

FOR STEAMED: Lay the spears in a steamer basket set over ½ inch or so of boiling water. Cover tightly and steam for 3 to 5 minutes or until almost tender; it will continue to cook a little as it cools. Remove the steamer basket from the pan and spread the asparagus out on a towel to cool.

Sauce the asparagus with orange mayonnaise, page 157.

Roasted Asparagus

Put the asparagus spears in a shallow ovenproof dish and toss with a little olive oil and salt and pepper. Roast at 400°F until tender, about 15 minutes. Scatter some grated Parmesan cheese over the top for the last 5 minutes or until the cheese is golden brown.

Bell Peppers

Red, green, yellow, purple—whatever color, they're all loaded with vitamin C and also have some vitamin A and some minerals. Look for firm peppers; farmers' markets will have thin-walled peppers, which are especially delicious. Red bell peppers are cheapest in late summer and fall when they're in season—a good time to make a lot of fried peppers. One-half cup of chopped bell pepper is 2.4 carbs.

Roasted Bell Peppers

Cut off the stem end of the peppers and pull out the seeds. Either slice them or cut them in half for roasting and put them on a baking sheet lined with foil. Roast skin side up for 20 minutes at 400°F, then take them out of the oven and fold the foil up around them so they steam for 10 minutes. Remove the foil and pull off the blistered skin.

Bell Pepper Hors d'oeuvres

For a snack, spread raw bell pepper slices with seasoned cream cheese (chives, smoked salmon, mixed herbs, etc.). For another hors d'oeuvre, spread red bell pepper slices with a little tapenade, page 164.

Garlic Pepper Strips

Grill some peppers over the dying coals after you've finished grilling dinner. Refrigerate them and cut them into strips the next day. Drizzle with olive oil; add a clove of minced garlic and salt and pepper. Let stand 1 hour to develop flavor.

Cheese-stuffed Roasted Peppers

Take two roasted pepper halves and put a fat slice of smoked mozzarella on each one. Crumble a little oregano over the top and run under the broiler until the cheese is bubbling.

Tunisian Pepper Salad

Make two peppers of different colors the heart of a Tunisian-style salad: Cut them in very small dice, then add a small cucumber cut the same way, some scallions, a few chopped mint and parsley leaves, some olive oil and lemon juice. Add salt and ground black pepper to taste and a pinch of cumin. Let the salad sit for half an hour to develop flavor.

Broccoli

The champion cruciferous vegetable, broccoli is thought to have strong anticancer compounds. Broccoli is also strong in vitamins A and C, as well as calcium, phosphorus, potassium, and zinc. Choose broccoli with tightly closed buds, the greener the better. You can eat the stems as well as the florets; peel them and cut them into ½-inch pieces, then cook them about 3 minutes before you add the florets—4 or 5 minutes more and they should be done, firm but tender. Broccoli is also a champion in the carb department: you can have a whole cup of it for a mere 2.2 carbs.

Broccoli Purées

Cook the broccoli stems in boiling salted water for 5 minutes, then add the florets and cook for another 5 minutes or until tender. Drain and purée the broccoli in a food processor or in a food mill; add enough cream to make a thick purée. Add salt and pepper to taste.

♦ Finish with a little butter and grated nutmeg.
♦ Or finish with a little butter, some grated Parmesan cheese, and a touch of roasted garlic purée.

Leftover Broccoli

Make extra broccoli and cook the chopped leftovers in a generous tablespoonful of olive oil to which you've added a smashed clove of garlic. Add salt and pepper to taste and toss in a few red pepper flakes, to taste. Remove the garlic before serving.

Broccoli With Sun-dried Tomatoes

Microwave chopped broccoli florets and toss them with grated Parmesan and some slivered sun-dried tomatoes.

Broccoli and Cauliflower With Lemon Butter

Cook broccoli with cauliflower. Boil or microwave—don't steam it or it will turn a terrible color—and sauce it simply with butter, lots of lemon juice, salt, and pepper.

Savory Sautéed Broccoli

Try broccoli sautéed in olive oil and garlic with a little anchovy paste tossed in. A few black olives would be good with this.

Sautéed Broccoli Rabe

Broccoli rabe (also known as rape, broccoli raab, or rapini) is a different creature, but also very good for you. It requires a brief dunk in boiling water before sautéing with olive oil, garlic, and red pepper flakes.

Cabbage

Another anticancer vegetable hero, cabbage has vitamins A and C, phosphorus, and folic acid. It comes in plain green, in red, and in the elegant savoy and Chinese cabbages. All of them are high fiber and delicious. Look for firm heads that feel heavy. They'll keep for about a week in the refrigerator. The rule for cabbage is to cook it either briefly or for a long time—or just have it raw, as in coleslaw. You can have 1½ cups of cabbage for 4.5 grams of carb.

Coleslaw

Coleslaw is the easiest, fastest, tastiest way to go. It tastes better if it has a half hour to develop flavor, but even fresh-made coleslaw is very good. If you're used to sweet coleslaw, you may need to add some Equal for a while, but soon that will taste too sweet. Add snipped dill, celery seed, slivers of green pepper, scallion rounds, even hunks of cheese and ham to make a main course.

Sautéed Red Cabbage

Sauté sliced red cabbage in olive oil in a wide skillet. When it begins to wilt, add a couple of drops of pure orange oil (page 41) in a big spoonful of champagne vinegar. If you have any orange zest, add some too. Add a spoonful of drained capers and taste for seasoning.

Curried Cabbage

Add some mild curry powder to butter before sautéing sliced cabbage in it. Cover and cook for several minutes or until tender and add salt and pepper to taste.

Steamed Cabbage

Steam wedges of cabbage in a steamer basket over 2 inches of boiling water for a few minutes. Be careful not to overcook. Serve with melted butter into which you've stirred some paprika. Add salt and pepper.

Roasted Cabbage Strips

The Queen of Roasting, Barbara Kafka, likes to roast cabbage strips, which are delicious. She slices a 1-pound head in ½-inch strips, tosses the strips with a couple of spoonfuls of melted butter, puts them on a large baking sheet, and roasts them at 500°F for half an hour, turning to expose all the cabbage halfway through. Add a spoonful of caraway or cumin seeds to this mix, and add salt and pepper when it's finished.

Sautéed Cabbage

Sliced cabbage simply sautéed in butter is delicious finished with a little cream and snipped dill.

Cauliflower

Almost everything you can do with broccoli you can also do with cauliflower, yet they're completely different in character. Broccoli could never masquerade as potatoes, for instance, as cauliflower can. Cauliflower has a lot of vitamin C and some iron. Look for creamy white firm heads with no yellowing or bruises. You can eat cauliflower raw as a crudité. A whole cup of cauliflower florets is just 2.6 carbs—a long way from potatoes.

Cauliflower Purée

(This is a lot like mashed potatoes.) Steam cauliflower florets or microwave them until soft. Purée in a food processor or food mill and add butter and cream to taste. Season with salt and pepper and warm briefly in a saucepan.

Cauliflower Gratin

Make the purée above, spread it in a shallow baking dish, and cover it with grated Parmesan cheese. Run under the broiler until the cheese is golden brown.

Sautéed Cauliflower

Steam florets and then sauté them in olive oil with garlic and red pepper dice.

◆   Or sauté steamed florets in a little sizzling butter, then add sour cream and snipped dill.

Giant Cauliflower Pancake

Steam florets until soft. Melt clarified butter or Plugra (page 48) in a skillet; when it's warm, add a minced garlic clove. Add the cauliflower and mash it down with a potato masher until it sticks together in a pancake about half an inch thick. Sprinkle grated nutmeg over the top and add salt and pepper. Turn up the heat and fry the pancake on both sides until golden. Drain on paper towels and salt again; serve immediately.

Celery

Crisp is mostly what celery is—there are a few nutrients, but none of much note. The sweet inner ribs are a very different thing from the tougher outer ones; save the inner ones for eating raw if you're cooking the celery. Don't worry about strings; just cut the celery on the diagonal and they'll go away. The leaves are delicious in salad, but in a simple soup, such as chicken soup, a lot of celery leaves can turn bitter. A celery rib is less than 1 carb gram.

Celery Salad

Chop the ribs and some leaves and add some crumbled blue cheese and a few toasted cashew nuts. Toss with a red wine vinaigrette.

Celery as Hors d'oeuvres

Dip the inner celery ribs in olive oil, then in salt and pepper for a very informal hors d'oeuvre.

- ◆ Mix blue cheese with butter and fill inner celery ribs with it. Chopped toasted walnuts would be good with this, too.
- ◆ Serve a bouquet of celery ribs—the sweet inner ones—with your cheese course.

Celery Braised in Butter

Cut celery into ¼-inch pieces, toss in melted butter, and cook over low heat in a covered saucepan for 20 minutes or until tender. Salt and pepper to taste.

Eggplant

Some people shy away from eggplant because they don't want to deal with the salting and draining to draw out the bitter juices. You don't have to worry about that with truly fresh eggplant from the farmers' market—otherwise you can use Japanese eggplant, the skinny Easter-egg-colored ones that don't need salting. Eggplant isn't a nutritional powerhouse, though it does have some potassium and folic acid. Look for firm, shiny light-in-the-hand eggplant and use them right away—it's old, stored eggplant that gets bitter. One-half cup of diced eggplant is 3.2 grams of carb.

Grilled Eggplant Slices

Just brush eggplant slices with olive oil, add salt and pepper, and grill on both sides until they take on a golden brown color in spots.

Eggplant Cannelloni

Slice an eggplant lengthwise ¼-inch thick and grill it. Mix up a little ricotta cheese with herbs—parsley, oregano—and roll the grilled eggplant around it. Put the eggplant rolls in an oiled baking dish and sprinkle a little grated Parmesan on top. Run the rolls under the broiler until the cheese melts and serve them with a simple tomato sauce, page 194.

Grilled Eggplant Salad

Prepare eggplant slices for the grill, then make up a batch of garlicky red wine vinaigrette. Cover the eggplant slices with a few spoonfuls before grilling. When the slices are grilled, toss them with more vinaigrette and let cool to room temperature.

Grilled Japanese Eggplant

Prick whole Japanese eggplant in several places so they won't burst. Grill them on all sides until tender and the skin is charred. Split and serve with butter, salt and pepper, and a little lemon juice.

Eggplant Mozzarella Sandwiches

Make the roasted eggplant slices on page 276 and cover each slice with a thin slice of mozzarella. Sprinkle a little oregano on top. Run under the broiler until the cheese melts.

Sautéed Eggplant

Cut an eggplant into 1-inch cubes and salt it; leave it to drain in a colander for 30 minutes to 1 hour. Dry the cubes with paper towels. Heat olive oil with a smashed garlic clove in a wide nonstick skillet; when it's hot, remove garlic and add the eggplant. Sauté until golden brown and tender, about 8 minutes. Add salt and pepper to taste and serve immediately.

Green Beans

Although they have some vitamin A and C, green beans and their ilk—wax beans, Italian beans, yard-long beans, etc.—aren't big on nutrients. But they're delicious and lend themselves to interesting preparations. Look for crisp but flexible beans. They're not called string beans anymore because the strings have been bred out of them, so all you have to do is snap off their tops and either steam them or cook them briefly in a lot of boiling salted water. Run them under cold water in the sink and dry well before proceeding with the recipe. One-half cup of green beans is a little less than 4 carbs.

Green Beans With Nuts

Serve hot cooked green beans with a sauce of sizzling butter with chopped toasted hazelnuts. Or use pecans or walnuts.

- Try steamed green beans served hot with pesto and chopped toasted walnuts.

Roasted Green Beans

Make a dressing of olive oil with lots of smashed garlic and some thyme and let it sit for a few hours to develop flavor. Remove the garlic before tossing the beans in the flavored oil. Add salt and pepper, and roast in a single layer on a baking sheet at 450°F for 15 minutes, stirring every now and then.

Asian Roasted Green Beans

Proceed as for roasted green beans above, but use light sesame oil and a little soy sauce for the flavored oil. Toss the cooked beans with toasted sesame seeds before serving.

Leftover Green Beans

These can be used for salad or heated up in olive oil or butter and served with lemon juice. Don't add the lemon

juice or any other acid until just before serving or the
beans will discolor.

- ◆ If you have leftover beans and cauliflower, toss
  them together with some fresh slivered mint and
  a lemony vinaigrette.

- ◆ Lightly steamed beans that still have a little
  crunch are delicious on the crudité platter.

Greens

These are everything from beet greens to collard
greens—they're inherently delicious and endlessly good
for you, so they're one of the backbones of the low-carb
diet. They work as side dishes, as salads, or as a bed for
the main dish in place of noodles or potatoes or some
other starch. Spinach (just over ½ gram of carb for 1 cup,
which means you can eat endless amounts) may be the all-
time favorite, but arugula (less than ½ gram for ½ cup)
and mustard greens (4 grams for 1 cup) and bok choy
(under 1 gram per cup) aren't far behind. Kale and collard greens and chard are just under 4 grams for ½ cup.
Try mixing cooked greens together.

Frozen greens are obviously a big convenience, but
fresh ones are incomparable. Once you get used to wash-
ing spinach—two or three rinses in warmish water in a
big bowl—it seems like no work at all for such taste and
nutritional dividends. Strip off the heavy stems of collards, kale, and spinach. It's worth keeping frozen greens
around for emergencies—you never want to be caught
without vegetables.

Almost all greens are improved by an element of acid:
vinegar or lemon juice. They also flourish with butter or

olive oil or peanut oil or light sesame oil. Hot peppers are great with greens and so is a smoky taste—from bacon, liquid smoke, or chipotle peppers (page 38).

Spinach Salad

Use only small young spinach leaves, flat or crinkled. For a main-dish salad, add smoked turkey or ham or both, cubes of Swiss cheese, chopped hard-cooked eggs, and scallions sliced in rounds. Make a creamy lemon dressing with Dijon mustard—just add a little mayonnaise with Dijon to a lemon dressing, page 119.

Spinach or Chard With Garlic and Lemon

Cut off the heavy spinach stems or the white chard stems (cook the chard stems separately, and longer). Chop the greens and put them in a big pot with just the water that still clings to them. Cook them down over medium heat until they begin to wilt into a clump. Drain in a colander and, when they're cool enough, squeeze dry with your hands. In a wide skillet, heat several sliced garlic cloves with olive oil until they just turn golden. Add the greens and cook, stirring, for a couple of minutes. Add a splash of red wine vinegar or balsamic vinegar and salt and pepper to taste. Red pepper flakes would be a good idea here, too.

Simple Spinach Gratin

Rub a large gratin dish with olive oil. Chop 2 pounds of clean dried spinach, toss it with salt and pepper, and put it in the gratin dish. Drizzle with ¼ cup of olive oil and bake uncovered at 375°F for 40 minutes. Add a layer of grated Parmesan and ¼ cup of crumbled croutons; bake for 10 more minutes.

Baby Bok Choy

This is vegetarian cook Deborah Madison's wonderful
way with these little bundles of green. Cut the bok choy
in half lengthwise and soak them in a bowl of water for 15
minutes. Rinse carefully, especially at the base. Set them
cut side down in a skillet of simmering salted water for 4
minutes, or until tender. Remove to a platter with a pair
of tongs. Season with a little salt and drizzle with a few
teaspoons of peanut oil.

Southern Collard Greens

Put a ham hock on to simmer in a big pot of water for
half an hour. Meanwhile, cut out the big ribs on the collard greens and slice the greens in big pieces. Add them
to the pot along with a dried red pepper if you like. Cook
the greens slowly, uncovered, for a couple of hours or
until completely tender. Drain and serve with hot pepper
vinegar.

Instant Collard Greens

Cut the washed leaves into skinny ribbons and dry
them in a salad spinner. Heat some olive oil in a wok and,
when it's hot, add the collards. Stir-fry over high heat for
just a minute, until the greens are wilted. Add salt and
pepper and hot pepper vinegar.

Leftover Greens

These can go into an omelet or frittata, be served at
room temperature with a simple olive oil and lemon juice
dressing, or jump into a skillet with some olive oil,
roasted peanuts, and hot pepper flakes.

Mushrooms

These are among the biggest carb bargains at just a little over 2 grams for 1 cup of chopped mushrooms—2 shiitakes add up to 5 grams. They have a little niacin but not much else in the way of nutrients. Cremini (baby shiitake) mushrooms are tastier than button mushrooms, but regular market mushrooms have their place too. If the mushrooms seem dirty, wipe them with a damp paper towel; otherwise just brush them off and pull off the stems. Slice them raw into salads. Sauté them in a little butter with salt and pepper over medium-high heat for just 2 or 3 minutes, until they begin to brown. To broil them, paint the caps with melted butter and put them 4 inches below the flame for 2 minutes. Turn them over, paint the interior with more melted butter, and grill them for another 2 or 3 minutes, until golden brown. Try stuffing the mushrooms with cooked sausage or cheese—Gorgonzola on shiitakes is particularly good. All mushroom leftovers are delicious in omelets or meat loaf.

Spaghetti Squash

This weird vegetable has a lot to offer the low-carb cook. For starters, ½ cup is only 5 carbs, not bad for a pasta pretender. It's a good source of folic acid and also has some potassium. Every time I cut into a spaghetti squash and pull away the layers of pastalike strands, I'm amazed all over again. Still, spaghetti squash doesn't really taste like pasta (or like much of anything, for that matter), so don't set your expectations too high, and you won't be disappointed. When you're dying for pasta with pesto, though, you can be considerably cheered by spaghetti squash with pesto. I particularly like spaghetti squash baked into a gratin with a pasta sauce and grated Parmesan on top. You can also use it for cold "noodle" salads: just soak it in ice water for 15 minutes to crisp it once it's cooked, then drain and dry the strands and proceed with a favorite Asian noodle recipe.

You'll most likely find a 2- to 2½-pound squash, which will give you about 4 cups of squash spaghetti. The easiest way to cook it is to bake it for an hour at 350°—be sure to puncture it a few times with a cooking fork so it won't explode. Cut it open right away when it's cooked and take out the seeds and their darker yellow strings. The seeds tend to hide, so feel around for them. Pull away the layers of strands one at a time, or they'll be too thick. If you're not using the squash right away, store it in the refrigerator, where it will keep well for several days.

Tomatoes

The absolute joy of summer tomatoes leaves us feeling bereft the rest of the year. But there are some other possibilities: toward the end of the year some wonderful little Italian tomatoes still on their stems find their way into some markets—they're expensive, but a great treat. Cherry tomatoes are often better than any others out of season, especially the ones that come from Baja California. Israeli tomatoes are good, with thick skins. Plum tomatoes are good for baking, as are not-so-ripe supermarket tomatoes—just punch them up with balsamic vinegar and salt before you proceed. Tomatoes have a lot of vitamin C and some A and B, as well as potassium and other minerals. A medium tomato has only 4.3 carbohy-drate grams; count on 1 gram for a cherry tomato.

Slow-baked Tomatoes

Slice tomatoes in half horizontally and put them on an oiled baking sheet, cut side up. Drizzle with olive oil and sprinkle with salt and pepper. Bake at 325°F for 2 to 3 hours or until the tomatoes collapse and begin to caramelize. Sprinkle with snipped basil and serve warm or at room temperature.

- Variation: Sprinkle the tomatoes with oregano when you add the salt and pepper; then add crumbled feta cheese on top when you serve.

Tomato and Mozzarella Salad

This classic is to be made only with vine-ripened tomatoes and really good mozzarella. You can either al-ternate slices of cheese and tomato on a platter and insert leaves of basil so they look perky—or serve everyone their own tomato, sliced almost all the way through, with cheese slices tucked into the tomato and basil added. Ei-ther way, drizzle with best-quality olive oil and sprinkle salt and pepper on top. The whole thing can be served on a bed of arugula, if you like.

Baked Tomatoes With Cheese

Put sliced tomatoes in a buttered shallow baking dish and sprinkle with sherry vinegar. Bake at 300°F for half an hour. Add a layer of snipped basil, sprinkle with a little cream, and top with a thatch of grated cheddar. Bake 15 minutes longer or until the cheese is melted and golden brown.

Skillet Tomatoes With Cheese

Cut tomatoes in half horizontally and put them in an ovenproof skillet with a little olive oil on the bottom. Sprinkle with salt, pepper, and oregano or basil. Cook over low heat for 10 minutes, moving the tomatoes around so they don't stick. Sprinkle the tops of the tomatoes with grated mozzarella and run the skillet under the broiler until the cheese melts.

Zucchini

This humble vegetable is low in both flavor and nutrients, except potassium. To bring out the flavor, slice zucchini or dice it and sprinkle with salt. Leave it to drain in a colander for at least half an hour, preferably an hour. Dry it off and proceed with the recipe. Little zucchini are by far the best; look for shiny firm ones without any blemishes. You can eat zucchini raw, but it's not much more than a novelty. One cup of zucchini is 4 grams of carb.

Oven-roasted Zucchini With Parmesan

Trim off the stem end of small zucchinis and slice them in half lengthwise. Put a little olive oil in a baking dish just large enough to hold the squash in one layer and add them, turning to coat the zucchini with the oil. Start the zucchini cut side down and salt and pepper the tops. Roast at 500°F for 15 minutes. Turn the zucchini cut side up, add salt and pepper, and top with a scattering of grated Parmesan. Return to the oven for 10 more minutes.

Pan-roasted Zucchini

For this you use whole baby zucchini and coat them with olive oil in a skillet the same way you would oven-roasted zucchini. Cook them slowly, uncovered, for 25 minutes or half an hour, until browned all over and tender, turning so they cook evenly. Sprinkle with snipped basil.

Sautéed Zucchini

Salt very thin slices of zucchini for 30 minutes to an hour; drain and pat them dry. Sauté in melted butter over high heat for about 4 minutes or until crisp-tender. Add some thin slices of pepperoni and some chopped parsley along with salt and pepper. You can also turn this into a shallow baking dish and top it with grated cheese, then run it under the broiler.

Fried Zucchini Salad With Mint

Cut the zucchini in half lengthwise and then into 2-inch pieces. Salt and drain as above. Rinse and pat dry with paper towels. Fry in a skillet with olive oil and sliced garlic until tender and browned, about 15 minutes. Put the zucchini in a shallow serving bowl and pour a little red wine vinegar over it. Add salt and pepper and lots of chopped mint. Let sit for several hours to develop flavor.

Desserts

Life without dessert seems unthinkable, and yet it's dessert that gets us into the most trouble. In the old low-fat-diet school, fruit was the right answer, and it's still a very delicious answer, but only some fruits—the low-carb ones like berries, melons, peaches, coconut, grapes (a few), oranges (limited), and of course rhubarb. If you're serving plain fruit, or slightly gussied-up fruit, add a plate of low-carb cookies—your own, or store-bought ones such as amarettini, pizzelle, Destrooper almond thins, or rich Pepperidge Farm cookies.

Dessert (and rhubarb in particular) brings up the troubling sweetener question (even vanilla is sweetened, but see Sources for an unsweetened version). Until sucralose (the left-handed sugar called SPLENDA® in Canada) is approved in this country, there really isn't a good alternative to sugar in delicate recipes (see page 33 for more on this subject). The recipes in this section use aspartame in the form of Equal packets and Equal Spoonful—but if you're serving dessert at a party, you should either make the same dish using sugar as well as the diet version or warn your guests that aspartame has been used and offer an alternative, since some people are allergic to it.

You can minimize both the artificial sweeteners and the addiction to dessert (in case you're one of those people who react to any kind of sweet sensation adversely—

i.e., by gaining weight and losing control) by serving good cheese with crackers for the guests and just a few slightly sweet tidbits: chocolate-covered coffee beans, spiced nuts, chocolate-covered almonds, little nut meringues, chunks of Australian candied ginger.

However you work this out day to day, I'm a firm believer in having the birthday blowout once a year, which includes a favorite dessert for both lunch *and* dinner, along with pasta, bread, and whatever else your heart most desires. Meantime, enjoy these alternatives, which will keep you where you need to be.

RICOTTA PUFFS

California cook Susan Costner makes a savory version of
this dish that's also very good—just add lots of chopped
fresh herbs to the ricotta and drizzle a little olive oil on
top. (Leave out the lemon zest and Equal, obviously.) This
wonderfully airy dish goes with almost everything.

SERVES 6

>   Butter for the baking dishes
>   3 large egg whites
>   ½ teaspoon salt
>   2 cups whole-milk ricotta cheese
>   Minced zest of 1 lemon
>   6 packets Equal
>   Freshly grated nutmeg
>   Raspberry-orange sauce, page 377

Per Serving: Protein: 16.5g   Fat: 16g   Carbohydrate: 4g

Preheat the oven to 375°F. Have ready 6 buttered
ramekins or custard cups.

Beat the egg whites in a mixing bowl until you have
soft peaks. Mix the salt, ricotta, lemon zest, and Equal,
and fold the mixture into the egg whites. Pour the mixture into the ramekins and dust with nutmeg.

Bake for 30 minutes. The ricotta will rise, then settle
when the puff cools. Unmold and serve slightly warm or
at room temperature with raspberry-orange sauce.

SIMPLE RHUBARB

This basic buttery rhubarb is good on its own, as a sauce,
or as a stand-in for syrup. SERVES 4

2 tablespoons butter
2 cups chopped rhubarb in ½-inch pieces
2 to 4 packets Equal to taste, or see Note below

Per Serving: Protein: 0g   Fat: 5.5g   Carbohydrate: 3.5g

In a heavy saucepan over medium heat, melt the butter and add the rhubarb. Stew it slowly, stirring to coat
the pieces with butter. Stir again after 5 minutes and
check to see if the rhubarb is tender. Keep cooking until
it is. Add Equal to taste. Serve warm with cream and add
a little minced ginger to the cream if you like.

Note: If you add ¼ teaspoon of baking soda, you can
cut the amount of sugar substitute in half. It will foam up
and turn the rhubarb a slightly different color.

MELON WITH CARDAMOM

This refreshing melon dessert goes together in a moment. You can of course use different colors of melon—green, yellow, orange. It tastes best with chilled melon. The pepper is delicious here and the lime itself is sweet—but if you think you need it, you can add some Equal or liquid stevia. SERVES 4

> 1 cantaloupe, chilled
> ¼ teaspoon ground cardamom
> 1 tablespoon fresh lime juice
> A grinding or two of pepper
> Optional: 1 packet Equal to sweeten, mint sprigs to
>   garnish

Per Serving: Protein: 0g   Fat: 0g   Carbohydrate: 6g

Using a melon baller, cut the melon into balls—or just dice it if you have no melon baller. Toss with the remaining ingredients and serve in glass dishes with a sprig of mint.

AMBROSIA

The old classic from the Southern dessert table is always in style. Don't bother segmenting the oranges—you're just losing fiber in the name of refinement—but do slice down the sides of the peeled oranges to be sure you've got all the white pith removed. And take out the fuzzy plug in the middle of the slices. Save any juice that accumulates while you're preparing the oranges and add it to the ambrosia. SERVES 6

>   4 Valencia or navel oranges, peeled, seeded, and
>   sliced thin
>   1 cup grated fresh coconut
>   1 tablespoon brandy, optional

Per Serving: Protein: .4g   Fat: 4.5g   Carbohydrate: 8.5g

Arrange the orange slices and the grated coconut in alternate layers in a glass bowl. Sprinkle the brandy over the fruit, cover, and chill for at least 2 hours to develop flavor.

PEACHES WITH AMARETTINI CREAM

The best peaches always seem to be the white ones, even
when they come from as far away as Italy. But any peach
that smells delicious is the one to choose. The amarettini
cream dresses up this simple dessert. SERVES 4

> 4 perfectly ripe peaches, preferably white
> Sweetener to taste—Equal or stevia
> 1 cup heavy cream
> 2 drops pure almond extract
> 9 amarettini cookies (the tiny ones in the Italian
>   red tin), crushed

Per Serving: Protein: 4g   Fat: 22g   Carbohydrate: 12g

Peel and slice the peaches into a serving bowl and add
sweetener. Mix gently to combine.

Beat the cream until it's nearly stiff, then fold in more
sweetener, almond extract, and the crumbed cookies.
Serve the peaches with the cream in a bowl to pass at the
table.

BERRIES WITH TREMBLING CREAM

This rich, elegant silky cream is sensational with fresh berries, even in winter with imported berries. It's a perfect dish to volunteer to bring to a party, since you can easily sweeten half a recipe with ⅓ cup of sugar for the other guests. SERVES 6

THE CREAM

2 cups heavy cream

1 envelope unflavored gelatine

1 pint sour cream

16 packets Equal

1 tablespoon pure vanilla extract

A grating of fresh nutmeg, optional

THE BERRIES

3 pints mixed berries or all one kind

1 packet Equal

Dash of balsamic vinegar for out-of-season
        strawberries, optional

Per Serving: Protein: 5g   Fat: 45g   Carbohydrate: 12.3g

Pour the cream into a small saucepan and sprinkle the gelatine over. Let stand for 2 minutes. Heat very slowly over very low heat, whisking from time to time, until the gelatine dissolves, about 5 minutes.

Pull off any skin that forms on the surface of the cream. Add the sour cream, Equal, and vanilla and mix well to blend. Pour the cream into a serving bowl and sprinkle with nutmeg. Cover the bowl with plastic wrap and chill for 3 hours before serving.

The berries: Clean 2 pints of berries and mix them with the Equal. Mash the third pint—strawberries or raspberries work best—to make a rough sauce.

Serve the cream in small bowls surrounded with berries and sauced with the berry sauce.

SPIRITED WATERMELON

It's hard to beat watermelon with crescents of lime to squeeze over it, but if you need something more exotic, try this: serve each guest a wedge of watermelon and pass a bottle of chilled Gewürztraminer at the table to splash onto the fruit.

Per Serving: Protein: 0g   Fat: 0g   Carbohydrate: about 10g

PEACH AND BLUEBERRY CRUNCH
WITH ALMONDS

Ripe local peaches in season are so good served simply
with cream that it seems silly to mess around with them
and add more carbs in the bargain. But sometimes you
want a little crunch with juicy warm fruit—and this is
the answer. SERVES 6

FRUIT
Butter for the baking dish
4 ripe peaches, peeled and sliced
1 pint blueberries
⅓ cup Equal Spoonful
Dash of cinnamon

CRUNCHY TOPPING
2 cups almonds
½ cup Equal Spoonful
Pinch of salt
1 large egg white
2 teaspoons cornmeal, optional

Per Serving: Protein: 9.5g   Fat: 23.5g   Carbohydrate: 19.6g

Preheat the oven to 375°F. Butter a 9-inch baking
dish. Mix the fruit ingredients together in a bowl, then
arrange them in the baking dish. Bake the fruit for 15
minutes.

Meanwhile, chop the nuts fine in a food processor.
Combine in a bowl with the sweetener and salt. In a separate bowl, whisk the egg white until it's quite foamy,

then pour the dry ingredients into the beaten white and mix well, stirring in the cornmeal if you're using it. Rub the topping through your fingers to be sure it's thoroughly combined. Spread the topping on a large plate and let it sit at room temperature until you're ready to use it.

After the fruit has cooked 15 minutes, remove the dish from the oven and spread the topping evenly over it. Bake on the lowest oven shelf for another 25 to 30 minutes, or until the fruit is bubbling hot. Cool on a rack for at least 10 minutes before serving.

RUM-COCONUT BALLS

Bourbon would also be very good in these little nuggets—a good thing to pass with after-dinner coffee. You can easily double the recipe, to make four dozen.
MAKES 24, TO SERVE 12

  1 cup pecan pieces
  ¾ cup unsweetened dried coconut
  1 cup Equal Spoonful
  2 tablespoons unsweetened cocoa powder
  Pinch of salt
  3 tablespoons butter
  2 tablespoons rum or bourbon, or more to taste
  2 teaspoons Just Whites egg white powder or 1 egg
      white, beaten
  2 tablespoons warm water to dissolve egg white
      powder

Per Serving: Protein: 2.7g   Fat: 10.6g   Carbohydrate: 3g

Preheat the oven to 350°F. Spread the pecans on a baking sheet and roast in the oven for about 10 minutes, or until they begin to smell good. Set aside to cool a bit. Meanwhile, in a large mixing bowl, combine the coconut, sweetener, cocoa, and salt. Melt the butter.

When the pecans have cooled a bit, put them in the workbowl of a food processor and chop in several short bursts, leaving a little texture. Add the pecans to the coconut mixture. Mix the rum with the melted butter and stir into the combined ingredients.

Put the egg white powder in a small bowl and add the warm water. Beat with a fork for 2 minutes, until frothy and dissolved. Mix the egg white into the combined ingredients.

Form the mixture into little balls—you should have 24. Leave the candies on a baking sheet to dry out a bit—about an hour. Store in a tin.

How Sweet It Is . . .

In the sometimes bewildering world of aspartame, it takes a while to figure out what's what. It seems logical that Equal would be in fact equal to sugar, but no, that's Equal Spoonful, which can be used measure for measure to replace sugar. Equal comes in tiny packets, and loose, as Equal Measure. Here's how they compare to sugar measures.

SUGAR	EQUAL PACKETS	EQUAL MEASURE
2 teaspoons	1	¼ teaspoon
1 tablespoon	1½	½ teaspoon
¼ cup	6	1¾ teaspoons
⅓ cup	8	2½ teaspoons
½ cup	12	3½ teaspoons
¾ cup	18	5½ teaspoons
1 cup	24	7¼ teaspoons

PECAN MERINGUES

These are excellent—crisp, light meringues flavored with
finely chopped toasted pecans. They're good with ice
cream or fresh berries, and you can even make the whole
recipe into a pie shell to make a delicious base for an ice
cream pie. Making meringues with aspartame is tricky;
the key to producing crisp, dry meringues is using just a
touch of real sugar and long baking in a low oven.

SERVES 8

> ½ cup toasted pecans, page 180, cooled to room
> temperature
> ½ cup Equal Spoonful
> 3 large egg whites, at room temperature
> 1 tablespoon sugar
> Big pinch of cream of tartar

Per Serving: Protein: 1.8g   Fat: 4.3g   Carbohydrate: 5g

Preheat the oven to 250°F. Line a baking sheet with
cooking parchment or brown paper. Chop the pecans fine
with the Equal in a food processor. Using an electric
mixer, beat the egg whites until they start to gain some
volume, then gradually add the sugar and cream of tartar
with the mixer still running. Stop beating just when the
egg whites hold firm peaks.

Sprinkle the nut mixture over the egg whites and fold
in. You can spoon the meringue mixture into 8 little
mountains on the baking sheet or shape them into little
cups—good for holding berries or ice cream—by using
a smaller spoon to make a depression in the center of
each mound.

Bake the meringues on the center rack of the oven for 1¼ to 1½ hours; they should be a little brown and very dry. Turn off the oven and leave them in until the oven cools down. Or put them in another dry, warm spot for a couple of hours. Peel them off the paper when you're ready to serve them. Store in an airtight container.

Pecan Meringue Pie Shell

Pile the meringue mixture into a lightly buttered 9-inch glass pie plate, covering the bottom and sides but not the rim of the plate. Bake for 1¼ to 1½ hours, until the pie shell sounds hollow when flicked with a finger. Let dry completely in the turned-off oven.

ALMOND COOKIES

These are a little like the traditional Mexican wedding cakes. They're somewhat crumbly, bite-size, and quite addictive. MAKES ABOUT 20 COOKIES

>   8 tablespoons (1 stick) unsalted butter, at room
>   temperature
>   1 large egg yolk
>   1 cup Equal Spoonful
>   ½ teaspoon vanilla extract
>   ¼ teaspoon almond extract
>   2 cups almond flour, page 47
>   ¼ teaspoon baking powder
>   ¼ teaspoon salt
>   ¼ teaspoon cinnamon

Per cookie: Protein: 2.8g   Fat: 11g   Carbohydrate: 3.6g

Using an electric mixer, cream the butter, then blend in the egg yolk, sweetener, and extracts. In a separate bowl, break up the almond flour with your hands, then mix it with the remaining ingredients. Add the dry mixture to the butter mixture and stir until evenly blended. Cover and refrigerate the dough for 1 hour.

Shape the dough into 1¼-inch balls and place them on a large cookie sheet, evenly spaced. Refrigerate the cookies on the sheet for 15 minutes while you preheat the oven to 350°F.

Bake the cookies for 20 minutes. Cool them on the sheet for a minute or so, then transfer to a rack to finish cooling.

PINCH PIE

This old-fashioned meringue pie shell can be filled with
fresh berries or peaches or a combination of fruits and
served with whipped cream. Or use it as the base for the
delectable lemon Pavlova, page 338. But don't try it on a
rainy day. SERVES 8

5 large egg whites
¼ teaspoon cream of tartar
2 tablespoons sugar
18 packets Equal

Per Serving: Protein: 2g   Fat: 0g   Carbohydrate: 5.5g

Preheat the oven to 225°F. Beat the egg whites and
cream of tartar in an electric mixer until you have soft
peaks. Add the sugar a tablespoon at a time, then the
Equal one packet at a time as you continue beating
the egg whites. When the whites are glossy and reach the
stiff peak stage, the meringue is finished.

Generously butter a 9-inch pie plate, including
the rim. Using a rubber spatula, spread the meringue
over the pie plate, building up the sides about an inch
above the rim. Smooth out the interior to make the pie
shell and finish the rim by making little swoops with the
rubber spatula.

Bake the pie shell on the middle rack of the oven for
an hour. It should be firm and crisp on the outside. Let it
stay in the turned-off oven for another hour.

Let the pie shell cool to room temperature before filling. If you're using a fruit filling, serve at once or spread
with a layer of whipped cream before adding the fruit.

ORANGE CAKE

When you need a birthday cake that's low-carb, here's a good choice. Serve it with clouds of whipped cream, flavored with a drop of almond extract and a little mace. This is a variation on a cake developed by the NutraSweet folks. SERVES 16

1¼ cups cake flour
1 cup almond flour (page 46)
24 packets Equal
¼ cup sugar
1 tablespoon baking powder
½ teaspoon salt
¾ cup cold water
⅓ cup vegetable oil
4 large egg yolks
1 teaspoon pure vanilla extract
1 teaspoon pure orange oil, page 41
2 teaspoons grated orange zest
8 large egg whites
½ teaspoon cream of tartar

Per Serving: Protein: 4.7g   Fat: 10.4g   Carbohydrate: 16g

Preheat oven to 325°F. Have ready a 12-cup Bundt pan, ungreased.

Combine the flours, Equal, sugar, baking powder, and salt in a mixing bowl and beat in the water, oil, egg yolks, vanilla, orange oil, and orange zest.

In an electric mixer, beat the egg whites until you have soft peaks. Add the cream of tartar and beat until they stand in stiff peaks. Stir ⅓ of the egg whites into the flour mixture, then add the flour mixture back into the egg whites, folding in with a rubber spatula. Pour the batter into the pan and bake for 1 hour or longer, until the surface springs back when touched lightly.

Cool the cake in the pan on a baking rack for 10 minutes, then invert and release the cake onto the rack to continue cooling.

ALMOND POUND CAKE

This pound cake is excellent alone or with fruit and whipped cream. It has a pleasant grainy texture, and like the best traditional pound cakes, a dense, moist interior. The cream cheese gives the cake just a slight tang. The oat flour can be found in most natural foods stores. For the almond flour, see Sources. SERVES 10

> 8 tablespoons (1 stick) unsalted butter, at room
>   temperature
> 4 ounces cream cheese, at room temperature
> 1½ cups Equal Spoonful
> 5 large eggs, at room temperature
> 1 teaspoon vanilla extract
> 1⅓ cups almond flour, page 46
> 1 cup oat flour
> ½ teaspoon baking powder
> ¼ teaspoon salt
> ¼ teaspoon grated nutmeg
> ¼ teaspoon cinnamon

Per Serving: Protein: 7.4g   Fat: 24.8g   Carbohydrate: 12g

Preheat the oven to 350°F and butter an 8½ × 4½–inch loaf pan. Line the pan with waxed paper, allowing about 4 inches of overhang on each of the long sides. Butter the waxed paper.

Using an electric mixer, cream the butter, cream cheese, and sweetener. Add one of the eggs and the vanilla and beat until smooth.

Put the flours, baking powder, salt, and spices in a large sieve or sifter and sift them, breaking up any clumps by rubbing the mixture with your hands. Anything that can't go through the holes can just be dumped back into the pile.

Add the remaining 4 eggs and the dry ingredients alternately to the creamed mixture, beating until smooth after each addition, beginning and ending with dry ingredients. Scrape the batter into the prepared pan and smooth the top with a spoon.

Bake the cake for approximately 45 to 50 minutes, until a tester inserted in the center comes out clean. Cool the cake in the pan, on a rack, for 30 minutes, then lift the cake out by the paper and place it on the rack. Peel down the sides of the paper and cool the cake thoroughly. Slice the cake after it has cooled. Store leftovers, wrapped in plastic wrap, in the refrigerator.

LEMON PAVLOVA

This is a bit like lemon angel pie and reminiscent of lemon meringue pie—it's delicious, and deliciously rich, a good dessert to serve after a relatively light meal. You can gild this lily by adding a border of fresh raspberries just inside the rim. SERVES 8

> 5 large egg yolks
> ¼ cup fresh lemon juice
> 1 tablespoon sugar
> Zest of 1 lemon, minced
> ½ cup Equal Spoonful
> 1 cup heavy cream
> Dash of pure vanilla extract
> 1 baked Pinch Pie, page 333

Per Serving: Protein: 5g   Fat: 14.5g   Carbohydrate: 9.5g

In the top of a double boiler, whisk the egg yolks until thick. Add the lemon juice, sugar, and lemon zest, and stir together. Heat the mixture over simmering water, stirring frequently, until it's thick. Remove from the heat, let cool for a few minutes, and stir in the sweetener.

Whip the cream until it's stiff, adding a little vanilla toward the end of the beating. Spread a thin layer of whipped cream over the pie shell, then spread the lemon filling on top. Spread the remaining whipped cream over the pie, cover carefully with plastic wrap, and refrigerate for 2 hours before serving.

The Ice Cream Problem

Sugar isn't just another sweetener; it has complex roles to play in baking and even in ice cream making. If you try using your favorite ice cream recipe and just substitute aspartame (Equal, etc.) for sugar, you'll end up with a rock-hard substance that's likely to break the plastic paddle on your manual ice cream maker—I ruined my Donvier this way. Sturdy electric models should be able to cope, though.

There are several ways around this problem: making soft ice cream in the food processor, making semifreddo slices, adding a tablespoon of liquor to the ice cream mix, or using gelatine. If you add, say, a tablespoon of rum to the vanilla ice cream, you can use a manual ice cream maker and it will produce soft ice cream in just a couple of minutes, not the usual 20 to 30 minutes it takes to make ice cream. If you go beyond the soft ice cream stage, though, you'll be jamming the paddle and producing the hard rocks. (By the way, adding egg whites, a traditional solution to the problem, doesn't work with aspartame.)

If you don't mind using gelatine, that will also work to keep the ice cream relatively soft. Just dissolve 1 packet of gelatine per cup of cream this way: sprinkle over 1 cup of cream in a saucepan and let stand 5 minutes. Over medium heat, bring just to a boil before adding slowly to the eggs. Try this simple frozen custard recipe as your ice cream base. Sprinkle two packets of gelatine over ¼ cup water in a small bowl. Let stand 2 minutes. Then microwave for 40 seconds to dissolve gelatine. Beat 4 eggs well with 1 tablespoon vanilla; strain. Add ¾ cup Equal Spoonful and 2 cups heavy cream. Mix well with the gelatine and freeze in

your ice cream maker. Or puree frozen chunks in the food
processor for soft frozen custard. Serves 4.

If you really want pure ice cream that isn't soft, make
the soft ice cream and then return it to the freezer for 15
minutes or longer until you have the texture you want.
You'll have to experiment and see what timing works for
your freezer. The more acid there is in the ice cream, the
less problem with aspartame icing up.

WARM BERRY COMPOTE

When berries are in high season, make this simple but delicious warm berry dessert. Serve it with plain vanilla ice cream, page 346, or with pouring custard, page 342. If you can get your hands on any lemon verbena, snip a few leaves into the warm custard to flavor it, then strain before serving. SERVES 6

> 1 cup blueberries
> 2 cups hulled and quartered strawberries
> 1 cup raspberries
> ¼ cup Equal Spoonful or more to taste
> 4 tablespoons (½ stick) butter

Per Serving: Protein: 0g   Fat: 7.3g   Carbohydrate: 8g

Put ½ cup of water in a large saucepan and heat until it boils. Reduce the heat to a simmer, add the blueberries and strawberries, and cook for 2 minutes. Add the raspberries, the sweetener, and the butter to the pan and stir well. The compote is ready when the butter is melted.

Remove the pan from the heat, stir one more time, and divide the compote among 6 small bowls. Top with ice cream or pass a pitcher of pouring custard at the table.

POURING CUSTARD

Variously called crème anglaise, stirring custard, or the title it has here, this is a sauce for berries or other fruit that can be turned into frozen custard by using the method described on page 341. It's particularly delicious made with the seeds from a real vanilla bean; if you have one, slit the bean and scrape the seeds into the cream when it first goes onto the heat.

You're always on the verge of making scrambled eggs when you're cooking the custard, so be sure to keep it from boiling—whisk it constantly, and take it off the fire from time to time if it threatens to boil. But don't worry; even if you get a bit of scrambled egg in the pan, it will disappear when the custard is sieved.

MAKES 2 CUPS, SERVES 6

1 cup heavy cream
½ cup milk
5 large egg yolks
6 packets Equal
1 tablespoon vanilla extract

Per Serving: Protein: 4.5g   Fat: 19.6g   Carbohydrate: 4.5g

Mix the cream and milk in a heavy saucepan and place it over medium heat. In a mixing bowl, preferably one with a spout, whisk the egg yolks together with the sweetener and vanilla until they're pale yellow. When the cream begins to have a bubble or two rising at the edge of the pan, take it off the heat and slowly pour it into the eggs, whisking all the time. Pour the custard back into the pan and return it to the heat.

Cook the custard at a bare simmer—don't let it boil—whisking constantly, especially around the edges of the pan. When the custard thickens, take it off the fire and continue to whisk for a minute or two. Pour the custard through a sieve into a glass measure. While still hot, place a sheet of plastic wrap directly on the surface to prevent a skin from forming. Let it cool, then cover and refrigerate until ready to serve.

RASPBERRY CRÈME BRÛLÉE

Here's the perfect dessert for a dinner party or a special
brunch. Just remember to make the custards the day before—a plus for the busy cook—so they have plenty of
time to chill. If no fresh raspberries are in sight, use
frozen ones and defrost them for half an hour before
using. Sweetened rhubarb makes a great alternative to
the raspberries. SERVES 6

- 2 cups heavy cream
- 1 cup light cream
- ⅔ cup Equal Spoonful
- 7 large egg yolks
- ¼ teaspoon vanilla extract
- 1 pint fresh raspberries or 1 cup defrosted frozen
    raspberries
- 2 packed tablespoons light brown sugar

Per Serving: Protein: 6g   Fat: 40g   Carbohydrate: 15g

Put a kettle of water on to boil and get out 6 ramekins
(these look like tiny soufflé dishes). Preheat the oven to
325°F and adjust the oven rack to the lowest setting.

In a medium-size nonreactive saucepan, bring the
creams and sweetener to a near boil over medium heat,
stirring occasionally. While that heats, stir—don't
whisk—the egg yolks in a large mixing bowl until evenly
blended. Remove the cream from the heat and cool
briefly. Using about ¼ cup for starters, stir the cream
into the egg yolks. Add several more small batches of
cream, then gradually stir in the rest of the cream. Stir in
the vanilla extract. Strain the mixture through a sieve
into a large pitcher.

Arrange a single layer of tightly fitting raspberries in the bottom of each ramekin. Slowly fill each one with custard. Don't be concerned if some of the berries float to the top.

Put the ramekins in a large roasting pan or shallow casserole, evenly spaced. Place the roasting pan in the oven, then carefully—so it doesn't splatter—pour enough of the boiling water into the pan to come halfway up the sides. Loosely cover with a sheet of tented foil.

Bake the custards for 40 to 50 minutes; when done, the custards will be just slightly wiggly and loose in the center but not wet. Transfer the ramekins to a rack. Cool to room temperature, then cover with plastic wrap and refrigerate overnight. Just before serving, add brown sugar topping.

A quick way to caramelize the brown sugar on top is with a propane torch from the hardware store. Just spread a teaspoon of brown sugar over the custard, then light the torch and wave it over the custard so the tip of the flame just hits the sugar.

Otherwise, spread the sugar over the custards and place them in a shallow casserole. Surround them with ice to protect the custard from the heat, then run the casserole under the broiler. The tops should be about 6 inches from the flame. When the sugar melts and turns bubbly, they're done. Remove and serve at once.

VANILLA ICE CREAM

Here's a basic method for making soft ice cream, which
can be flavored several ways. If you'd rather, instead of
soft ice cream you can serve what the Italians call a semifreddo—ice cream frozen in a loaf pan, then allowed to
soften slightly before it's sliced and served. Either way,
this ice cream is easy and delicious. Because the ice cream
is soft after it comes out of the food processor, be sure to
chill small serving bowls ahead of time to keep it from
getting too soft. SERVES 4

> Butter for the pan
> 1½ cups heavy cream, chilled
> 4 large eggs, separated
> ¾ cup Equal Spoonful
> 1 teaspoon vanilla extract
> ⅓ to ½ cup light cream, chilled

Per Serving: Protein: 8.7g   Fat: 42g   Carbohydrate: 13g

Butter a 9 × 5–inch metal loaf pan. Line the pan with
a double layer of plastic wrap, leaving at least a 4-inch
overhang on the long sides. Chill the pan for half an hour.

Using an electric mixer, whip the heavy cream until it
thickens. Beat in the egg yolks, sweetener, and vanilla
until the mixture is not quite as thick as regular whipped
cream but close.

In a separate bowl, beat the egg whites until they hold
soft peaks. Fold the egg whites into the whipped mixture until uniformly blended. Scrape the mixture into
the chilled pan, cover with foil, and refrigerate for 12 to
24 hours, until solid.

Note: Unless you have a very large-capacity food processor, make the ice cream in half batches.

To make regular soft ice cream: Chill your food processor workbowl and blade. Put 1 inch of very hot water in a small shallow casserole. Lower the loaf pan into the hot water, wait 5 seconds, then remove. Firmly pull up on the plastic wrap and remove the ice cream loaf. Peel off the plastic wrap.

Cut the loaf into thick slices with a large knife, then cut each slice into 4 or 5 chunks. Immediately put these chunks in the chilled workbowl of the food processor and begin to process in 5-second bursts, adding as much of the light cream as needed to make the ice cream smooth. Scrape down the sides of the bowl as necessary. When the ice cream has a smooth texture, but before it's too soft, serve in chilled bowls.

To serve as semifreddo: Unmold and slice the loaf into ¾-inch slices. Lay the slices flat on serving plates and let stand at room temperature 5 to 7 minutes before serving. Garnish with fresh fruit.

To make strawberry or raspberry ice cream: Halve a handful of frozen strawberries and add them to ice cream chunks. Process as above. Or use a large handful of frozen raspberries.

To make ginger ice cream: Mince four ½-inch chunks of Australian candied ginger and stir into the soft ice cream just before you serve it.

To make coffee-hazelnut ice cream: Add 1 tablespoon instant powdered espresso to the egg yolk/cream mixture. Toast 1 cup hazelnuts on a baking sheet in a 350°F oven for 15 minutes, or until they smell delicious. Cool slightly and rub between two kitchen towels to remove skins. Chop nuts coarsely and stir into soft ice cream before serving. For semifreddo, fold into ice cream mixture before it goes into the pan.

CRÈME FRAÎCHE ICE CREAM

Once you get into the habit of making ice cream, it's a
snap. This one is particularly delicious, with a subtle
tang—good with berries or berry syrups.

MAKES 1 QUART, SERVES 8

> 3 cups crème fraîche, page 161
> 8 large egg yolks
> ¼ cup Equal Spoonful

Per Serving: Protein: 5g   Fat: 31.1g   Carbohydrate: 5.3g

Put the crème fraîche into a heavy saucepan. Whisk
the egg yolks and the sweetener together in a bowl, then
pour the mixture into the crème fraîche. Heat the mixture over medium heat for 3 minutes. Use the directions
on page 347 to freeze the ice cream.

RUM-COCONUT ICE CREAM

If you keep coconut milk on hand, you can rustle up this
ice cream in no time. SERVES 6

> 2 cups half-and-half
> 1 (14–ounce) can unsweetened coconut milk
> ¾ cup Equal Spoonful
> 2 tablespoons dark rum

Per Serving: Protein: 3.3g   Fat: 20g   Carbohydrate: 4.3g

In a heavy saucepan, bring the half-and-half to a boil,
stirring occasionally. Remove from the heat and let cool.

Stir in the coconut milk, sweetener, and rum. Follow
the freezing directions in the vanilla ice cream recipe on
page 346.

STRAWBERRY SHERBET

This is convenience food—if you have a package of frozen unsweetened strawberries in the freezer, a few minutes' work will give you a fresh-tasting, refreshing dessert. If you'd rather have instant gratification, just throw the frozen berries into the food processor (hang on; it's a rough ride in the beginning) and add the lemon juice and sweetener to the strawberry slush to serve 3. SERVES 6

    1 (1-pound) package unsweetened frozen
        strawberries, thawed
    1 tablespoon fresh lemon juice
    ¼ cup Equal Spoonful
    4 large egg whites, beaten stiff

Per Serving: Protein: 4g   Fat: 0g   Carbohydrate: 7g

Put the strawberries in the workbowl of a food processor and purée. Add the lemon juice and the sweetener. Fold the berries into the egg whites and mix thoroughly. Spoon into a plastic container and freeze for 4 hours.

FROZEN COFFEE

Somewhere between granita and coffee ice cream, this is
a great thing to have lurking in your freezer on a hot day.
It's also the right thing to do with leftover coffee—just fill
ice cube trays with it. You can sweeten it or not, add
cream or not, serve it with clouds of flavored whipped
cream or just enjoy it straight. SERVES 6

> **4 cups strong brewed coffee, espresso or regular**
> **Optional: Equal or liquid stevia, to taste**
>
> TOPPING
> **¾ cup heavy cream, whipped**
> **½ teaspoon vanilla extract**
> **Optional: Equal or liquid stevia to taste, 2**
> **teaspoons brandy**

Per Serving: Protein: .5g   Fat: 10g   Carbohydrate: .8g

Pour the coffee and optional sweetener into ice cube
trays and freeze hard. If you're using the topping, prepare
it right before you're ready to serve the dessert. Whip the
cream and blend in the other ingredients. Refrigerate.
Empty the frozen coffee cubes into the food processor—
you may have to do this in batches—and process until you
have a chunky slush. Serve immediately with the flavored
whipped cream, if using.

STRAWBERRY-RHUBARB MOUSSE

The affinity of these two fruits (well, actually rhubarb's a vegetable) for each other is an almost endless delight. Once you have the fruit mixture together—before you add it to the cream—you can purée it for a syrup. So you might want to make a double recipe of the fruit part.
SERVES 8

  4 cups diced rhubarb
  Pinch of salt
  1 pint strawberries, in small pieces
  11 packets Equal
  1 pint heavy cream

Per Serving: Protein: 1.2g   Fat: 22g   Carbohydrate: 7.5g

Cook the rhubarb in the microwave until soft, then add the salt—or add the salt to the rhubarb and stew it gently, uncovered, on top of the stove. You may need to add a tiny amount of water. Add 9 packets of Equal. Add the strawberries and put the mixture in the freezer for 20 minutes while you whip the cream.

Whip the cream until you have stiff peaks. Mix in the remaining 2 packets of Equal, and gently fold in the rhubarb-berry mixture. Pile the mousse into a serving dish, cover with plastic wrap, and refrigerate until ready to serve.

CHOCOLATE MOUSSE

This goes together in just a few minutes and it can be made up to four hours ahead. Instead of the orange flavoring, you could use a spoonful of Kahlúa. Saco is the brand of cocoa powder used here, but you could also use Hershey's—just add 2 grams of carbs. SERVES 4

1½ cups heavy cream
6 packets Equal
Minced zest of 1 orange
½ teaspoon vanilla extract
¼ cup unsweetened cocoa powder

Per Serving: Protein: 1.8g   Fat: 33g   Carbohydrate: 3.7g

Beat the cream in an electric mixer or by hand until it begins to get thick, then add the Equal a packet at a time. Add the orange zest, vanilla, and cocoa powder and beat until almost stiff. Turn off the mixer and scrape down the sides and bottom of the bowl. Mix again. Divide the mousse among 4 ramekins or small dessert dishes, cover, and refrigerate for ½ hour or up to 4 hours.

PUMPKIN MOUSSE

This is the perfect Thanksgiving dessert—but it's so delicious that you'll find it works all year long. For a special touch, use mace instead of nutmeg, or just dust the top of the mousse with powdered mace (the outer covering of the nutmeg, which has a particularly delicate flavor).
SERVES 8

> 2 envelopes unflavored gelatine
> ¼ cup water
> 2 cups heavy cream
> 1 tablespoon vanilla extract
> 8 packets Equal
> 1½ cups canned pumpkin
> 1 tablespoon dark brown sugar
> 1 teaspoon cinnamon
> ½ teaspoon grated nutmeg or mace
> ⅛ teaspoon allspice
> 1 tablespoon bourbon
> Garnish: a dusting of mace

Per Serving: Protein: 5.5g   Fat: 22g   Carbohydrate: 7.5g

Sprinkle the gelatine over the water in a small bowl. Let stand 2 minutes, then microwave for 40 seconds. In a small saucepan, warm 1 cup of the cream with the vanilla until it bubbles. Then stir in the pumpkin and sugar and cook for 3 minutes. Add the sweetener, the spices and the bourbon. Stir in the gelatine. Beat the remaining cream to soft peaks and fold into the pumpkin mixture. Scoop into a glass or ceramic serving bowl and refrigerate covered until ready to serve, up to 6 hours. Decorate the top of the dish with sprinkled mace.

POTS DE CRÈME

These intense little cups of chocolate are deeply satisfying, and just a few carbs more than a true diet dessert.
SERVES 6

4 ounces semisweet chocolate
4 large eggs, separated
1 teaspoon pure vanilla extract
2 teaspoons very strong brewed black coffee
Pinch of salt

Per Serving: Protein: 4.7g   Fat: 9g   Carbohydrate: 11g

Melt the chocolate in the microwave and cool for 5 minutes. Beat the egg yolks slightly with the vanilla and coffee and stir in the cooled chocolate. In a separate bowl, beat the egg whites with the salt until they form stiff peaks. Using a rubber spatula, fold—do not beat—the chocolate into the egg whites. Pour into 6 small ramekins, cover, and chill from 4 to 24 hours.

SPANISH CREAM

This is a classic dessert from the first half of the century but it's almost entirely disappeared, more's the pity. If you grew up in the forties, you may have had Spanish cream as a nutritious treat when you were sick. It's quite delicious: a glassy custard subtly flavored with sherry supports little clouds of meringue. SERVES 6

2 envelopes of gelatine
¼ cup water
3 cups milk
3 large eggs, separated
¼ teaspoon salt
1 teaspoon pure vanilla extract
2 tablespoons sherry or madeira
½ cup Equal Spoonful

Per Serving: Protein: 9g   Fat: 6.8g   Carbohydrate: 7.9g

Sprinkle the gelatine over the water in a small bowl and let stand for 5 minutes. Put the milk in a saucepan. Put the egg yolks in the top of a double boiler and beat lightly with a whisk.

Mix the gelatine into the milk and stir to dissolve over low heat. Scald the milk, but don't let it come to a simmer (no bubbles). Off the heat, pour the milk very slowly into the eggs in the top of the double boiler. Heat the water in the bottom of the double boiler over medium heat and put the egg-milk mixture on top. Stirring almost constantly, cook until the mixture thickens enough to coat a spoon. Be sure to stir around the edges of the pot so the egg doesn't collect there and cook.

Take the custard off the fire and let cool for about 10 minutes. Meanwhile, beat the egg whites stiff. When the custard has cooled, add the remaining ingredients and stir well. Strain into a mixing bowl and fold in the egg whites, leaving little mounds of them on top of the custard. Pour the Spanish cream into a 1-quart serving dish and chill for 2 hours. Serve cold.

COFFEE GELATINE

Like all other gelatine desserts, this one seems to have
fallen out of our cookbooks. But it's an elegant light
dessert and a good pick-me-up on a sultry afternoon.
You can use espresso or regular coffee; if you'd rather, you
can brew your own and use that instead of the 3 cups of
cold water. The cardamom is a delicate flavoring; you can
also use sugar-free amaretto or regular amaretto or sam-
buco, but they'll cost you a few more carbs. SERVES 6

- 2 envelopes gelatine
- 3 cups cold water
- 3 tablespoons instant espresso or coffee
- 3 to 6 packets Equal, to taste
- ¼ teaspoon cardamom, optional
- 2 tablespoons sugar-free amaretto syrup (page 42),
    optional

Per Serving: Protein: 6g   Fat: 0g   Carbohydrate: 3g

Sprinkle the gelatine over 1 cup water in a medium
saucepan. Let stand for 5 minutes. Add the remaining
water and stir well. Set the saucepan over low and stir
until the gelatine is dissolved, about 5 minutes. Add the
instant coffee and stir until dissolved. Remove from heat
and cool for 10 minutes.

Add the sweetener and the optional flavorings, if
using. Stir well and pour the mixture into a 1-quart serving dish. Refrigerate for 2 to 3 hours to set.

The gelatine tastes best after it's been at room temperature for half an hour, to soften a bit and let the flavors
develop. Serve with vanilla-flavored whipped cream.

PASKHA

This is a traditional Russian cheesecakish spread made to serve with kulich, the tall Russian sweet bread. But mold it in a flowerpot, slice and serve it the next day as an enriched cheesecake, and you'll have no complaints. You can also make this molded in a basket if flowerpots are out of the question. Just remember to make the cheese a day ahead. SERVES 16

> 1 pound cream cheese, at room temperature
> 2 sticks (½ pound) butter, at room temperature
> 24 packets Equal
> 1 cup almonds, toasted and chopped, page 180
> 1 tablespoon vanilla extract
> Minced orange zest from 2 oranges
> 1 cup sour cream

Per Serving: Protein: 7g   Fat: 27.8g   Carbohydrate: 3.5g

Push the cream cheese through a sieve and drain off any liquid that appears. In an electric mixer, beat the butter with the cream cheese until fluffy. Add the remaining ingredients and beat until thoroughly combined.

Line a clean new 5-inch clay or plastic flowerpot—or a basket—with a tea towel and add the cheese mixture. Fold the towel up over the top of the cheese, add a plate that just fits the pot, and weight the cheese down with a small can or other heavy object. Set the whole thing on the top shelf of the refrigerator and put a dish on the shelf directly underneath it to catch any drips. Let drain overnight.

Unmold the cheese and turn it out onto a serving plate. Let it ripen in the refrigerator, loosely covered, until ready to serve. Slice in skinny slices and serve on small plates.

CHEESECAKE

Forbidden on every other diet known to man, cheese-cake is the great reward of low-carb dieting. It's so good and so tempting, in fact, that I try not to make it too often, since I can easily eat several pieces without even noticing. To dress up this cheesecake, see the note on the chocolate drizzle below. SERVES 12

Butter for the pan
2 pounds cream cheese, at room temperature
1½ cups Equal Spoonful
4 large eggs, at room temperature
Zest of 1 lemon, minced, optional
Zest of 1 orange, minced, optional
2 tablespoons heavy cream
1 teaspoon pure vanilla extract

Per Serving: Protein: 8.2g   Fat: 28g   Carbohydrate: 4g

Preheat the oven to 350°F. Butter a 9-inch springform pan and set aside.

Using an electric mixer, beat the cream cheese well on medium speed until it's absolutely smooth. Slowly beat in the sweetener. Add the eggs one at a time and beat well after each addition. Add the remaining ingredients, scrape down the bowl, and stir to combine.

Pour the cheesecake into the prepared pan and smooth the top. Bake for 10 minutes. Turn the heat down to 275° and bake for 1 hour, or until the edges are lightly brown. Turn off the oven.

Run a knife around the edge of the pan and return the pan to the oven to cool slowly. Don't worry if the center of the cheesecake looks a little wiggly; it will firm up in the oven.

Cover the cooled cheesecake with plastic wrap and refrigerate overnight, or up to 3 days. To serve, run a knife around the edges again and remove the sides of the pan.

Chocolate-drizzled Cheesecake

Just before serving the cheesecake, melt 1 cup of semisweet chocolate chips in a glass measure in the microwave at 70 percent power for 1 minute. Stir every 20 seconds and stop the moment the chocolate is liquid. Drizzle the liquid chocolate over the cheesecake in a random pattern. Refrigerate for 15 minutes to set before serving.

Per Serving: Protein: .8g   Fat: 4g   Carbohydrate: 8.7g

FATHER SARDUCCI'S CHEESECAKE

The origin of this cake is lost—as is Father Sarducci—but the cake itself has survived in books, cheesecake contests, and the treasured recipe collections of home cooks from Texas to Queens. Have all the ingredients at room temperature. SERVES 12

> Butter for the pan
> 1 (15-ounce) container whole-milk ricotta
> 2 cups sour cream
> 16 ounces cream cheese
> 1½ cups Equal Spoonful
> 8 tablespoons (1 stick) butter, melted
> 3 extra-large eggs
> 3 tablespoons flour
> 3 tablespoons cornstarch
> 2 scant tablespoons vanilla extract
> 2 scant tablespoons fresh lemon juice

Per Serving: Protein: 10g Fat: 34g Carbohydrate: 9g

Preheat the oven to 350°F and set a baking rack in the middle of the oven. Butter a 10-inch springform pan.

Put the ricotta in the workbowl of a food processor and process until smooth. Add the sour cream and cream cheese and process until smooth. Add the remaining ingredients through the feed tube and process until well combined.

Pour the mixture into the prepared pan and bake for 1 hour. Turn off the heat and leave the cheesecake in the oven with the door ajar for one more hour. Cool on a rack. The cheesecake can be made two or three days in advance and kept, covered with plastic wrap, in the refrigerator. You can also freeze it for up to three weeks; defrost before serving.

Note: If you forgot to put out the eggs and cream cheese ahead of time so they'll be room temperature when you're ready to make the cheesecake, just drop the cream cheese in its foil packets into a bowl of warm water for a few minutes—same thing with the eggs.

Lemony Cheesecake

Add 2 teaspoons of minced lemon zest.

Lime Cheesecake

Use lime juice instead of lemon and add 2 teaspoons of minced lime zest.

THE RICOTTA DESSERT

Ricotta is one of the most satisfying homey desserts imaginable, and a half-cup serving of whole-milk ricotta will set you back only 4 carbs. Of course, the better the ricotta, the better the dessert, so it's worth seeking out a good Italian brand. For a velvety texture, whip the ricotta in a food processor briefly. Keep ricotta on hand and you have instant dessert—just add one of the following:

Raspberries

Minced lemon or orange zest

Warm Berry compote, page 341

A dusting of cinnamon

A dusting of espresso powder

A dusting of cocoa powder

Mini chocolate chips: 10 for 3 carbs

5 chocolate-covered coffee beans tucked inside

2 Hershey's Almond Kisses, roughly chopped: 4.5
    carbs

Chocolate sauce, page 366

CHOCOLATE SAUCE

When the lily—vanilla ice cream, for instance—needs gilding, try this intense chocolate sauce, just 2 carbs for a tablespoonful. MAKES 18 TABLESPOONS, SERVES 9

⅓ cup heavy cream
1 tablespoon butter
1 tablespoon sugar
4 ounces semisweet chocolate, chopped
1 packet Equal or more to taste

Per Serving: Protein: .4g   Fat: 4g   Carbohydrate: 3.8g

Combine the cream, butter, and sugar in a small saucepan and bring to a boil. Place the chocolate in a mixing bowl and pour the hot cream over it. Stir well and add the Equal. Stir every 5 minutes until the chocolate is dissolved. Store in the refrigerator and serve at room temperature.

CHOCOLATE PEANUT BUTTER DROPS

If you absolutely have to have a little sweet after dinner, try these, for just 2 carbs apiece. Not elegant, but not bad—these don't keep more than a day. Try them with homemade toasted hazelnut butter. MAKES 12

    1 ounce unsweetened chocolate
    ⅓ cup chunky peanut butter
    2 tablespoons butter
    ⅓ cup whole-milk ricotta
    12 packets Equal
    1 teaspoon pure vanilla extract

Per Serving: Protein: 2.8g   Fat: 5.3g   Carbohydrate: 2g

Melt the first 3 ingredients in a bowl in the microwave. Stir well to combine. Add the remaining ingredients, stir again and drop by the tablespoon on waxed paper—you should have 12 drops. Chill until firm—at least 1 hour—and keep in the refrigerator.

THE CHEESE PLATTER

This popular European finale to a great meal has been largely forgotten on this side of the pond, but it's as wonderful as ever. For your carb-eating guests, serve wholemeal biscuits and thin slices of dark nut bread. Low-carb crackers are fine with cheese. You need at least four different kinds of cheese to make this work, with contrasting flavors and textures. Serve them on a large board, a platter, a tray, whatever works. Real grape leaves—or the fake paper ones sold in specialty stores—look terrific under the cheeses. Serve the cheese with a mixed green salad. Or go in a different direction and add several bunches of grapes—again, different kinds—a couple of kinds of nuts, and a jar of sweet celery sticks cut from the inner stalks. If your guests aren't sure how to cut the cheese, show them: in general, you follow the shape of the cheese for wedges; small rounds or squares are cut in wedges, and logs are cut in small circles. Using a real cheese knife—which has hollow areas in the blade—makes a big difference. Ask your cheesemonger for suggestions on felicitous combinations. Here are some possibilities:

> Hard cheese: Gouda, cheddar
> Blue cheese: Gorgonzola, Maytag blue, Roquefort
> Goat cheese: Boucheron, Montrachet
> Soft cheese: Brie, Camembert, cambozola, St.
>   Andre
> Sheep cheese: manchego, pecorino

Serve the cheese just slightly cool, with wine.

Breakfast

⋔

In some ways, this is the most difficult meal of the day for low-carbers, even though there may be some extra leeway on carbs in the morning (see page 23). Juice has way too many carbs to spend frivolously—much better to eat the whole fruit and get the fiber too, unless you're such a juice nut that you're willing to spend all your carbs on juice. The traditional breakfast favorites—cereal, bagels, muffins, pancakes, waffles—hit the carb budget too hard to enjoy, except for the low-carb whole-grain toasts. Then too, you need to remember to have enough protein.

For an on-the-run breakfast, which is what most everyday breakfasts turn out to be, you may turn to cottage cheese or one of the high-protein low-carb bars (Biozone, Balance, Protein 21—see Sources). More fun is the smoothie, made with soy milk and perhaps protein powder in the form of egg white plus some delectable fruit. Use the smoothie recipe on page 375 as a guide and play with the fruits and the flavorings. You can make a chocolate smoothie with cocoa powder and sweetener and vanilla, a mocha one by adding powdered espresso, or just have plain vanilla, with a little sour cream and grated nutmeg blended in.

Eggs and breakfast meats or fish (lox, smoked or kippered salmon, sable) are great solutions and there are a number of ideas here as well as in the Main Dish category.

You can make skinny 2-egg flat omelets and stack them with fillings like creamed spinach, mushrooms, ratatouille, etc., to make a big omelet cake. Top it with grated Parmesan and minced parsley; run it under the broiler briefly to melt the cheese, and serve in wedges. Sausage patties or bacon or Canadian bacon or sliced ham is a perfect accompaniment.

For a big-treat breakfast, try the three-grain waffles with raspberry-orange syrup. They beg for some sausage or bacon—or both; add those and you've got a memorable breakfast feast.

THE FORTY-SECOND OMELET

Howard Helmer is Mr. Egg, the spokesperson for the American Egg Board—and he really wants you to learn how to make an omelet. This is his way. He likes cheap 10-inch nonstick pans with sloping sides and he uses a pancake turner, so there's no big-deal equipment. Inside his omelets can be half a cup of just about anything: grated cheese, vegetables, smoked salmon with cream cheese and chives—whatever you can think of. For each omelet, here's what you need to know. SERVES 1

> 2 large eggs
> 2 tablespoons water or soda water
> ⅛ teaspoon salt
> Pepper to taste
> 1 teaspoon olive oil or butter (I say butter, or Plugra)
> Optional: ½ cup filling

Per Serving: Protein: 12.2g   Fat: 8.6g   Carbohydrate: 1.2g

Break the eggs into a glass measuring cup. Add the water, salt, and pepper and beat with a fork until combined.

Put the oil or butter in the omelet pan and set over medium-high heat. When the fat starts to sizzle, swirl the pan to distribute it evenly. Pour in the eggs, which will immediately begin to set.

Using an inverted pancake turner, push the cooked eggs toward you to the center and turn the pan so that the raw eggs run into their place. Keep doing this until the omelet has thickened and very little liquid egg remains. At this point spread the optional filling over half the omelet. Using the pancake turner, flip the other side of

Scrambled Egg Tips

- Add a little crunch by tossing in a few croutons briefly sizzled in butter for each serving.

- The great French gastronome Escoffier liked to scramble his eggs with a fork on which he'd impaled a garlic clove—good idea.

- Use half eggs, half crumbled soft tofu for a lighter version of scrambled eggs—good with hot pepper sauce. Add tofu during the last minute of cooking.

- To make a lot of scrambled eggs ahead of time for a crowd:

Preheat the oven to 225°F. Beat a dozen eggs with ¼ cup of cream and add salt and pepper to taste. Melt 3 tablespoons of butter in a skillet; when it's foaming, add the eggs. Stir well until the eggs are heated through completely but not cooked. Put the eggs in a buttered mixing bowl and set it in a pan of warm water in the oven. The eggs will finish cooking and hold well for about 15 minutes. Turn the bowl upside down on a round serving plate and unmold the eggs. Cover the mound of eggs with snipped chives and surround it with strips of crisp bacon and grilled tomatoes.

the omelet over the filling and slide the whole thing onto a waiting plate. Ambitious cooks can simply invert the omelet onto the plate with a quick flip of the wrist—a nice flourish.

KILLER SCRAMBLED EGGS

These are pretty exciting fare, considering that they're basically just scrambled eggs. They have chive or scallion cream cheese folded into them and then they're topped with caviar or chopped smoked salmon. Perfect for a late-night supper or brunch. SERVES 1

> *For each serving:*
> 2 large eggs
> 2 tablespoons cream
> Salt and pepper to taste
> 1 teaspoon butter
> 1 tablespoon chive or scallion cream cheese
> 1 tablespoon caviar or chopped smoked salmon

Per Serving: Protein: 15g   Fat: 17g   Carbohydrate: 2.4g

In a glass measuring cup, beat the eggs and the cream together with a fork and add salt and pepper to taste. Heat the butter in a skillet until a drop of water sizzles when it hits the butter. Pour in the eggs and stir them around with an inverted pancake turner so that the cooked eggs come to the surface and the liquid eggs go to the bottom of the pan.

When the eggs are beginning to thicken, add the cream cheese and stir it into the eggs. When the eggs are firm but still moist, turn them out onto a plate and top with the caviar or smoked salmon.

BAKED EGGS WITH SPINACH

A good little informal supper or breakfast dish. It's worth
making extra spinach so you'll have it left over to make
these eggs. If you don't have individual ramekins, you can
use a baking dish; just spread the spinach over the bottom, then slide the eggs on top. Try adding a little freshly
grated nutmeg to the spinach. SERVES 1

> *For each serving you'll need:*
> **2 teaspoons butter**
> **¼ cup cooked buttered spinach, squeezed dry**
> **2 large eggs**
> **Salt and pepper to taste**
> **1 tablespoon heavy cream**
> **1 teaspoon grated Parmesan cheese**
> **Dash of paprika**

Per Serving: Protein: 13.3g   Fat: 24.8g   Carbohydrate: 3.6g

Preheat the oven to 325°. Butter a ramekin and add a
layer of the spinach. Put the ramekin on a baking sheet
and into the oven to heat for a few minutes. Crack the
eggs into a saucer and slide them into the ramekin, add
salt and pepper to taste, and pour over the cream. Sprinkle the cheese and paprika on top and send the ramekin
back to the oven for 5 minutes under a loose tent of foil.
The whites should be set; the yolks won't look done at
this point, but they will be by the time they get to the
table.

MANGO SMOOTHIE

If you really miss mangoes, remember that your insulin problems are at their lowest in the morning, so breakfast is the time to indulge. This heavenly drink provides 27 grams of protein and satisfies the mango longing perfectly. SERVES 1

½ cup diced mango
2 tablespoons sour cream
1 cup unsweetened soy milk
2 heaping tablespoons protein powder, preferably
    egg white
½ teaspoon vanilla extract
1 packet Equal
Zest of 1 lime
Dash of salt
¾ cup water

Per Serving: Protein: 23.4g   Fat: 9.6g   Carbohydrate: 16g

Mix everything together in a blender until smooth and drink immediately.

THREE-GRAIN PANCAKES WITH
RASPBERRY-ORANGE SAUCE

An excellent Sunday breakfast with Canadian bacon or
sausage. Yes, these are a little high in carbs, but remember, your insulin is more sensitive in the morning and
you should be able to handle the extra carbs with no
problems—try these and see.

To save time in the morning, mix up the dry ingredients the night before and set them aside, mix up the wet
ingredients and refrigerate them—the next day, all you'll
have to do is beat the egg whites and mix everything together. SERVES 4

½ cup fine yellow cornmeal
½ cup oat flour
½ cup barley flour (or use oat flour)
2 teaspoons baking powder
¼ teaspoon salt
Large pinch of cinnamon
1 cup milk
3 large eggs, separated
4 tablespoons (½ stick) unsalted butter, melted

Per Serving: Protein: 10.2g   Fat: 18.5g   Carbohydrate: 28.8g

In a mixing bowl, combine the flours, baking powder, salt, and cinnamon—don't bother sifting. In a separate bowl, whisk the milk, egg yolks, and butter. Make a
well in the dry mixture, add the liquids, and stir until
evenly blended.

In a clean bowl, beat the egg whites until they hold soft peaks. Fold the whites into the batter, just until evenly blended. Using about ¼ cup of batter each, cook the pancakes on a hot griddle, about 1 to 1½ minutes per side, flipping once. Serve hot, with the raspberry-orange sauce.

RASPBERRY-ORANGE SAUCE

SERVES 4

1½ cups frozen raspberries
1 tablespoon grated orange zest
2 drops pure orange oil, page 41, optional
Equal, to taste

Per Serving: Protein: 0g   Fat: trace   Carbohydrate: 3.1g

Combine the raspberries and orange zest plus the optional oil in a small nonreactive saucepan. Bring to a gentle boil, then reduce the heat slightly and simmer for 2 minutes. Stir in the sweetener and taste—you may need more sweetener or orange. Transfer the sauce to a food processor workbowl and process until smooth. Serve the sauce warm to spoon over the pancakes.

SIMPLE WAFFLES

These crispy, delicate waffles can be served with sliced
strawberries and a dollop of sour cream or with butter
and berry syrup or ersatz maple syrup. If you don't have
a waffle iron, you can make them into pancakes—though
they're so light that turning them is a bit tricky.

SERVES 4

> 4 large eggs, separated
> 4 tablespoons (½ stick) unsalted butter, slightly
>   chilled
> ¼ cup oat flour
> 1 cup sour cream
> ½ teaspoon pure vanilla extract
> ½ teaspoon salt
> Grating of nutmeg, optional

Per Serving: Protein: 7.9g   Fat: 28.6g   Carbohydrate: 7.3g

Beat the egg whites in an electric mixer until they
form soft peaks. Set aside in another bowl. In the same
mixer bowl, cream the butter until fluffy and beat in the
yolks one at a time. Add the flour and sour cream alternately, beating well after each addition. Stir in the vanilla,
salt, and nutmeg. Fold in the egg whites. Bake in a preheated waffle iron according to manufacturer's directions.

RICOTTA PANCAKES

These high-protein low-carb pancakes are at least reminiscent of the high-carb pancakes we all used to love. If you decide to leave out the powdered egg whites, the batter will be thin, so you should make little silver-dollar pancakes. If you're really hungry, two people can divide these pancakes for 33 grams of protein, 26.2 grams of fat, and 12.5 carbs each. SERVES 3

4 large eggs
1 cup ricotta
½ teaspoon vanilla extract
⅓ cup oat flour
1 tablespoon melted butter or vegetable oil
Pinch of salt
Big pinch of grated nutmeg
1 packet Equal, optional
2 tablespoons powdered egg whites (Just Whites, page 44)
1 teaspoon butter for the griddle

Per Serving: Protein: 22g   Fat: 17.5g   Carbohydrate: 8g

Set a griddle or a large skillet over high heat. Put all the pancake ingredients (except the butter for the griddle) in a blender or food processor and blend well. When the griddle is hot enough so that a drop of water jumps when it hits the surface, grease the griddle with the butter. Drop the batter by spoonfuls, large or small as you like, onto the griddle. Turn the pancakes when the edges lose their shine and bubbles begin to appear. Cook briefly on the other side and serve immediately. Butter and Vermont Sugar-Free Syrup are the right accompaniments.

BLUEBERRY SYRUP

You can use fresh or frozen blueberries here. This is good
on pancakes or ricotta for dessert or just spooned over
cottage cheese when you want a little treat. SERVES 4

    1 cup blueberries
    ½ cup water or more as needed
    2 packets Equal
    Dash of cinnamon
    1 teaspoon grated lemon zest or 2 drops lemon oil

Per Serving: Protein: 0g   Fat: 0g   Carbohydrate: 4.3g

In a small saucepan, bring the blueberries and water to
a gentle simmer over medium heat. Crush the berries a
bit with a cooking spoon and add the remaining ingredients. Let the syrup thicken a little and take off the heat.
You can either purée it or serve it chunky.

MENUS

MENUS

Thanksgiving Menu

Smoked Trout on Watercress

Roast Turkey with Wild Rice Stuffing

Cranberry Sauce

Broccoli Purée

Spaghetti Squash with Roasted Pecans

Salad of Winter Greens with Pomegranate Seeds

Pumpkin Mousse

Christmas

Smoked Salmon Canapés

Standing Rib Roast of Beef with Horseradish Cream

Turnip Gratin with Blue Cheese

Wild Rice

Spinach with a Ton of Butter

Watercress Salad with Orange and Toasted Walnuts

Pecan Meringue Ice Cream Pie

New Year's Eve Supper

Caviar on Cracked Pepper Crackers

Radishes with Sweet Butter and Sea Salt

Oyster Stew with Mushrooms

Salad of Winter Greens with Orange and Avocado

Cheese Platter with Celery Sticks

Tidbits: Chocolate Almonds, Chocolate Coffee Beans,

Candied Ginger, Cracked Walnuts

Casual Winter Supper

Eggplant and Pepper Dip with Endive

Sauerkraut Soup

Spicy Cheese Wafers with Caraway Seed

Big Green Salad

Ambrosia with Amarettini

Mexican Dinner

Mexican Shrimp Cocktail

Carnitas

Tortillas, Large Romaine Leaves, Pickled Onions, Salsa, Sour Cream, Cilantro Sprigs, Tomato Chunks, Lime Wedges

Mixed Melon Balls with Mint

Almond Cookies

Texas Supper

Fried Cheese on Greens

Oven Barbecued Brisket

Tex-Mex Coleslaw

Potato Salad

Green Chile Soufflé

Southwest Zucchini Pancakes with Salsa

Watermelon with Lime Wedges

Quick Dinner

Smoked Salmon Rolls with Hazelnut Cream Cheese

Nut-Crusted Swordfish with Romesco Sauce

Spinach with a Whiff of Garlic

Broccoli Purée

Chocolate Mousse

Elegant Spring Dinner

Walnut Parmesan Lace Crisps

Crudités with Cucumber Dip

Salmon with Garlic Cream Spinach and Chanterelles

Herb Salad with Lemon Vinaigrette

Raspberry Crème Brûlée

A Simple Dinner

Zucchini Pasta

Crispy Chicken Cutlets

Green Bean Pie

Greek Salad, No Tomatoes

Father Sarducci's Cheesecake

A Grilled Dinner

Lime Scallops

Tuna with Mint, Garlic, and Soy

Skillet Watercress

Zucchini Pancakes

Ricotta Puffs with Raspberry Sauce

A Southern Feast

New Orleans Spicy Shrimp

Southern-Style Smothered Pork Chops

Country-Style Greens

Cauliflower Purée

Corn Crisps

Peach and Blueberry Crisp with Almonds

Summer Lunch

Vichyssoise

Salmon and Green Bean Salad with Dill

Spicy Cheese Wafers

Cherry Tomatoes

Berries with Trembling Cream

A Middle Eastern Dinner

Cheese Balls

Leg of Lamb with a Tapenade Crust

Slow-Baked Tomatoes with Feta Cheese

Tabbouleh

Melon Balls with Cardamom

Pecan Meringues

South American Grill

Provoleta

Steaks with Chimichurri Sauce

Potato Skins

Swiss Chard with Chiles

Peaches with Amarettini Cream

Italian Dinner

Olives / Caponata

Tricolored Pepper Crescents

Roast Leg of Pork

Zucchini Pancakes

Fennel and Orange Salad with Frico

Fresh Fruit: Cherries, Grapes, Forelle Pears

Pecan Meringues

Sources

Bacon: My favorite bacon to date is the hickory-smoked peppered one from Wright's in Vernon, Texas. It's distributed in the middle of the country and they'll tell you where if you call 817-553-1811. The bacon will keep in the freezer for 6 months, so it's worth importing it.

Candy: Chocolate Mocha Beans are a little less than 1 carb each. From Williams-Sonoma, 1-800-541-2233.

Blueberries: Little wild Maine blueberries come frozen from L. L. Bean at 1-800-221-4221. Keep them in your freezer.

Chile powder: New Mexico chile and chipotles and other hot stuff can be ordered from Coyote Cocina, 1-800-866-HOWL, and Mo' Hotta, Mo' Betta, 1-800-462-3220. Try also M & S Produce, at 1-505-852-4368.

Citrus oils: Boyajian pure lime, lemon, and orange oils can be mail-ordered from Williams-Sonoma, 1-800-541-2233. King Arthur Flour also sells a sampler collection, 1-800-827-6836.

Gourmet products: A great source is Zingerman's, 1-313-663-3354. Also Dean and DeLuca, 1-800-221-7714. For Asian foods, Kam Man Chinese Supermarket, 212-571-0330.

Low-carb prepared food: D'lites Emporium, 1-954-433-
5865. They offer cheesecakes at 6 carbs for the entire cake, protein bread at 12 carbs per slice,
flatbread, cookies for 1 carb each, etc. Also The
Sugar-Free Marketplace on the internet at
www.icaneat.net/sugarfree.

Low-carb on the Net: Check out lowcarb-list-
request@maelstrom.stjohns.edu.

Meats: For lamb, Jamison's is sold by Williams-Sonoma,
1-800-541-2233. They also carry Niman-Schell's
exemplary beef. These meats are organic. For pork,
S. Wallace Edwards at 1-800-222-4267 sells excellent ham, country ham, and bacon. Ham I Am! (1-
800-742-6426) has a huge number of fans for its
Texas pork products, including Ozark Trails peppered bacon. Nueske of Wisconsin (1-800-392-
2266) carries applewood-smoked turkey and
chicken as well as pork. Aidell's excellent low-fat
sausage is widely distributed; if you can't find it, or
their cocktail franks, call 1-415-285-6660.

Nuts: Ann's House of Nuts in Jessup, Maryland, has excellent, very fresh nuts. 1-410-813-0080. For
peanuts, the ultimate source is Nuts D'Vine, 1-
800-334-0492. They carry hot and spicy nuts,
extra large buff blanched peanuts, cashews, oil-
roasted redskins, and peanut pieces for making
peanut butter. They also have a wonderful virgin
cold-pressed peanut oil that's intensely aromatic,
and a bargain.

Pork rinds: Exemplary are St. Michael's, distributed by
Jade King in Seattle. They'll send you a case of 24
packages by UPS for a little over $50.00. Fax them
at 1-206-763-8026 or call 1-203-763-8212.

Protein Bars: There are Biozone bars and Balance bars but

the best low-carb bar is the Protein 21 Nutritional Bar at only 12 carb grams and 21 protein grams, no artificial ingredients. A 14-bar box is available from Nutritional Assistance Inc. at 1-800-965-9008.

Protein Shakes: For breakfast or an alternative meal, the High Protein Nutritious Beverage Powder from Take Care is a good bargain at 4 to 8 carb grams and 20 protein. It comes in plain (not recommended), chocolate, vanilla and strawberry, from 1-800-445-3350.

Radish Recipes: From the indefatigable North American Radish Council—their best recipes for this spunky little low-carb vegetable. Call 212-420-8808.

Splenda: Be first on your block to be notified when Splenda goes on sale: call 908-524-6336 and leave your phone number.

Stevia: Order plants from Richter's, 905-640-6677. For information on plants, call Log House Plants at 1-541-942-2288. You can order stevia in powder form from Body Ecology at 1-800-STEVIA. For stevia leaves: Jean's Greens, 518-239-8327.

Stevita: A mix of powdered stevia and maltodextrin (which is also the sugar packaged with aspartame in Equal), this is very easy to use—½ teaspoon equals 2 teaspoons of sugar. It still has the stevia taste in delicate dishes like custard, but it's muted compared to the other stevia powders on the market. It's also quite expensive, but the company promises the price will be coming down soon. If this product isn't in your local health food stores, call 817-483-0044 to order.

Sugar-free syrups: The delicious Italian syrups from DaVinci are to be found at your local Barnes & Noble—but you can also call DaVinci directly and

find out all their flavors and where their nearest
distributor is. 1-800-640-6779.

Tejava: This elegant, almost addictive mineral-water tea
is made by Crystal Geyser Water Company in Cal-
istoga, California. For a source near you, call 1-
800-GEYSER.

Thyroid information: The Broda Barnes, M.D. Foundation, Inc., P.O. Box 98, Trumbull, CT 06611. 1-
203-261-2101.

Toast: These very good low-carb breads are even better
toasted. Alvarado Street Bakery's Sprouted Multi-
grain Bread at 9 carb grams (as is Sprouted Soy
Crunch) or their California Style Complete Protein Bread at 8 grams are distributed nationally at
natural food stores—call 707-585-3293.

Trout, Smoked: The very best smoked trout in America
comes from Mt. Walden. You can order it direct
from 540-622-2800.

Tortillas: The excellent low-carb tortillas (get the fat-
free ones) from La Tortilla Factory can be ordered
from 1-800-446-1516.

Vanilla: For top-quality, unsweetened pure vanilla extract
call Lochhead Vanilla Company at 314-772-2124.

Index